Learning from Victims' Family Narratives

Offering a new perspective on intimate partner abuse and homicide, this book recognises the families of victims as legitimate agents of knowledge in terms of the harm experienced by their family members, and considers how this harm is extended to the families themselves.

Examining harm from both an offline and online point of view, the book explains the multipurpose roles of offline and online harm and how these roles do not occur in isolation in terms of the victims' and families' abusive experiences. In doing so, it demonstrates the range of harm experienced in the context of intimate partner abuse and homicide, and outlines the overlapping nature of offline and online harm without prioritising one form of harm over the other; instead, considering the harm experienced as a continuum.

Providing theoretical and empirical contributions that are largely absent from existing victimology and harm literature, *Learning from Victims' Family Narratives: The Impact of Offline and Online Harm in Cases of Intimate Partner Homicide* will be of interest to scholars, researchers, students, and practitioners exploring the modern conceptualisation of harm and its impact on individuals beyond the victim and perpetrator.

Morag C. Kennedy is Senior Lecturer at Nottingham Trent University, focusing on intimate partner abuse and homicide involving digital harm. This work primarily considers co-victim perspectives. Key publications include the book chapters "Digital Coercive Control: A Male Perspective" (2022) and "'They Didn't Want to Upset the Client': Stalking in Hands-On Occupations" (2023), and the book *Victimisation in the Digital Age: An Online/Offline Continuum Approach* (Routledge, 2024). Her research seeks to empower vulnerable and marginalised people through the lens of feminism.

Routledge Studies in Crime and Society

Extremism and Radicalization in the Manosphere
Beta Uprising
Deniese Kennedy-Kollar

Neoliberalism and Punishment
Ignacio González-Sánchez

Victimisation in the Digital Age
An Online/Offline Continuum Approach
Edited by Tine Munk and Morag Kennedy

Disability Hate Crime
Perspectives for Change
Edited by Leah Burch and David Wilkin

Crime, Criminal Justice and Ethics in Outer Space
International Perspectives
Edited by Yarin Eski and Jack Lampkin

Youth Involvement in Street Gangs in California's Central Valley
Huan Gao

Pauline Tarnowsky's Les Femmes Homicides
Part I
Edited by Lin Huff-Corzine and Kayla Toohy
Translated by Kayla Toohy and Boniface Noyongoyo

Crime, Violence and Masculinities
Research Paths and Understanding
Stephen Tomsen

Learning from Victims' Family Narratives
The Impact of Offline and Online Harm in Cases of Intimate Partner Homicide
Morag C. Kennedy

For more information about this series, please visit:
www.routledge.com/Routledge-Studies-in-Crime-and-Society/book-series/RSCS

Learning from Victims' Family Narratives

The Impact of Offline and Online Harm in Cases of Intimate Partner Homicide

Morag C. Kennedy

Routledge
Taylor & Francis Group
LONDON AND NEW YORK

First published 2026
by Routledge
4 Park Square, Milton Park, Abingdon, Oxon OX14 4RN

and by Routledge
605 Third Avenue, New York, NY 10158

Routledge is an imprint of the Taylor & Francis Group, an informa business

British Library Cataloguing-in-Publication Data
A catalogue record for this book is available from the British Library

ISBN: 978-1-032-73495-8 (hbk)
ISBN: 978-1-032-73496-5 (pbk)
ISBN: 978-1-003-46448-8 (ebk)

DOI: 10.4324/9781003464488

Typeset in Sabon
by Taylor & Francis Books

Contents

List of Tables vi
Acknowledgements vii
List of Abbreviations viii

1 Introduction 1
2 Current Context 18
3 Offline Harm: Existing Risk Factors in the Web of Abuse 50
4 Online Harm: Emerging Risk Factors in the Web of Abuse 91
5 Overspill of Abuse 117
6 Concluding Thoughts 133

Index 146

Tables

1.1 Participant Sample 9
2.1 UK Responses to Online Harm 37
3.1 Different Contexts for Jealousy 53
3.2 Examples of Active and Passive Threats 65
4.1 Conceptualising Online Harm and Coercive Control 101

Acknowledgements

This book has been a labour of love with the empirical research incorporated within it beginning with the support of the Centre for Applied Criminology at Birmingham City University. As such, I would like to thank my doctoral supervisors, Dr. Charlotte Barlow and Dr. Sarah Pemberton, for their support and guidance at this very early stage of the research. Although Dr. Martin Glynn has always been on the sidelines in terms of my research, he has continued to champion me in all of my endeavours.

Hard work, dedication and a lot of soul searching has brought this book to fruition. It has not been an easy journey. I would like to extend sincere thanks to my colleagues in the Criminology and Criminal Justice Department at Nottingham Trent University, with particular attention to Dr. Tine Munk whose work ethic and passion for research inspired me to take the plunge with this book. I owe a debt of gratitude to her. In addition, a special thanks go to Dr. Thais Sardá, Dr. Ian Mahoney, Dr. Becky Thompson, Dr. John Whitehead, Dr. Leah Cleghorn, Dr. Paul Hamilton, Ellen Harris, Michelle Cunliffe, Elliot Doornbos, Neil Radford, Joe Hale, Jordan Cashmore and others who have continued to humour me by listening and advising me throughout this entire process. A huge thank you to Morwenna Scott and the rest of the Routledge team for helping get this project off the ground.

On a more personal note, I would also like to express my heartfelt gratitude to my family and friends who have helped me on this journey including my mother, Heather, Kaylee, Sundas, Shona, Tanya, Rhona, Sapphire, Moe, Somia, Kirsty and Paul OB. I would also like to thank my husband, Warren, for continuing to believe in me even when I did not have any belief left in myself. His unwavering support has allowed me to finish this book. Without it, the book would never have materialised.

Lastly, I would like to thank the victims' families who took the time to discuss their loved ones with me. Your stories will stay with me, forever.

List of Abbreviations

Abbreviation	*Full Name*
AAFDA	Advocacy After Fatal Domestic Abuse
CPS	Community Safety Partnerships
DFVDRU	Domestic and Family Violence Death Review
DHR	Domestic Homicide Review
DVCVA	Domestic Violence, Crime and Victims Act 2004
DVFR	Domestic Violence Fatality Review
DVMPA	Domestic Violence and Matrimonial Proceedings Act 1976
LGBTIQA+	Lesbian, Gay, Bisexual, Transgender, Intersex, Queer/Questioning, Asexual
CPS	Crown Prosecution Service
PTSD	Post-Traumatic Stress Disorder
ONS	Office for National Statistics

1 Introduction

Introduction

The book, *Learning from Victims' Family Narratives: The Impact of Offline and Online Harm in Cases of Intimate Partner Homicide*, is a result of empirical research carried out with the families of victims who were murdered by an intimate partner, where digital coercive control was used as a tool of coercion. This book is not exploring perpetrator accounts of offline and online harm. Instead, it seeks to consider victimisation and impact from a perspective which rarely receives attention. This looks to co-victims for their valuable insights into risk factors for intimate partner homicide. As such, it does not cover all risk factors but rather those which are associated with their observations. It also considers harm which spills over into the lives of co-victims, particularly family of the victim, and the impact this has on supporting those experiencing coercive control which turns fatal.

While the research data used within this book originates from England and Wales, it has global appeal. Intimate partner abuse and homicide are the most common forms of abuse (Garcia-Moreno et al., 2006; Pereira et al., 2013; Smith et al., 2017; Spencer et al., 2022; Toprak & Ersoy, 2017) and fatal abuse worldwide (Petrosky et al., 2017; Stöckl et al., 2013; Spencer, 2018; Spencer & Stith, 2020). Within victimology, there is a tendency for constructions of victimhood to be considered in two ways: victims and perpetrators (Jankowitz, 2018). These social constructions give rise to other binary distinctions such as innocence and guilt, good and bad, legitimacy and illegitimacy (Jankowitz, 2018). As such, some victims are considered more or less deserving of victim status than others (Carrabine et al., 2004; McGarry & Walklate, 2015). Part of this book's purpose is to elevate the status of victims' families' by recognising them as legitimate agents of knowledge. As narrators of the lives of victims of intimate partner homicide, they are uniquely placed to observe and document harms which have led to their loved ones' deaths.

Research on co-victims has existed for over 30 years, focusing on the psychological challenges of reconciling homicide (Rock, 1998), the concept of forgiveness (Hourigan, 2020), clinical observations of families that have experienced homicide (Browning et al., 2017; Rynearson, 2013), the impact of

DOI: 10.4324/9781003464488-1

homicide on and responses to homicide survivors (Davies et al., 2013), and accounts from co-victims themselves (Browning et al., 2017; Rynearson, 2013; Spungen, 1998). However, these texts consider the murder of young or adolescent children (Rock, 1998), are practitioner focused (Spungen, 1998) or only provide a snapshot of homicide co-victimisation, including perhaps a tokenistic chapter concerning this victim group (Browning et al., 2017; Davies et al., 2013; Holt, 2021). Therefore, this book aims to provide a more nuanced understanding of harm, co-victimisation and the impact on those supporting victims of intimate partner abuse which has resulted in homicide. In addition, it intends to centralise the narratives of victims' families' unreservedly by making their accounts the main focus of the book.

Zemiology in a Nutshell

Zemiology is the study of social harms, largely speaking to acts of abuse which do not necessarily constitute crime (Treadwell, 2016). This discipline emerged in the late 1990s where it was separated from the wider social science discourse before being associated with criminology (Hillyard et al., 2004; Hillyard, 2013; Pemberton, 2015). The argument for such a merge was to capture social harms which were not recorded or regulated by lawmakers (Hillyard et al., 2004). As such, criminologists broadened the focus of harm, from both a public and sociological perspective, by going beyond harms which were considered the most damaging in society (Treadwell, 2016). Instead, they focused on everyday occurrences which could incur more harm than those caused by criminal activity (Treadwell, 2016). Zemiology also acknowledges that the criminal justice system and lawmakers are contributors of harm (Pemberton, 2015; Treadwell, 2016). They reinforce social divisions, encourage punishment and contribute towards injustice (Treadwell, 2016). This is where zemiology differs from traditional criminological approaches.

With that being said, this is a fairly new discipline which is still establishing itself. As such, there are concerns regarding accountability, how social harms can be categorised and what methodological approaches are best suited to this discipline (Pemberton, 2015; Treadwell, 2016). Similarly, as this field of study grows and develops, it has shone light on the neoliberal capitalist regime and how this impacts harm in addition to other schools of thought (Treadwell, 2016). Typically, criminology has created two contrasting ideologies, the study of crime and the study of harm, but perhaps these are more closely related than first thought (Brown, 2006; Kotzé, 2018). In considering the origins of zemiology, Kotzé (2018: 92) has found that the terms used to describe crime and harm are part of the same complex dyad, suggesting that "it seems illogical to force an artificial cleavage between crime and harm". This is in tune with the broader understandings of crime and harm, and their importance as two intersecting elements within the same scholarly camps (Paoli & Greenfield, 2013).

The rationale for using the term harm within this book as an overarching concept is to incorporate forms of harm which are yet to be recognised in any legal sense (Copson, 2018; Kennedy, 2024). It is also to capture and catalogue those harms which differ from those that are criminalised. This book does not necessarily suggest that the harms discussed throughout the rest of the book should be criminalised, but it does follow the same thought process as zemiologists who believe all harms should be acknowledged (Walklate et al., 2018).

Co-victims of Intimate Partner Homicide

Arguably, anyone can be impacted by the death of a loved one with the term 'co-victim' encompassing a range of different people within the victim's life (van Wijk et al., 2017). However, MacVane et al. (2003) have suggested that co-victims are more likely to be related to the victim, thereby sharing a familial link with them. On the other hand, Hertz et al. (2005: 289) have indicted that co-victims can include "surviving family, friends and loved ones" which favours a broader approach to co-victimisation. While the aforementioned research involved unsolved homicides, it could be argued that it also applies to solved homicides or those undergoing prosecution. Nevertheless, MacVane et al.'s (2003) work presumes that the family's grief is more profound than that of friends or others involved in the victim's life. It is this author's opinion that this unfair categorisation does not take into account other intersections related to 'family' structure which will be considered in more detail in Chapter 2. Nor does it consider the complexities associated with the grieving process. Furthermore, it fails to address more complicated relationships where victims may be estranged from family. Bastomski and Duane (2019) have gone further to suggest that co-victims are survivors of homicide that have a familial, kinship or friendship link with victims. This may include parents, grandparents, children, grandchildren, cousins, partners or ex-partners of the victim, friends or other individuals who identify as a chosen family members (Jackson et al., 2022). This consideration is fuller and more inclusive of changes to family structure and the intricacies involved in family dynamics. As such, this book embraces the newer conceptualisations of co-victims which include victims' wider social circles such as family, friends and co-workers (Bastomski & Duane, 2019; Hertz et al., 2005). However, its contribution focuses on the immediate family, including the parents and siblings of victims.

It must be noted that some research exists involving friends of victims. Of that research, much of the participant samples comprise of family members with only a few friends being considered (see Discola, 2020; Mastrocinque et al., 2015). For instance, in Discola's (2020) study 11% of the participant sample identified as a "best friend". Similarly, four participants were categorised as "other" which could indicate a friendship rather than a familial link (Mastrocinque et al., 2015). With that being said, both studies considered homicide more generally rather than looking at specific types of homicide such as intimate partner homicide. However, where co-victims are referred to as "informal supporters" the research field expands to some extent (Gregory, 2017: 63). In Gregory's (2017) study, the majority of participants identified as the victim's "friend" or "co-worker". Similar proportions of the sample were found in Latta's (2008) doctoral research and subsequent publication (Latta & Goodman, 2011: 973) where co-victims were termed "informal network members". Accordingly, the lack of research into friends may be due to recruitment issues or perhaps scholars researching co-victims sharing the same view as MacVane et al. (2003), i.e., that friends of the victim cannot provide a full enough picture of the victim's experience and are, therefore, discredited as participants or legitimate agents of knowledge.

While there appears to be research concerning others who are not necessarily considered 'family', the age-old debate concerning terminology surfaces again. Consequently, there is little consensus in terms of the language used to refer to co-victims within the academic community. In addition to this, a large proportion of research regarding co-victims considers the impact from the perspective of intimate partner abuse victim-survivors (Riger et al., 2002; Swanberg & Logan, 2005; Wolf et al., 2000), whilst some takes a statistics-only approach by analysing domestic violence fatality cases (Hobart, 2002) and coroner and police investigations (McLachlan & Harris, 2022), and other research has reviewed the literature (Gregory et al., 2017a). At any rate, the studies that do exist in this area are valuable for understanding the impact of supporting co-victims of intimate partner abuse (Gregory et al., 2017a; Gregory et al., 2017b) but they rarely consider intimate partner homicide (Cadwallader & Kennedy, 2024). This will be discussed in more depth in Chapter 5.

Older literature has sought to explain how families respond to a traumatic event, with Vesper and Cohen (1999) and Miller (2009) providing a typology for understanding post-traumatic stress disorder (PTSD) in families who undergo litigation. They suggest that there are five specific patterns of reaction to litigation: (i) the functional family, (ii) the contemptuous family, (iii) the brittle family, (iv) the enduring family, and (v) the hierarchical family. These patterns of reaction explore families' coping mechanisms and responses to litigation. The functional family supports and bolsters each other, problem solving to overcome or confront stressors. The contemptuous family blame each other, blame the victim and are unsupportive of each other. The brittle family are unlikely to seek support from inside the family unit instead relying on others, thereby emphasising their lack of cohesion and flexibility in the face of adversity. The enduring family relies on religion and spirituality to cope with the traumatic event. The hierarchical family is rigid in their decision-making processes, relying on elders to consult on family matters; there is little flexibility in terms of the roles and responsibilities in this family type but they do band together when faced with challenges. Miller (2009) also mentions this reaction pattern typology can be applied to families who have experienced the murder of a loved one. However, the original typology focused on traumatic events more generally where the victim had survived. Furthermore, it is situated in outdated psychotherapy and psychiatry literature where sources date back to the 1970s. Miller's (2009) discussion of this typology also very much mirrors its previous iteration, thereby lacking critique. While the typology goes some way to explaining or describing families' reactions to litigation, it is reductionist in its approach.

Impact on Co-victims of Intimate Partner Homicide

Homicide has far-reaching repercussions not only for the victim but also for those left behind. People close to the victim are deeply affected by the devastating and, often, sudden loss (Costa et al., 2017; Stretesky et al., 2010). Persons (1990) describes the tragic loss of a family member by homicide as all-encompassing as it touches every aspect of that individual's life. In many cases, families can struggle to come to terms with the death (Prigerson et al., 1999). This is often made worse by the circumstances surrounding the murder being unknown, uncertain and ongoing (Connolly & Gordon, 2015). Consequently, many turn to the criminal justice system for answers as a way of helping with the bereavement process (Stretesky et al., 2010). For the most part, this is detrimental to the process, usually leading to further victimisation.

It is estimated that around six to ten family members are likely to be affected by homicide, as well as countless friends, neighbours and co-workers (Connolly & Gordon, 2015; Costa et al., 2017; Gross, 2007; Kilpatrick & Acierno, 2003). Given the current estimates of intimate partner abuse and the risk of homicide in these relationships, this may affect one in four families in the UK alone, without considering global perspectives. The incidence of intimate partner abuse and homicide is discussed further in Chapter 2. Families often receive little to no support in the aftermath of the homicide and can, in many contexts, be considered outcasts due to the stigma attached to their loss (Costa et al., 2017; Hertz et al., 2005). This alienates them from colleagues and friends, diminishing their support networks.

In addition to the social and occupational effects of homicide, the entire family dynamic can change. The family environment becomes a source of distress as daily tasks can act as a reminder of the homicide (Costa et al., 2017). Often the anniversary of the family member's death, birthdays and other special occasions can bring back particularly painful memories (Soares et al., 2006). Other significant psychological effects include depression, aggression, anxiety, suicidal thoughts and somatisation – where psychological distress manifests as physical symptoms (Gregory et al., 2017a; Norris et al., 1998). Co-victims are also more likely to present with PTSD (Burke et al., 2010; Gregory et al., 2017a; Hertz et al., 2005; Clements & Vigil, 2003; Costa et al., 2017). As part of their PTSD, family members report having recurrent dreams regarding the homicide which can involve the victim being saved or instead the most distressing part of the homicide (Miller, 2009). Emotional anaesthesia is also commonly reported by co-victims where they feel incapable of feeling any type of emotion (Connolly & Gordon, 2015). Memory loss, attention problems and sleep disturbance are other common issues associated with the murder of a loved one (Charmaine & Mahoney, 2004; Connolly & Gordon, 2015). Lastly, family members may have a diminished interest in important activities in their lives as well as avoiding anything which may remind them of the painful memories associated with the murder of their relative (Hertz et al., 2005).

Understandably, the grieving process of co-victims does not follow the same stages as those mourning a non-violent death (Connolly & Gordon, 2015; Malone, 2007; Wellman, 2017). Malone (2007) suggests the duration and intensity can differ. Many family members blame themselves for the homicide or are self-critical in terms of the help they provided the victim prior to their death (Hardesty et al., 2008; Latta, 2008; McNamara, 2008). They may even blame themselves for not predicting the homicide (Connolly & Gordon, 2015; Wellman, 2017). This emotional reaction to the homicide can be described as 'survivors' guilt' and is mostly experienced by those who witnessed the homicide but were left unharmed (Gross, 2007). As discussed earlier, the grieving process can be complicated by legal, financial and social issues raised as a result of the homicide (Malone, 2007). Furthermore, criminal justice proceedings can impede co-victims' abilities to mourn (Englebrecht et al., 2014; Malone, 2007; Miller, 2009; Stretesky et al., 2010). As such, many co-victims have no other option but to postpone their grief until the criminal justice system's involvement comes to an end (Riches & Dawson, 1998).

Secondary victimisation by the criminal justice system is not the only source of re-victimisation for families. The way in which the media portrays the murder, if it gains local and/or national attention, can also impact the families negatively (Connolly & Gordon, 2015; Costa et al., 2017). The media print stories for readership so often the death of murder victims are reported with a lack of sensitivity, thereby dehumanising and trivialising the victim's death and the family's suffering (Connolly & Gordon, 2015). This distorted depiction can leave families feeling like they have lost their "own truth about the victim" (Costa et al., 2017: 3092). As such, this can have a significant impact on the family's ability to grieve. In addition, stories sensationalising the victim's death, involving graphic media coverage, prevent families from focusing on the more pleasant memories of their loved ones.

One way in which families positively adjust to their new life is through sense-making (Armour, 2003; Currier et al., 2006; Stretesky et al., 2010). This process involves families having a greater understanding of the murder which results in or aids post-identity loss reconstruction (Stretesky et al., 2010). It is also extremely important for the grieving process (Currier et al., 2006). Often relatives who have lost a loved one through a traumatic event need to ascribe meaning to their loss (Costa et al., 2017). It is argued that this can have positive emotional effect for the family members in question (Stretesky et al., 2010). The interviews with victims' families used for this book have facilitated this notion of sense-making to some extent.

Research with Victims' Families

The Underpinning Principles of Qualitative Feminist Research

Research for this book took a qualitative feminist approach which involved: (i) a women-centred perspective with reflexivity being a critical part of the research process (Harding, 1991; Letherby, 2003); (ii) a recognition that victims' families' are legitimate agents of knowledge in terms of victims' experiences of intimate partner abuse; (iii) a desire to create researcher-participant relationships that followed a non-hierarchal and non-manipulative approach using a 'participatory model' (Reibharz, 1983); and (iv) an acknowledgement of the importance of politics in terms of understanding the experiences of women (Harding, 1987, 1991; Marshall, 2006). It relied on feminist standpoint and feminist postmodern epistemological assumptions which focus on illuminating the experiences of women whilst recognising that there are no absolute truths as knowledge and truth exist in relation to culture, society and/or history (Harding, 1987, 1991). This approach favoured subjectivity and was heavily influenced by the work of Marx in terms of the role of the proletariat, with women being the oppressed class (Harding, 1991; Waugh, 1998).

Having said that, both feminist standpoint and feminist postmodernism have their critiques. For example, Harding (1991) argued that standpoint theory may be better understood as a sociology of knowledge. It also fails to distinguish between different women's experiences in terms of intersectionality, grouping all 'women' into one category (Smith, 1990; Stoetzler & Yuval-Davis, 2002). Other scholars have rejected standpoint theory, stating no overarching 'truths' exist and that these 'truths' can only be made up of partial knowledge as they are constructed at a particular time and place (Letherby, 2003; Millen, 1997; Williams, 1996). Moreover, feminist postmodernism disregards objectivity, maintaining that knowledge can only be grounded in the interests and values of particular groups (Letherby, 2003; Waugh, 1998). With that being said, it suggests there are no discrete categories within society, meaning there is no such thing as a 'woman' or 'patriarchy' as these concepts are governed by a set of relations. Alcoff (1988) went further by arguing that if women were reduced to categories, the very androcentric ideologies feminism sought to eliminate would simply be replicated. As such, if gender was considered a social construct and feminism sought to speak for 'women', the interests of women could not be stood up for as they did not exist. In addition, Millen (1997) suggested postmodernism undermines the political role of feminist research which focuses specifically on gender and inequality.

Despite the limitations underpinning the qualitative feminist approach used to collect empirical data for this book, it was deemed the most appropriate method for researching within the feminist paradigm. Owing to the subjective nature of qualitative research, it allowed for the worlds of women and families to be studied without the typical objective and value-free nature of quantitative research (Harding, 1991; Letherby, 2003; Stanley & Wise, 1993; Westmarland, 2001). However, there are known drawbacks to qualitative research including issues relating to a lack of transparency, generalisability, transferability, dependability and confirmability (Bryman, 2012; Caulfield & Hill, 2014; Shenton, 2004). Many of these issues stem from the notion that qualitative research cannot be replicated but this is not the point of qualitative research. Instead, it seeks to understand a particular social phenomenon from an individual perspective and illuminating this perspective would be hampered if strict scientific guidelines were adhered to, as per quantitative research.

This approach also enabled a more equal relationship between the author and her participants (Harding & Norberg, 2005; Stanley & Wise, 1990). This was facilitated by using a participatory model, which was achieved by maintaining contact with victims' families' throughout the entire research process (Reibharz, 1983). Usually contact with participants ceases after data collection with many remaining uninformed of the research findings. However, it was important for this author that the families were an integral part of the research. During data collection, research progress was communicated to participants every three to four months via email so they were kept appraised of research development, and had the opportunity to comment on or question the data they provided. A summary of the findings was also circulated to the participants via email to allow them time to reflect on what was found. Participants were encouraged to discuss the findings with the author in order to create a mutually reciprocal relationship (Fontana & Frey, 1994; Oakley, 1981). In doing so, it was the intention of the author to reduce the risk of secondary victimisation, where possible (Campbell & Raja, 1999; Doerner, 2012).

Gatekeeper Access

Advocacy After Fatal Domestic Abuse (AAFDA) acted as the gatekeeper for recruitment of participants. This national charity, situated in England and Wales, specialises in guiding families and friends through inquiries including Domestic Homicide Reviews (DHRs), domestic abuse related suicides and unexplained deaths. It also provides training, information, guidance and advice to professionals involved in cases of fatal domestic abuse. An initial meeting was set up with this gatekeeper to discuss the research in more detail. Thereafter, contact was limited to emails and phone calls. As a result of attending a conference hosted by the charity, more participants were approached and recruited. In addition, a small number of individuals were contacted over social media platforms (e.g., Facebook and Twitter/X) for recruitment. All of the participants were then given the relevant information prior to taking part in the research. This involved making phone calls and emailing potential participants.

The criteria used to identify participants for the research involved individuals having a familial link to the victim who was murdered as a result of intimate partner abuse. The harm needed to be perpetrated both offline and online, and families had to be prepared to discuss all aspects of their loved one's murder including the circumstances leading up to it, the murder itself and how online harm was a factor.

The Research Sample

This book is based exclusively on the narratives of eight co-victims from six families (see Table 1.1, Participant Sample). As mentioned above, AAFDA was approached and agreed to act as a conduit for recruitment of victims' families. Participants' initial contact was, therefore, with the gatekeeper. The gatekeeper sent out emails to those they thought were suitable for the research, outlining the aims and objectives of the research, and the participants who were willing to take part emailed the author directly with their interest. As the gatekeeper had an existing relationship with families bereaved by intimate partner homicide, they selected many of the participants for the research (six out of seven families). The gatekeeper's role in this research was twofold: an enabler and a participant (Boden et al., 2009; Davies, 2011).

Table 1.1 Participant Sample

Participant	*Relationship to Victim*	*Victim Characteristics*			
		Gender	*Age*	*Ethnicity*	*Year of Death*
Suisan	Mother	Female	33	White	2012
Niall & Mia	Father & Mother	Female	20	White	2014
Fergus	Brother	Female	47	White	2003
Tam & Mairi	Father & Mother	Female	17	White	2013
Nelson	Brother	Female	24	White	2016
Jen	Sister	Female	31	White	2016
Shena*	Mother	Female	17	White	2013

Note: Scottish pseudonyms and locations were used to anonymise the research data captured in England and Wales.
* Shena's daughter was pregnant with her first child when she was murdered.

Interviews with Victims' Families

An unstructured interviewing approach was taken in order to collect insights from victims' families. This flexibility afforded more opportunities to probe participants further than other more standardised approaches to interviewing, thereby enabling them to reveal or prioritise concerns of real or symbolic value (Holstein & Gubrium, 2004; Lofland et al., 2006). This resulted in seven unstructured interviews conducted over a ten-month period commencing August 2017 until May 2018. Prior to interview, all participants were informed that their participation was voluntary and they could withdraw from the research at any time within the process. This was demonstrated in their ability to participate (or not) in the research.

All participants had a familial connection to the victim. Each family was interviewed separately at a place convenient to them. In all but two cases, this was in the victim's family home. These interviews were conducted in the family home in order to make the participants feel as comfortable as possible (Elwood & Martin, 2000; Letherby, 2003). Each interview varied in length but the majority averaged at approximately one hour. Permission was granted to audio record all interviews, with care and sensitivity being key considerations during the research process.

As coercive control is a major risk factor for intimate partner homicide, the aim was to give the victims' families as much control over the interviews as possible to enable them to have more control over the whole research process. This, in turn, broke down the hierarchical barrier between the author and interviewees, allowing the participants to play an active role in the research rather than being objectified. This achieved a non-hierarchal and non-manipulative relationship which is indicative of the 'participatory model' discussed previously (Harding, 1987; Reibharz, 1983). Of course, power cannot be eliminated completely from the interview process as it is the researcher who walks away with the data (Cotterill, 1992). This was overcome by ensuring that participants had someone independent to talk to during the course of the research.

Nearing the start of the interviews, the author disclosed the reason for choosing this research topic, thereby revealing her own experiences of coercive control and intimate partner abuse. It was important that the victim's families were aware of the rationale for studying this topic from the offset. It also fostered common ground and enabled participants to open up more about their own experiences and the experiences of their loved ones. Stanley and Wise (1993) advocate that researchers must be seen to be making themselves vulnerable in order to equalise the power dynamics of the interviewer-interviewee relationship. Despite, the limited number of interviews, they still produced rich, in-depth data.

Methodological Limitations

Methodological limitations predominantly related to the inability to ensure full anonymity of the research participants. Anonymity was challenged due to all the interviewees' stories receiving widespread media attention. In particular, this related to media interest in a crime resulting in the death of a loved one (e.g. homicide), campaign or fundraising activity for the families' charities, or in a court judgement (e.g. the sentence for the offender) (Saunders et al., 2015). Many of the families had also contributed to or appeared in television programmes discussing the death of their loved one. As such, the concern was not that the participants would be identified in the mass media because of the research but rather that they may be identifiable in the research used for this book because they had already appeared in the media. Despite the participants choice to 'go public' by sharing their stories with journalists, anonymity was still afforded to participant data to the fullest extent.

Terminologies

Specific terminology is used within this book to describe or name the harm caused to victims and their families. These terms are in line with feminist understandings of the harms caused as well as the gendered nature of this abuse. Given the numerous definitions of domestic abuse and violence within the literature, it is important to situate the terminology used in this book within the wider academic discourse. All definitions related to this type of abuse are universally gender neutral in England and Wales, thereby failing to consider the most dominant forms of abuse which are predominantly perpetrated against women by men (Boyle, 2018; Monckton Smith, 2012). This continues to be the case when it comes to the *Domestic Abuse Act 2021* which follows this gender neutral approach, maintaining the inadequate criminal justice system's response to this crime. However, there have been some improvements with the implementation of the *Domestic Abuse Act 2021* in terms of intersectionality of victims and/or survivors (*Domestic Abuse Act*, 2021).

As this book considers research pertaining to male-perpetrated abuse by a male partner, ex-partner or acquaintance, the term intimate partner abuse is used instead of domestic abuse or domestic violence (Dobash & Dobash, 2015; Monckton Smith, 2012). This terminology is used as both domestic abuse and domestic violence are problematic in a number of different ways. For example, the term *domestic* trivialises the abuse with police and other agencies not responding to 'domestics' with the same diligence as other crimes. It implies crimes like these are less serious even though they manifest the same rationality and legitimisation by perpetrators as other crimes (Hammer, 2002; Lawoko, 2008; Mullender, 2002; Pain, 2014). In many cases, the perpetrator and victim may have separated but the abuse continues so the term *domestic* is not applicable in these situations (Mullender, 2002). In a similar vein, the term *violence* does not adequately reflect the harm being perpetrated towards to victims and/or survivors. This term speaks to physical injury which is not always present within abusive relationships (Monckton Smith, 2012). The violence or assault model is one school of thought which has since been replaced with a concept encompassing a pattern of controlling and abusive behaviour which leaves the victim feeling perpetually frightened (Monckton Smith, 2012; Stark, 2007, 2018). As such, the term *abuse* better reflects the ongoing pattern of behaviour associated with coercive control (Geffner, 2016; Stark, 2007, 2023). Therefore, intimate partner abuse situates the harm within a specific context.

Furthermore, similar issues surround the terms *homicide* or *murder* which are also considered gender neutral. They were created by men as a result of heteronormative values within a patriarchal society, with their purpose being to continue to embed this gendered ideology within society (Ingala-Smith, 2018; Monckton Smith, 2012). As these terms fail to consider the misogynistic killing of women, Radford and Russell (1992) suggested the term femicide was more inclusive of the gendered nature of this crime. As *domestic homicide* or *family homicide* do not fit with characterisation, assuming a family connection between the perpetrator and victim(s) through blood or marriage, the term *intimate partner homicide* is used in this book (Websdale, 1999). It brings the terms *homicide* and *murder* in line with the feminist focus of the book and is considered a derivative of femicide, thereby taking into account the gender dynamics involved in the killing of women (Ingala-Smith, 2018).

Outline of the Book

This book is about offline and online harm in cases of intimate partner homicide where digital coercive control was a contributing factor in fatal abuse. It considers the experiences of harm from the perspective of victims' families. Together with their own experiences of harm, the families adopt the role of narrators, bringing to life their loved one's ordeal. This first chapter conceptualises the study of harm, explaining how this relates to the book. It outlines co-victimisation, identifying whom fits this criteria. It also provides the methodological underpinnings for this research. Chapter 2 covers context more broadly, exploring global estimates of intimate partner abuse and homicide, theoretical perspectives, conceptual understandings and legal remedies. In Chapter 3, there is an in-depth discussion of existing risk factors for intimate partner homicide constructed from victims' families' accounts and incorporated case studies. The same approach is taken with Chapter 4 with the focus being on online harm. Chapter 5 considers the overspill of harm towards victims' families themselves, and finally Chapter 6 concludes the book, drawing attention to its contribution and suggesting future research trajectories.

References

Alcoff, L. M., 1988. Feminist theory and social science: new knowledges, new epistemologies. In: Duncan, N. ed. *Body Space*. London: Routledge, pp. 13–27.

Armour, M., 2003. Meaning making in the aftermath of homicide. *Death Studies*, 27, pp. 519–540.

Bastomski, S., & Duane, M., 2019. *Losing a Loved One to Homicide: What We Know About Homicide Co-victims from Research and Practice Evidence* [online]. Washington, DC: Center for Victim Research. Available at: https://justiceresearch.dspacedirect.org/server/api/core/bitstreams/879bb0ce-3fc7-4215-b2ba-68dc3bae9090/content [Accessed 15 January 2025].

Boden, R., Epstein, D. & Latimer, J., 2009. Accounting for ethos or programmes for conduct? The brave new world of research ethics committees. *The Sociological Review*, 57 (4), pp. 728–749.

Boyle, K., 2018. What's in a name? Theorising the inter-relationships of gender and violence. *Feminist Theory*, 20 (1), pp. 19–36.

Brown, S., 2006. The criminology of hybrids: Rethinking crime and law in technosocial networks. *Theoretical Criminology*, 10 (2), pp. 223–244.

Browning, S. W., & Van Eeden-Moorefield., B., 2017. *Contemporary Families at the Nexus of Research and Practice*. Abingdon: Taylor & Francis.

Bryman, A., 2012. *Social Research Methods*. 4th ed. Oxford: Oxford University Press.

Burke, L. A., McDevitt-Murphy, M. E., & Neimeyer, R. A., 2010. African American homicide bereavement: Aspects of social support that predict complicated grief, PTSD, and depression. *Journal of Death and Dying*, 61, pp. 1–24.

Cadwallader, M., & Kennedy, M. C., 2024. When cyberspace turns deadly: The significance of online harassment in intimate partner homicide. In: Munk, T., & Kennedy, M. C., eds. *Victimisation in the Digital Age: An Online-Offline Continuum Approach*. Oxon: Routledge, pp. 151–168.

Campbell, R., & Raja, S., 1999. Secondary victimization of rape victims: Insights from mental health professionals who treat survivors of violence. *Violence & Victimology*, 14 (3), pp. 261–275.

Carrabine, E., Iganski, P., Lee, M., Plummer, K. & South, N., 2004. *Criminology: A Sociological Introduction*. Oxon: Routledge.

Caulfield, L., & Hill, J., 2014. *Criminological Research for Beginners: A Student's Guide*. Oxon: Routledge.

Charmaine, P. C., & Mahoney, A. M., 2004. Understanding the psychosocial sequelae of the murder of a grandparent/caregiver: Cases of Jamaican school-age children. *Journal of Loss and Trauma*, 9, pp. 299–313.

Clements, P. T., & Vigil, G. J., 2003. Child and adolescent homicide survivors: Complicated grief and altered worldviews. *Journal of Psychosocial Nursing & Mental Health Services*, 41, pp. 30–39.

Connolly, J., & Gordon, R., 2015. Co-victims of homicide: A systematic review of the literature. *Trauma, Violence, & Abuse*, 6 (4), pp. 494–505.

Copson, L., 2018. Beyond "criminology vs. zemiology": Reconciling crime with social harm. In: Boukli, A., and Kotzé, J., eds. *Zemiology: Reconnecting Crime and Social Harm: Critical Criminological Perspectives*. Switzerland: Springer International Publishing, pp. 33–56.

Costa, D. H., de Njaine, K. & Schenker, M., 2017. Repercussions of homicide on victims' families: A literature review. *Ciência & Saúde Coletiva*, 22 (9), pp. 3087–3087.

Cotterill, P., 1992. Interviewing women: Issues of friendship, vulnerability and power. *Women's Studies International Forum*, 15 (5/6), pp. 593–606.

Currier, J. M., Holland, J. M. & Neimeyer, R. A., 2006. Sense-making, grief, and the experience of violent loss: Toward a mediational model. *Death Studies*, 30 (5), pp. 403–428.

Davies, P., 2011. Doing interview in prison. In: Davies., P., Francis, P. & Jupp, V., eds. *Doing Criminological Research*. London: Sage, pp. 161–178.

Davies, R. C., Lurigio, A. L. & Herman, S., 2013. *Victims of Crime*. London: Sage Publications.

Discola, K. L., 2020. Emerging narratives in the wake of homicide: Victim, survivor and transgender. *Journal of Victimology and Victim Justice*, 3 (2), pp. 202–218.

Dobash, R. P., & Dobash, R. E., 2015. *When Men Murder Women*. New York: Oxford University Press.

Doerner, W., 2012. *Victimology*. Burlington, MA: Elsevier, Inc.

Domestic Abuse Act 2021 (c.17). Available at: https://www.legislation.gov.uk/ukpga/2021/17/contents [Accessed 24 March 2025].

Elwood, S. A., & Martin, D. G., 2000. "Placing" interviews: Location and scales of power in qualitative research. *The Professional Geographer*, 52 (4), pp. 649–657.

Englebrecht C. M., Mason D. T., & Adams, M. J., 2014. The experiences of homicide victims' families with the criminal justice system: An exploratory study. *Violence and Victims*, 29, pp. 407–421.

Fontana, A., & Frey, J. H., 1994. Interviewing: The art of science. In: Denzin, N., & Lincoln, Y., eds. *The Handbook of Qualitative Research*. Thousand Oaks: Sage Publications, pp. 361–376.

Garcia-Moreno, C., Jansen, H. A., Ellsberg, M., Heise, L. & Watts, C. H., 2006. Prevalence of intimate partner violence: Findings from the WHO Multi-Country Study on Women's Health and Domestic Violence. *The Lancet*, 368, pp. 1260–1269.

Geffner, R., 2016. Partner aggression versus partner abuse terminology: Moving the field forward and resolving controversies. *Journal of Family Violence*, 31 (8), pp. 923–925.

Gregory, A. C., 2017. "The edge to him was really, really nasty": Abusive tactics used against informal supporters of domestic violence survivors. *Journal of Gender-Based Violence*, (1), pp. 61–77.

Gregory, A. C., Williamson, E., & Feder, G., 2017a. The impact on informal supporters of domestic violence survivors: A systematic literature review. *Trauma, Violence, & Abuse*, 18 (5), pp. 562–580.

Gregory, A., Feder, G., Taket, A., & Williamson, E., 2017b. Qualitative study to explore the health and well-being impacts on adults providing informal support to female domestic violence survivors. *BMJ Open*, 7, doi: 10.1136/bmjopen-2016-014511.

Gross, B., 2007. Life sentence: Co-victims of homicide. *Annals of the American Psychotherapy Association*, 10, pp. 39–43.

Hammer, R., 2002. *Antifeminism and Family Terrorism: A Critical Feminist Perspective*. Lanham, MD: Rowman & Littlefield.

Harding, S., 1987. *Feminism and Methodology*. Bloomington, IN: Indiana University Press.

Harding, S., 1991. *Whose Science? Whose Knowledge?: Thinking from Women's Lives*. Ithaca, New York: Cornell University Press.

Harding, S., & Norberg, K., 2005. New feminist approaches to social science methodologies: An introduction. *Signs*, 30 (4), pp. 2009–2015.

Hardesty, J., Campbell, J., McFarlane, J. & Lewandowski, L., 2008. How children and their caregivers adjust after intimate partner femicide. *Journal of Family Issues*, 29, pp. 100–124.

Hertz, M. F., Prothrow-Stith, D. & Chery, C., 2005. Homicide survivors: Research and practice implications. *American Journal of Preventive Medicine*, 29(5S2), pp. 288–295.

Hillyard, P., Pantazis, C., Tombs, S. & Gordon, D., 2004. *Beyond Criminology: Taking Harm Seriously*. London: Pluto Press.

Hillyard, P., 2013. Zemiology revisited: Fifteen years on. In: Gilmore, J., Moore, J. M., & Scott, D., eds. *Critique and Dissent: An Anthology to Mark 40 Years of the European Group for the Study of Deviance and Social Control*. Ottawa: Red Quill Books Ltd, pp. 219–233.

Hobart, M., 2002. *"Tell the World What Happened to Me": Findings and Recommendations from the Washington State Domestic Violence Fatality Review 2002* [online]. Washington, DC: Washington State Coalition Against Domestic Violence. Available at: https://www.baylor.edu/content/services/document.php/29323.pdf [Accessed 3 January 2025].

Holstein, J. A., & Gubrium, J. F., 2004. The active interview. In: Silverman, D., ed. *Qualitative Research: Theory, Method and Practice*. London: Sage, pp. 140–161.

Holt, A., 2021. *Family Criminology: An Introduction*. London: Palgrave Macmillan.

Hourigan, K. L., 2020. *Redefining Murder, Transforming Emotion: An Exploration of Forgiveness After Loss Due to Homicide*. Oxon: Routledge.

Ingala-Smith, K., 2018. Femicide. In: Lombard, N., ed. *The Routledge Handbook of Gender and Violence*. Oxon: Routledge, pp. 185–198.

Jackson, C. L., Margolius, S., & Browning, S., 2022. The impact of intrafamilial homicide on the family system. *Journal of Family Violence*, 37, pp. 573–583.

Jankowitz, S., 2018. Intergroup struggles over victimhood in violent conflict: The victim-perpetrator paradigm. *International Review of Victimology*, 24 (3), pp. 259–271.

Kennedy, M. C., 2024. Introduction. In: Munk, T., and Kennedy, M., eds. *Victimisation in the Digital Age: An Online/Offline Continuum Approach*. Oxon: Routledge, pp. 3–13.

Kilpatrick, D. G., & Acierno, R., 2003. Mental health needs of crime victims: Epidemiology and outcomes. *Journal of Traumatic Stress*, 16, pp. 119–132.

Kotzé, J., 2018. Criminology or zemiology? Yes, please! on the refusal of choice between false alternatives. In: Boukli, A. and Kotzé, J., eds. *Zemiology: Reconnecting Crime and Social Harm*. London: Palgrave Macmillan, pp. 85–106.

Latta, R., 2008. Struggling to define my role: The experience of network members who intervened in intimate partner violence [online]. Ph.D. thesis, Boston College. Available at: https://www.proquest.com/openview/a7a88ceb2692e7eba34dfc1b539f3b5d/1?pq-origsite=gscholar&cbl=18750 [Accessed 3 January 2025].

Latta, R., & Goodman, L. A., 2011. Intervening in partner violence against women: A grounded theory exploration of informal network members' experiences. *The Counseling Psychologist*, 39 (7), pp. 973–1023.

Lawoko, S., 2008. Predictors of attitudes towards intimate partner violence: A comparative study of men in Zambia and Kenya. *Journal of Interpersonal Violence*, 23 (8), pp. 1056–1074.

Letherby, G., 2003. *Feminist Research In Theory and Practice*. Buckingham: Open University Press.

Lofland, J., Snow, D., Anderson, L., & Lofland, L. H., 2006. *Analyzing Social Settings: A Guide to Qualitative Observation and Analysis*. Belmont, CA: Thomson Wadsworth.

MacVane S. L., Miranda A. O. & Molina B. 2003. Coping with the murder of a loved one: Counseling survivors of murder victims in groups. *The Journal for Specialists in Group Work*, 28, pp. 48–63.

Malone, L., 2007. In the aftermath: Listening to people bereaved by homicide. *Probation Journal*, 54, pp. 383–393.

Marshall, J., 2006. Feminist jurisprudence: keeping the subject alive. *Feminist Legal Studies*, 14, pp. 27–51.

Mastrocinque, J. M., Metzger, J. W., Madeira, J., Lang, K., Pruss, H., Navratil, P. K., Sandys, M. & Cerulli, C. 2015. I'm still left here with the pain: Exploring the health consequences of homicide on families and friends. *Homicide Studies*, 19, pp. 326–349.

McGarry, R., & Walklate, S. 2015. *Victims: Trauma, Testimony and Justice*. Oxon: Routledge.

McLachlan, F., & Harris, B., 2022. Intimate risks: Examining online and offline abuse, homicide flags, and femicide. *Victims & Offenders*, 17 (5), pp. 623–646.

McNamara, P., 2008. Changed forever: Friends reflect on the impact of a woman's death through intimate partner violence. *Journal of Family Studies*, 14, pp. 198–216.

Millen, D., 1997. Some methodological and epistemological issues raised by doing feminist research on non-feminist women. *Sociological Research Online*, 2 (3), pp. 1–15.

Miller, L., 2009. Family survivors of homicide: I. Symptoms, syndromes, and reaction patterns. *The American Journal of Family Therapy*, 37 (1), pp. 67–79.

Monckton Smith, J., 2012. *Murder, Gender and the Media: Narratives of Dangerous Love*. London: Palgrave Macmillan.

Mullender, A., 2002. *Rethinking Domestic Violence: The Social Work and Probation Response*. Oxon: Routledge.

Norris, F. H., Ruback, R. B. & Thompson, M. P., 1998. Comparative distress levels of inner-city family members of homicide victims. *Journal of Traumatic Stress*, 11, pp. 223–242.

Pain, R., 2014. Everyday terrorism: connecting domestic violence and global terrorism. *Progress in Human Geography*, 38 (4), pp. 531–550.

Paoli, L., & Greenfield, V. A., 2013. Harm: A neglected concept in criminology, a necessary benchmark for crime-control policy. *European Journal of Crime, Criminal Law and Criminal Justice*, 21, pp. 359–377.

Pemberton, S., 2015. *Harmful Societies: Understanding Social Harm*. Bristol: Policy Press.

Pereira, A. R., Vieira, D. N. & Magalhães, T., 2013. Fatal intimate partner violence against women in Portugal: A forensic medical national study. *Journal of Forensic and Legal Medicine*, 20 (8), pp. 1099–1107.

Persons, R., 1990. Psychotherapist and widower. *The Psychotherapy Patient*, 6, pp. 71–80.

Petrosky, E., Blair, J. M., Betz, C. J., Fowler, K. A., Jack, S., & Lyons, B. H., 2017. Racial and ethnic differences in homicides of adult women and the role of intimate partner violence – United States, 2003–2014. *MMWR Morbidity and Mortality Weekly Report*, 66 (28), pp. 741–746.

Prigerson, H. G., Shear, M. K., Jacobs, S. C., Reynolds, C. F., Maciejewski, P. K., Davidson, J. R., Rosenheck, R., Pilkonis, P. A., Wortman, C. B., Williams, J. B., Widiger, T. A., Frank, E., Kupfer, D. J. & Zisook, S., 1999. Consensus criteria for traumatic grief. A preliminary empirical test. *The British Journal of Psychiatry*, 174, pp. 67–73.

Oakley, A., 1981. Interviewing women: a contradiction in terms? In: Roberts, H., ed. *Doing Feminist Research*. London: Routledge and Kegan Paul, pp. 30–61.

Radford, J., & Russell, E. H., 1992. *Femicide: The Politics of Woman Killing*. Buckingham: Open University Press.

Reibharz, S., 1983. Experiential research: A contribution to feminist theory. In: Bowes, G., & Klein, R. D., eds. *Theories of Women's Studies*. London: Routledge, pp. 162–192.

Riches, G., & Dawson, P., 1998. Spoiled memories: Problems of grief resolution in families bereaved through murder. *Mortality*, 3 (2), pp. 143–159.

Riger, S., Raja, S. & Camacho, J., 2002. The radiating impact of intimate partner violence. *Journal of Interpersonal Violence*, 17, pp. 184–205.

Rock, P., 1998. *After Homicide: Practical and Political Responses to Homicide*. Oxford: Clarendon Press.

Rynearson, E., 2013. *Retelling Violent Death*. United Kingdom: Taylor & Francis.

Saunders, B., Kitzinger, J. & Kitzinger, C., 2015. Anonymising interview data: Challenges and compromise in practice. *Qualitative Research*, 15 (5), pp. 616–632.

Shenton, A. K., 2004. Strategies for ensuring trustworthiness in qualitative research projects. *Education for Information*, 22, pp. 63–75.

Smith, D., 1990. *The Conceptual Practices of Power: A Feminist Sociology of Knowledge*. Boston, MA: Northeastern University Press.

Smith, S. G., Chen, J., Basile, K. C., Gilbert, L. K., Merrick, M. T., Patel, N., Walling, M. & Jain, A., 2017. *The National Intimate Partner and Sexual Violence Survey (NISVS): 2010–2012 State Report* [online]. Atlanta, GA: National Center for Injury Prevention and Control. Available at: https://stacks.cdc.gov/view/cdc/46305 [Accessed 17 January 2025].

Soares, R. R., 2006. The welfare cost of violence across countries. *Journal of Health Economics*, 25 (5), pp. 821–846.

Spencer, C. M., 2018. A meta-analysis of risk factors for intimate partner homicide: Examining male perpetration and female victimization [online]. Ph.D. thesis, Kansas State University. Available at: https://krex.k-state.edu/server/api/core/bitstreams/dbd914ee-c187-4cde-8f6f-73d9775e0cfc/content [Accessed 14 May 2024].

Spencer, C. M., & Stith, S. M., 2020. Risk factors for male perpetration and female victimization of intimate partner homicide: A meta-analysis. *Trauma, Violence & Abuse*, 21 (3), pp. 527–540.

Spencer, C. M., Stith, S. M. & Cafferky, B., 2022. What puts individuals at risk for physical intimate partner violence perpetration? A meta-analysis examining risk markers for men and women. *Trauma, Violence, & Abuse*, 23 (1), pp. 36–51.

Spungen, D., 1998. *Homicide: The Hidden Victims. A Guide for Professionals*. India: Sage Publications.

Stanley, L., & Wise, S., 1990. Method, methodology and epistemology in feminist research processes. In: Stanley, L., ed. *Feminist Praxis*. Oxon: Routledge, pp. 20–60.

Stanley, L., & Wise, S., 1993. *Breaking Out Again: Feminist Ontology and Epistemology*. Oxon: Routledge.

Stark, E., 2007. *Coercive Control: How Men Entrap Women in Personal Life*. New York: Oxford University Press.

Stark, E., 2018. Coercive control as a framework for responding to male partner abuse in the UK. In: Lombard, N., ed. *The Routledge Handbook of Gender and Violence*. Oxon: Routledge, pp. 15–27.

Stark, E., 2023. *Coercive Control: How Men Entrap Women in Personal Life*. 2nd ed. New York: Oxford University Press.

Stöckl, H., Devries, K., Rotstein, A., Abrahams, N., Campbell, J., Watts, C. & Moreno, C. G., 2013. The global prevalence of intimate partner homicide: A systematic review. *The Lancet*, 382(9895), pp. 859–865.

Stoetzler, M., & Yuval-Davis, N., 2002. Standpoint theory, situated knowledge and the situated imagination. *Feminist Theory*, 3 (3), pp. 315–333.

Stretesky, P. B., O'Connor Shelley, T., Hogan, M. J. & Prabha Unnithan, N., 2010. Sense-making and secondary victimization among unsolved homicide co-victims. *Journal of Criminal Justice*, 38, pp. 880–888.

Swanberg, J., & Logan, T., 2005. Domestic violence and employment: A qualitative study. *Journal of Occupational Health Psychology*, 10, pp. 3–17.

Toprak, S., & Ersoy, G., 2017. Femicide in Turkey between 2000 and 2010. *PLoS ONE*, 12 (8), pp. 1–16.

Treadwell, J., 2016. Z: Zemiology. In: Corteen, K., Morley, S., Taylor, P., & Turner, J., eds. *A Companion to Crime, Harm and Victimisation*. Bristol: Policy Press, pp. 172–173.

van Wijk, A., Van Leiden, I. & Ferwerda, H. 2017. Murder and the long-term impact on co-victims: A qualitative, longitudinal study. *International Review of Victimology*, 23 (2), pp. 1–13.

Vesper, J. H., & Cohen, L. J., 1999. Litigating posttraumatic stress disorder: Effects on the family. *Journal of Psychiatry and Law*, 27 (2), pp. 313–338.

Walklate, S., Fitz-Gibbon, K., & McCulloch, J., 2018. Is more law the answer? Seeking justice for victims of intimate partner violence through the reform of legal categories. *Criminology & Criminal Justice*, 18 (1), pp. 115–131.

Waugh, P., 1998. Postmodernism and feminism. In: Jackson, S., & Jones, G., eds. *Contemporary Feminist Theories*. Edinburgh: Edinburgh University, pp. 177–193.

Websdale, N., 1999. *Understanding Domestic Homicide*. Boston, MA: Northeastern University Press.

Wellman, A., 2017. Research on understanding the surviving families of homicide. In: Eeden-Moorefield, B. V., & Browning, S. W., eds. *Contemporary Families at the Nexus of Research And Practice*. Oxon: Routledge, pp.165–183.

Westmarland, N., 2001. The quantitative/qualitative debate and feminist research: A subjective view of objectivity [online]. *Qualitative Social Research*, 2 (1). Available at: http://dx.doi.org/10.17169/fqs-2.1.974 [Accessed 17 January 2025].

Williams, F., 1996. Postmodernism, feminism and the questions of difference. In: Parton, N., ed. *Social Theory, Social Change and Social Work: An Introduction*. Oxon: Routledge, pp. 61–76.

Wolf, M., Holt, V., Kernic, M., and Rivara, F., 2000. Who gets protection orders for intimate partner violence? *American Journal of Preventive Medicine*, 19, pp. 286–291.

2 Current Context

Introduction

This chapter begins by exploring the scale of intimate partner abuse and homicide before turning the reader's attention to the subject of victimology more broadly. It provides an overview of victimology literature by considering how victims and victimhood are understood and examining where the perspectives of co-victims fit within this field of study. In addition, it unpacks and deconstructs family, taking into account global perspectives which push the boundaries of Western nuclear families. This chapter covers legal responses situated within England and Wales relating to both offline and online harm. Finally, it establishes the theoretical framework for the book by introducing the topic of 'continuum thinking', with specific reference to the continuum of online-offline harm, relating this to the subject of intimate partner homicide.

Global Estimates

The problem of intimate partner abuse is endemic, with the extent being widespread and having global reach (Gregory et al., 2017a, 2017b; Rogers et al., 2023). Intimate partner abuse does not discriminate, affecting any age, culture, religion or socioeconomic group across the globe (García-Moreno et al., 2005; Gregory et al., 2017b; Pain, 2014; Rogers et al., 2023; Stark, 2007, 2023). It can be described as a chronic problem that has significant, far-reaching consequences (Gregory et al., 2017a). From the extensive research conducted in this area, we know it is a gendered crime which overwhelming impacts women (Stark, 2007, 2023). This is due to the pervasive patriarchal structural inequality which has manifested itself within the social, political, legal, economic and religious fabric of our societies worldwide (Dragiewicz & Lindgren, 2009; Dragiewicz et al., 2022; Johnson et al., 2019). However, others can also be affected by this crime (Rogers, 2020). It is estimated that 30% of women worldwide will experience abuse by an intimate partner in their lifetime (Gregory et al., 2017b; Smith et al., 2017). In England and Wals alone, this averages to around 6.6% of women (ONS, 2024). This abuse can involve a range of harmful behaviours perpetrated within an intimate or other relationship which

DOI: 10.4324/9781003464488-2

are of a physical, sexual, psychological, emotional, economic or coercive nature (Sardinha et al., 2022). Such behaviours can have lasting short-term and long-term consequences including physical injury, mental health concerns, unwanted pregnancies, sexually transmitted infections, etc., and can also result in death (Johnson et al., 2019; Rogers et al., 2023; Sardinha et al., 2022).

As such, intimate partner homicide has reached significant proportions worldwide (Spencer, 2018; Spencer & Stith, 2020; Stöckl et al., 2013). The rates of murder committed by an intimate partner are between 38–50% globally (Bacchus et al., 2018; Sardinha et al., 2022). Similarly, homicides of this nature disproportionately affect women with men primarily being identified as perpetrators (Johnson et al., 2019; Petrosky et al., 2017; Spencer, 2018; Spencer & Stith, 2020). Domestic homicide is still a term referred to when describing homicides involving the murder of an intimate or ex-partner and/or family member in England and Wales. This makes up around 65% of domestic homicides resulting in the death of a female victim (ONS, 2024). This equates to around 30% of all female homicide victims. Risk factors for intimate partner homicide have been investigated and will be discussed in more detail in Chapter 3. However, we know that not all perpetrators of intimate partner abuse will go on to commit homicide, and not all victims of intimate partner abuse will end up becoming victims of intimate partner homicide (Spencer, 2018). With that being said, the cost of intimate partner abuse and homicide is astronomical for governments, communities and the individuals affected (Walby, 2009; Sardinha et al., 2022).

Yet intimate partner abuse remains largely underreported by victims. This reluctance has been attributed to privacy concerns, a lack of confidence in the police and criminal justice system, and a fear of reprisal (Johnson, 2006; Monckton Smith, 2012; Monckton Smith et al., 2014; Stark, 2007, 2023). Furthermore, there is no means of recording reliable data for the prevalence of intimate partner abuse in England and Wales but the Crime Survey for England and Wales (CSEW) provides a glimpse into the scale of this problem (Bradbury-Jones & Taylor, 2013). When these figures are placed alongside the current estimates for male victims, the gendered nature of intimate partner abuse is lost. As such, the aforementioned statistics do not consider the context and impact of the abuse being experienced. Factors such as fear, repeat victimisation, power and control fail to be considered (Dobash & Dobash, 2004; Duggan, 2018; Hester, 2013; Myhill, 2015, 2017; Walby & Allen, 2004; Walby & Towers, 2017). With these factors in mind, the gendered nature of intimate partner abuse becomes evident.

It must be noted that this same criticism can be applied to fatal domestic abuse. Many intimate partner homicides are not classified in this manner and therefore go unnoticed (Monckton Smith et al., 2014), instead perhaps being misidentified as car accidents, suicides/suicide pacts, accidents and drug abuse (Ferguson & McKinley, 2019; Monckton Smith et al., 2014). Moreover, data collection in terms of intimate partner homicides globally has encountered problems, meaning comparative analysis is not possible (Sardinha et al., 2022).

For instance, South East Asia, Africa and the region of the Americas do not have the same homicide reporting mechanisms as the UK, resulting in large amounts of missing information about victim-perpetrator relationships (Stöckl et al., 2013). Similarly, prevalence rates of intimate partner homicide do not take into account attempted homicides (Spencer & Stith, 2020) or suicides which are a direct result of coercive control.

Theoretical Perspectives

Conceptualising Victims and Victimhood

The term 'victim' can be conceptualised in a number of different ways depending on who this relates to and who identifies someone as a victim. At its very basic level, a victim is someone who has experienced hurt, damage or been killed as a result of the actions of another individual(s) or something else such as an illness or a situation outside their control (Cambridge Dictionary, 2025). A victim's experience can be extensive and complex given the power relations that surround who is considered a victim, who secures the 'victim' label, and therefore who obtains victim status (McGarry & Walklate, 2015). Victimhood is arguably a highly debated topic. The term 'victim' is also gendered, particularly in French, where is it associated with being female. As such, feminists have made attempts to move away from the feminine label this term denotes as it suggests notions of powerlessness and passivity. Instead, they have adopted the term 'survivor' rather than 'victim' (McGarry & Walklate, 2015). However, using this binary either/or approach when it comes to victimhood suggests the process is static which is not necessarily the case (Boyle, 2018; Walklate et al., 2011). For example, Kelly et al. (1996) and Boyle (2018) have proposed that we consider victimisation and survival on a continuum rather than as binary "all-consuming identities" (Boyle, 2018: 26). Furthermore, this continuum should not be deemed one-way nor should it be considered sequential as victimisation and survival are more dynamic processes than this way of thinking (Boyle, 2018). It must be noted, though, that this discussion relates to women and girls' understanding of victimisation and survival of male violence.

Until recently the term 'victim' was not linked with crime, instead being regarded more generally with experiences of misfortune (Dignan, 2005; Furedi, 2013). With that being said, the word is problematic in criminal justice settings as it denotes innocence in the same way the term 'perpetrator' assigns guilt, when neither can be determined until the final outcome has been judged by criminal justice processes. This is certainly true when it comes to legal constructions of victimhood (McGarry & Walklate, 2015). Strobl (2010) has devised four ways in which victimhood could be conceptualised including: the actual victim (someone who regards themselves a victim and is regarded a victim by others), the non-victim (someone who does not regard themselves as a victim and is not regarded a victim by others), the rejected victim (someone who regards themselves as a victim but is not regarded a victim by others), and the designated victim (someone who does not regard themselves as a victim but is regarded a victim by others). Strobl's work shows that in addition to power relations, choice and gender, there is a process in which a victim is recognised. This process is dependent on how victims achieve recognition and who is involved in this process. This, therefore, has a significant impact on understandings of victim status and whether or not this is accurately depicted, particularly in policy (McGarry & Walklate, 2015).

An Overview of Victimology

Similar to criminology, victimology has not followed the same direction in every country. Nor has it advanced at the same rate. This also speaks to legislation in different countries across the world where some are much more developed than others (Fattah, 2000). Moreover, there are significant differences in terms of the study of victimology, where both qualitative and quantitative research methodologies have been used to investigate the discipline (Fattah, 2000). Arguably, Mendelsohn and Von Hentig have made the most significant contribution to this discipline, with Von Hentig moving beyond the one-dimensional study of perpetrators and proposing equal consideration to both the perpetrator and victim; and Mendelsohn being more concerned with culpability (Mendelsohn, 1956; McGarry & Walklate, 2015; Von Hentig, 1940/41). Von Hentig also suggested that the victim could have a motivational or functional role in their victimisation, with empirical studies following his publication on topics such as criminal homicide (Fattah, 1971; Wolfgang, 1958) and rape (Amir, 1971) to name a few.

After this point, the term victimology was conceived and more books and articles were written elevating the discipline (Rock, 1994; Wertham, 1949). As with many studies at this time, the assumption was that the perpetrator was male, heterosexual, white and middle-class. According to Von Hentig, the victim fell into one of the following groups: the elderly, the disabled or they were likely from a minority group. Mendelsohn (1956) suggested that the victim was an individual who could not be held responsible for their victimisation. As men were not considered vulnerable, they failed to meet the criteria for assignation of the 'victim' label and, as such, were not deemed victims. This larger discourse around culpability was regarded as victim blaming, with these practices being what feminists were most concerned with questioning (McGarry & Walklate, 2015). Largely speaking, there are four competing victimology narratives which seek to understand victimhood, including positivist victimology, radical victimology, critical victimology and cultural victimology (McGarry & Walklate, 2015).

While a brief account of each of these narratives is considered below, with the focus of this book being co-victims of intimate partner homicide, it aligns mostly with cultural victimology. The reason for its links to cultural victimology is that it foregrounds the experiences of victims in trauma, harm and power (Ferrell et al., 2008; McGarry & Walklate, 2015). It also bolsters the importance of making sense of victimisation, which is particularly important when considering co-victim narratives relating to intimate partner homicide (Ferrell et al., 2008; Hall, 2017; McGarry & Walklate, 2015).

Positivist Victimology

The term positivist victimology was first conceptualised in the 1980s and focuses on identifying factors contributing to victimisation, specifically concerning interpersonal violence (Miers, 1989). Its core is the notion that the victim may have caused their own victimisation in some way (McGarry & Walklate, 2015; Tapley & Davies, 2020). Hindelang et al. (1978) were increasingly interested in how lifestyle could contribute to victimisation and examined this through early criminal victimisation surveys. Often these victimisation surveys were an attempt to understand routine ordinary encounters which resulted in criminal victimisation such as robberies and violence against women. Such surveys have now been expanded to consider more wide-scale victimisation by ascertaining the nature and extent of genocide (Hagan & Rymond-Richmond, 2009). As such, the efforts of positivist victimology have mostly been felt within policy.

However, its quantitative nature prevents it from leading to an understanding of the impact on the victim. Positivist victimology believes that the term 'victim' is free from issue as it is situated within criminal law. The law, therefore, provides a foundation for which the nature of victimisation can be understood and also conceptualises victimhood in both a national and international sense (McGarry & Walklate, 2015). Despite the meso- and macro-level value of positivist victimology, it fails to explain how the victim's experience is actualised, thereby enabling harsher punishments for the perpetrator. Furthermore, the victim's voice is often stifled and absorbed into this agenda, thereby restricting or removing autonomy. Lastly, as the law addresses society as a whole and is arguably fixed in its understanding of victims, it does not take into account power or power relations (Tapley & Davies, 2020). Positivist victimology therefore furthers this notion that the victim and perpetrator are binary entities, rather than on a continuum where their identities may overlap (Boyle, 2018; Miers, 2007). Consequently, it neglects understandings around why particular victimisation patterns occur, why it occurs in the form that it does and, what the nature of this victimisation looks like for those affected (McGarry & Walklate, 2015).

Radical Victimology

Radical victimology, steeped in the work of Mendelsohn (1956) and Quinney (1972), is concerned with illuminating the experiences of those considered invisible by positivism (McGarry & Walklate, 2015; Rafter & Walklate, 2012). This includes victims of state crimes, corporate or white-collar crimes and victims of persecution. Its human rights approach to victimology is in opposition to the legal perspectives involved in positivist discourse. For state crimes, in particular, key scholars such as Kauzlarich et al. (2001) and Rothe and Kauzlarich (2014) have considered victimology from a different stance, taking into account power and suffering, especially where victims are held responsible for their own victimisation. For radical victimologists, their thought processes stem from the nature of harm as the foundation for victimology, considering harms that result from the proliferation of systematic violence, power and vulnerability (McGarry & Walklate, 2015; Tapley & Davies, 2020). They are also more inclusive in terms of victim status and victimhood, including those who may not have previously been considered under this label (McGarry & Walklate, 2011). There is also an acknowledgement that often victims of white-collar or corporate crimes are ignorant of their victimisation, considering instead that their victimisation is a result of bad luck (Box, 1983). Geis (1973) has termed this "victim-responsiveness" which relates to the recognition of victimisation and victims' ability to respond to it. Generally speaking, this type of victimisation has not been the focus of victimologists with the incidence of white-collar or corporate crime often being hidden in plain sight (Walklate, 2007). With that being said, it has afforded victimisation being considered on a wider frame of reference, especially concerning mass atrocities (Letschert et al., 2011).

However, as radical victimologists are concerned with power and power relations, their analysis stems from 'the powerful' or the State meaning that individual choice is minimised (Rafter & Walklate, 2012). Alleged victimisation, which voices are heard, and whether or not the State is responsible for this victimisation is considered from the State's point of view first rather than from those victimised. As such, this influences who can be victimised and what counts as victimisation depending on victims' social standing and their position in relation to 'the powerful' (McGarry & Walklate, 2015).

Critical Victimology

Critical victimology has been considered and explained by different scholars in different ways (Fattah, 2000; Mawby & Walklate, 1994). This account explores the work of Walklate (1990) and Mawby and Walklate (1994), grounding its suppositions in line with feminist understandings of victimology. Different from positivist and radical victimology, it is concerned with the underlying processes that assign victimhood to seen or unseen victims who can be considered active or passive depending on the power they have and the choices they make (McGarry & Walklate, 2015). Critical victimology considers the term 'victim' and the ways in which it can be applied. This approach to victimology examines the structural processes enabling victimisation, giving credence to patterns of victimisation actualised by positivist victimology and recognising the interest of the State in reproducing these structural processes. This impacts who is considered a victim and who is able to adopt or resist this identity (Rock, 2002; Walklate, 2011). As previously mentioned, this is difficult to determine and cannot be understood by the quantitative work of positivist victimology.

Nevertheless, critical victimology has not taken into account that the traditional binary approach to the victim and perpetrator can be interchangeable where there is a link between the those who are victimised and those who have offended (Boyle, 2018; Spalek, 2006). There are also issues in suggesting individuals are oppressed when they do not view themselves as oppressed. In doing so, critical victimologists are assigning assumptions which do not match individuals assumptions of themselves (Andrews, 2002). Arguably, this perpetuates the very structural processes which exist to strip those victims of their victimhood (Spalek, 2006).

Cultural Victimology

This specialism follows the same course as criminology where culture has become an integral part of victimology, with cultural victimology focusing on human agency and being responsive to "symbolic display and shared emotion" (Ferrell et al., 2008: 190). As such, victimisation is seen as a performance where the individuals affected express grief, thereby giving meaning to the way in which their victimisation is conceptualised. This creates symbolic environments where the victims, their families and others involved can make sense of their experiences (Ferrell et al., 2008). Other scholars have made similar suppositions (Furedi, 1997; Quinney, 1972). In the first instance, cultural victimology has considered the whole experience of victimisation including its aftermath and how it is considered publicly. Secondly, it appreciates in what manner grief, loss and trauma are charted throughout the criminal justice process (Hall, 2017; McGarry & Walklate, 2015). 'Courting compassion' is one way in which this has been conceptualised (Walklate, 2012). As such, cultural criminology is the most suited to the study of co-victimisation given it allows for the entire victimisation experience to be considered. Moreover, it takes into account other important factors such as trauma, harm and power in terms of making sense of victimisation more broadly (Ferrell et al., 2008; Hall, 2017; McGarry & Walklate, 2015).

Cultural victimology can therefore inform how we conduct work with victim-survivors and which concepts might influence that work (McGarry & Walklate, 2015). If the subject of trauma is also considered, perhaps cultural victimology can provide the opportunity for a more creative and critical study of victims of crime. Cultural victimology's wide-ranging ideology allows for harm to be centralised, for politics and power relations to be taken into account, and for the silencing of particular victim groups to be called into question. It arguably broadens the remit of critical victimology in its recognition of the State and how victimhood is situated within this capitalist system. Lastly, it considers the role of the media in constructing legitimate victimhood and who this construction serves (McGarry & Walklate, 2015).

While this more inclusive subdiscipline is helpful in merging the deeper facets of culture into victimology, it is important that the skewed impacts of crime are not dismissed or minimised across different communities (Mythen & McGowen, 2017). Moreover, we cannot assume that everyone is a victim, nor can we hold everyone's experience of victimisation to the same level. The meanings victims ascribe to victimisation – even with similar crimes – will differ significantly depending on demographic differences, prior experience and other factors (Mythen & McGowen, 2017). Fear of crime and the risks associated with victimisation still exist regardless of whether an individual is victimised or not. It is also important to recognise that the cultural dimension considered as part of this subdiscipline is not a magic formula through which victimisation experiences can be unpicked. Similar criticisms have been considered in line with cultural criminology (Hayward, 2016). These critiques have suggested that cultural criminology simply 'reinvents the wheel', thereby neglecting the very basis from which cultural studies are built (O'Brien, 2005). Cultural victimology should therefore encompass social, economic, political, geographical and technological factors in its approaches to victimology, with a caveat that "no solitary fix ... can be added to reinvigorate extant understandings of the victim" (Mythen & McGowen, 2017: 376).

Feminism and Victimology

Feminism seeks to disrupt the androcentric nature of victimology from which this discipline is based (McGarry & Walklate, 2015). Its one-dimensional approach to victimology, concerning the white heterosexual male, has left room for other interpretations of victimology which are considered more inclusive. As such, feminism recognises the concept of power in patriarchy highlighted by radical victimology and underpins critical victimology by emphasising an appreciation of how structure and context can play a part in our ability to see (or not see) particular victim groups (McGarry & Walklate, 2015). Despite the drawbacks to positivist victimology, victimisation surveys have enabled the nature and extent of victimisation of concern to feminists to be highlighted, including rape and domestic abuse (McGarry & Walklate, 2015). However, the methodology involved in criminal victimisation surveys is still problematic in terms of the victimisation counted. Again, this relates to who is considered a victim, what counts as victimisation and what happens to the data collected (Walklate, 2014).

Feminism also highlights the types of victimisation experienced by women which often remain hidden due to underreporting (Spalek, 2006). Furthermore, it concerns women's agency, stressing the importance of how women manage and resist their experiences of harm. Feminism considers women as more than just 'victims', instead considering them as active beings pushing back against the very conditions that victimise them (Spalek, 2006).

Yet, much of the work concerning feminism and victimology has considered white European perspectives (Spalek, 2006). This has neglected other groups of women including those from the Black community (Harris, 1997). As such, other structural inequalities related to race, class and culture have been omitted from much of this discourse (Mama, 2000). There needs to be an appreciation of ethnicity and cultural diversity in terms of victimisation to fully understand the spectrum of experiences. Postmodern feminism seeks to be more inclusive by considering this range of experiences rather than discussing the experiences of women more generally (Walklate, 2001).

Constructing the 'Ideal' Victim

At this point, it is important to consider Nils Christie's (1986) concept of the "ideal victim", drawing attention to who does or does not fit this label. Generally speaking, Christie suggested that either younger or older women tended to fit this characterisation, with the supposed 'ideal' perpetrator being considered a stranger. This is often what is reflected in rape cases. However, more often than not the perpetrator is someone known to the victim (Brooks-Hay, 2019). With that being said, this 'ideal' scenario continues to be perpetuated and is influential across cultures and societies in different parts of the world (McGarry & Walklate, 2015). Christie's concept attempts to acknowledge and explain a process, reinforced by assumptions, which results in some individuals being considered victims while others are not. If the victim label is obtained, victimisation is considered legitimate and is acknowledged by others. This thus allows victim status to be acquired, enabling those with such status to enjoy the benefits attributed to victimhood (McGarry & Walklate, 2015; Bradford-Clarke et al., 2022; Van Wijk, 2013).

The effectiveness of this concept has been considered in relation to international crimes. Van Wijk (2013) has stated that this concept can be applied within this context but that there is also a parallel process which takes place in terms of acknowledging victimisation. As such, victims of international crimes can only be assigned victim status when their victimisation is considered by the media. As readership is paramount, programmes or articles need to be easily understood. The conflict involved needs to be considered unique and short-lived, and timing is hugely important as the audience can only pay attention to a small number of conflicts at one time (Van Wijk, 2013). Van Wijk's (2013) work resonates with earlier discussions on victimhood considered by Furedi (1997). Within this discourse, there are clear ideas around 'innocence', 'legitimacy' and 'credibility' in terms of victimisation and the ability to acquire victim status. Carrabine et al. (2004) went further to discuss this notion of a 'hierarchy of victimisation' where some individuals are considered more deserving of victim status than others. For example, sex workers tend to be considered nearer the bottom of this hierarchy than others because of their employment, the assumption being that they put themselves in harm's way and therefore should not be considered legitimate victims (McGarry & Walklate, 2015). Vulnerability also plays a part here where some individuals are presumed to be more vulnerable than others based on their body, such as in the case of the elderly or infirm (Spencer, 2014). However, this is a one-dimensional view of vulnerability and can negatively impact how we understand victimhood (Walklate, 2011). Therefore, victimhood and the ability to ascertain victim status is a complicated process on both an individual and group level, with culture being a key factor within this process (McGarry & Walklate, 2015).

However, there are some drawbacks to Christie's (1986) influential work. For example, in discussing the *potential givers of victim status*, he is unclear in regards to who these individuals are by referring to them as 'us' or 'we', suggesting it is the 'social system' within a country that determines victim status (Van Wijk, 2013). Regardless of whether this 'social system' works on a local or national level, there are often competing perspectives within any given social system. Furthermore, if the inference is society as a whole, it is clear we do not speak with one voice. There are differences in privilege, culture, politics and opportunity preventing all voices from being heard equally (Van Wijk, 2013). The perspective of potential givers of victim status can also change over time depending on conflict or the legitimacy of victim status being reconsidered at a later date following an atrocity. Furthermore, the term 'victim' is non-specific meaning that is can be applied to a wide range of misfortunes and, as such, emphasises the interpretive process associated with conceptualising crime victims (Bradford-Clarke et al., 2022). Arguably, being labelled a 'victim' does not necessarily compute on the individual level, instead being considered a politicised notion to forward a punitive agenda, especially when considering right-wing reforms in the 1970s (Bradford-Clarke et al., 2022; Kenney, 2004).

Constructions of Family

The concept of 'family' is highly contested and could be considered indistinct (Holt, 2021). Arguably, defining 'family' is challenging as many definitions exist across different disciplines such as sociology and anthropology (Georgas et al., 2006). Families are defined by demographic characteristics such as class, culture, immigration status, religion, age and geographic area (i.e., urban/rural) (Crosbie-Burnett & Klein, 2009). A broad definition by the National Institute of Mental Health suggests 'family' is "a network of mutual commitment" (Pequegnat & Bray, 1997: 3). In addressing our understandings of 'family', it is important to consider whether we seek to describe or explain the purpose of 'family'. Similarly, we need to consider whether our explanations are deductive or inductive. For example, explanations may be applied to theories, or theories may be built as a result of interactions from diverse families. In applying explanations to theories, we need to decide if one or more than one theory should be considered within a framework. Using one or more theories to explain 'family' may be more inclusive than considering one overarching theory. Moreover, theoretical explanations too often consider one unit of analysis or one type of 'family', thereby homogenising all explanations and applying those to all 'family' types which can be unhelpful and reductionist (Crosbie-Burnett & Klein, 2009).

In the Western sense, 'family' can be considered synonymously with the 'nuclear' family which is steeped in patriarchal gender roles and always includes a mother, father and children (Georgas et al., 2006). From this outdated and incomplete view of 'family', Murdock (1949) suggested that the purpose of this social institution was sexual, economic, reproductive and educational. However, from a sociological point of view, Popenoe's (1988) went further by describing three important factors in the conceptualisation of 'family' including: (i) one adult and one dependant person, (ii) the parents being either same-sex or both sexes, and (iii) those in the relationship not necessarily being married. This construction of the 'family' was arguably more inclusive and modern. In the 'Majority World', 'family' or 'families' include grandparents, aunts, uncles and others non-related people, with the term 'Majority World' referring to the 90% of the population that falls outside of the Western world (Kağitçıbaşi, 1990, 1996). However, 'family' is more complicated than this as different societies across the world do not ascribe to one type of 'family'. This is very much dependent on culture. While the term 'family' is beneficial in a descriptive sense, it does not take into account the complexities considered as part of this "multifunctional institution" whereby cultural beliefs and meanings differ (Georgas et al., 2006: 5).

In the Global North, there have been generational changes to family structure over the past 50 years resulting in a shift in marriage, parenthood and life expectancy. Communities residing in the Global North are marrying later, sometimes choosing cohabitation over marriage, divorcing more often and living longer (Holt, 2021). This has all contributed to the changing structure and conceptualisation of 'family'. Legal constructions now encompass civil partnerships, same-sex marriage and reproductive advancements, thereby widening prior understandings of the term 'family' (Holt, 2021). Of course, understandings of 'family' differ significantly in non-Westernised communities. For example, it was the norm for polygynous families – one father with two or more wives/mothers – to exist in Islamic communities, although nowadays Islamic women are less inclined to enter into such a union. Similarly, in Nepal, Tibet and India, polyandrous families exist where one wife/mother marries two or more husbands/fathers. However, this is becoming less and less common due to the lack of women in these societies (Georgas et al., 2006; Pasternak et al., 1976). 'Family' for African Americans may involve the support of non-biological 'aunts', and Hispanic and Latino godparents are fundamental to 'family' in these communities (Crosbie-Burnett & Klein, 2009). Furthermore, deceased ancestors of Native Americans offer connection to previous generations, including tribal affiliations, histories, traditions and values which are considered essential for formulating identity (Swanson et al., 2022). In addition, advancements in reproductive medicine have enabled the use of sperm donors and surrogates which have further changed the landscape concerning 'family' or 'families' (Holt, 2021).

As outlined above, scholars in different disciplines have different definitions and understandings of family. For instance, sociologists consider 'family' as a social unit defined by social roles, hierarchical structure and pre-determined actions (Crosbie-Burnett & Klein, 2009; Holt, 2021). However, from a legal perspective, 'family' may be defined based on a group of individuals with rights supported by legislation relating to marriage, birth and death. For biologists, 'family' may be constructed of those biologically related to each other, whilst psychologists consider 'family' as those who are emotionally and cognitively linked even if deceased (Crosbie-Burnett & Klein, 2009; Holt, 2021). Anthropology, amongst other disciplines, has its own sources of reference for defining 'family' in addition to how knowledge is produced as part of this social institution (Crosbie-Burnett & Klein, 2009; Holt, 2021).

While newer conceptualisations of 'family' exist, *family criminology* reasserts the splitting of the discipline (Holt, 2021). Within the study of criminology, there have been attempts to go beyond the binary constructs of victim and perpetrator, and even further by considering models of criminology (e.g., the police), but this more inclusive approach to criminology is pointless if the discipline continues to be divided. Arguably, family criminology appreciates the challenges of criminology in recognising the importance of family, but by creating a new subdiscipline it places families apart from the larger discipline. This downplays and minimises the legitimacy of their knowledge as secondary or co-victims. It also follows the same thread as other subdivisions of criminology, and arguably victimology, where surviving relatives are considered irrelevant to the victim's experiences of harm.

Understanding the Family as Victims in Intimate Partner Homicide Cases

Victims' families' are considered a unique group of crime victims. Arguably, the term 'victim' is unhelpful and problematic as this terminology and the ideas associated with it restricts and limits the ability for this group to achieve full victim status (Bradford, 2019; Rock, 1998). Furthermore, there is a need to recognise how the victimisation of this group is socially constructed through interpretive and definitional processes, and how this reflects their location within the broader context of victimisation (Holstein & Miller, 1990; Kenney, 2004). It is important to remember that achieving the 'victim' label involves interpretive procedures whereby the term is not plainly applied. Instead, it is an "interactional activity that underpins victims' reality status", thereby becoming an inherent part of the social world, and represents that world itself (Holstein & Miller, 1990: 105). Moreover, defining victims as such in public discourse allows us to view them as "the dramatization of injury and innocence" (Holstein & Miller, 1990: 105). As discussed by Bradford (2019), the way in which crime victims are conceptualised is contingent on interactional processes that occur as a result of responses to them as part of their encounters with the criminal justice system. Kenney (2004: 230) suggests that "victim assignment practices" given by institutions, such as legal and therapeutic intervention providers, can perpetuate the "problem of helplessness", thus potentially having negative implications for victims interacting with criminal justice agencies.

As mentioned previously, co-victims of homicide cannot achieve full victim status given that the nature of their victimisation is 'indirect' (Bradford, 2019). With the 'direct' victim being murdered, the State becomes the "surrogate victim" where the harm perpetrated is handled as if the murder has occurred against the State (Amour, 2003: 519). As such, the processes co-victims of homicide endure are not clearly understood or expressed (Rock, 1998). Bradford (2019) argues that terminology is not in question here, but the symbolism around allocating the victim label, and therefore victim status, is of interest.

Research by Gekoski et al. (2013) and Casey (2011) suggests that co-victims of homicide are denied victim status by the interactional assignment processes allocated by the criminal justice system. It is also worth acknowledging that co-victims received little attention within the literature, history and empirical research until recently. This has influenced responses to them from an institutional and social perspective, with many remedies having the tendency to undermine their resilience post-homicide (Bradford, 2019).

It has already been established that the term 'victim' has a myriad of connotations which benefit or negate those perceived or not perceived in this way. Its passive portrayal discussed by McGarry and Walklate (2015) impedes those who have been impacted by crime. There is also a confusing element to this term given that the 'victim' has been murdered. This creates a misalignment in discourse for the police, criminal justice system and media (Bradford, 2019). Its generic and highly politicised nature often disregards the interests of 'victims', instead facilitating a particular political agenda (Kenney, 2004). Others have introduced the term 'secondary victims' which, again, constructs the impact experienced as *less than* the 'direct' victim (Bradford, 2019; Gekoski et al., 2013; Rock, 1998). Another term used to describe those bereaved by homicide is 'survivor' which, as previously mentioned, was introduced by feminist researchers (Boyle, 2018; McGarry and Walklate, 2015). Rock (1998) uses this term in his work, suggesting it empowers and enables autonomy in the adoption of a new identity for those who have lost a loved one to homicide. However, this conceptualisation calls into question who is empowering and enabling those affected by homicide. In an attempt to avoid the issues connected with these terms, this book adopts the term 'co-victims of intimate partner homicide', as it is more inclusive and suggests that the impact experienced by the 'direct' victim and 'co-victim' is comparable.

Legal Remedies to Domestic Abuse and Intimate Partner Homicide

There are a number of legislative and policy responses that are applicable to victims of crime in England and Wales. This section of the book seeks to outline these historical developments from the 1970s onwards to highlight the changes made to legislation once intimate partner abuse became a subject of public interest in the 1980s (Musgrove & Groves, 2007). It also underscores the gaps within legislation and policy when it comes to homicide and those who do not fit the usual 'victim' mould such as co-victims of intimate partner homicide.

Much civil and criminal legislation put in place since the 1970s and designed to support and protect women experiencing domestic abuse was incoherent, unclear and insufficient (Musgrove & Groves, 2007). Furthermore, little guidance was given to those expected to implement it. The two dominant pieces of legislation introduced to deal with the problem of domestic abuse extending to the mid-1990s were the *Domestic Violence and Matrimonial Proceedings Act 1976* (DVMPA) and the *Domestic Proceedings and Magistrates' Court Act 1978*. The DVMPA enabled judges to impose restrictions on one party from using violence against another and the *Domestic Proceedings and Magistrates' Court Act 1978* considered the financial support of one party by another (Graca, 2017). Although the DVMPA remit was on physical violence, as the name suggests, the legislation did extend beyond this to "threat(s) to sense of security" (Burton, 2022: 11). Similarly, the *Domestic Proceedings and Magistrates' Court Act 1978* also encompassed acts which transcended physical violence with its interpretation of molestation. Furthermore, the support provision available to victim-survivors under the later legislation also applied to cohabitees as well as spouses where violence was used or threatened (Burton, 2022).

Despite their attempts to improve the justice system's response to domestic abuse, both acts were insufficient in terms of their underlying rationale (Graca, 2017). This focus on the perpetrator intending to cause distress or harm to the victim(s) highlighted a lack of understanding regarding domestic abuse (Burton, 2022). Furthermore, the complexity of court orders was problematic. It was difficult to understand the rights of victim(s) and in what ways the law could protect them from future harm (Musgrove & Groves, 2007). Similarly, neither piece of legislation provided a legitimate power of arrest even for perpetrators who committed assault (Musgrove & Groves, 2007). With that being said, the DVMPA did allow for restraining orders or injunctions to be granted when a women was experiencing violence (Harwin & Barron, 2000). This meant that a power of arrest could be attached to court orders that were breached, but for injunctions there was a requirement for a warning letter to be sent to the home before an injunction order could go forward. This conflict of interest had clear implications for future harm in terms of victim(s) residing at this address. The *Domestic Proceedings and Magistrates' Court Act 1978* enabled magistrates to have the same jurisdictional rights as Crown Courts but they still did not have the power to sentence the perpetrator when court orders were breached (Bird, 1996).

Family Law Act 1996

In an attempt to address these concerns and consolidate existing legislation, the *Family Law Act 1996* was introduced and included a number of new measures to protect those experiencing domestic violence (Musgrove & Groves, 2007). These new measures included non-molestation orders which prohibited behaviours by the abusive partner, and occupation orders which supported the victim(s) in their own home (*Family Law Act 1996*). Occupation orders had the power to prevent the perpetrator from residing in the family home. While this was the first piece of legislation to clarify domestic violence and how it should be recognised in law, it did not consider every victim-survivor as equal. Couples who co-habited and those in same-sex relationships were not considered as part of this legislation. Moreover, until the *Family Law Act 1996* came into effect, civil remedies tended to be used for physical violence and this continued to be the case even after the implementation of this legislation (Burton, 2022). Around the same time the *Protection from Harassment Act 1997* was established, and though not directly linked to domestic violence, was an important addition to existing legislation. This act criminalised harassment, causing fear of violence, and breaching civil injunctions or restraining orders (Musgrove & Groves, 2007). However, the definitions of harassment and stalking within this statute proved unclear and did not fully appreciate the complexity of this type of abuse (Scarr & Kennedy, 2023).

Domestic Violence, Crime and Victims Act 2004

As part of the Labour government's plans to prioritise victims of domestic violence, the *Domestic Violence, Crime and Victims Act 2004* (DVCVA) was inaugurated to strengthen both general and domestic violence provision (Musgrove & Groves, 2007). It was also the first act to consider intimate partner homicide as a criminal offence under the umbrella of domestic violence (Home Office, 2004). The purpose of this legislation was to better support victims of domestic violence and enable better protection from the police and courts. Where previously legislation did not deem assault on an intimate partner an arrestable offence, this legislation did (Musgrove & Groves, 2007). Given that this law criminalised domestic violence more effectively, processes involved in procuring evidence had to follow the *Police and Criminal Evidence Act 1984*, which was then overtaken by the *Serious and Organised Crime and Police Act 2005*. It also bolstered civil law relating to domestic violence by enabling unmarried couples to have the same access to provision as married couples. This included those co-habiting, those who were in a relationship but did not share the same living space and same-sex couples (Musgrove & Groves, 2007). Moreover, it criminalised breaches of non-molestation orders.

However, the DVCVA did not provide a clear definition of domestic abuse and an intimate partner homicide offence was only recognisable when the defendant was a member of the same household and had frequent contact with the victim (Edwards, 2006; Home Office, 2004). This limited perpetrator accountability, particularly when considering online harm. Although subsequent intimate partner abuse and intimate partner homicide definitions have been outlined in the *Serious Crime Act 2015* and *Domestic Abuse Act 2021*, the initial components of the DVCVA made space for subjectivity, gaps and therefore contributed to a lack of understanding in future legislation. In addition, the DVCVA did not consider the needs of victim-survivors who may have immigration issues and therefore had no recourse to public funds. Nor did it consider the importance of suicide in the context of intimate partner abuse (Cadwallader & Kennedy, 2024; Musgrove & Groves, 2007). Moreover, it prevented co-victims from achieving legitimate victim status thereby impacting meaningful support (Reed & Caraballo, 2022).

Victims' Code

The *Code of Practice for Victims' of Crime* (Victims' Code) was issued as part of the *Domestic Violence, Crime and Victims Act 2004* which ensured all victims of crime were provided with access to services and a minimum standard for these services by organisations in England and Wales (Mawby, 2016; Ministry of Justice, 2020). This came into effect in 2006 with amendments to the Code expanding its remit in 2013 and 2015 (Clamp, 2022). This statute also developed a statutory Victims' Advisory Panel and a Victims' Fund, endorsed by fines and fixed penalties for motoring offences, to aid third sector agencies in managing the impact of serious offences. The Code was argued to be initiated as part of New Labour's 'rebalancing' agenda which ensured better services to victims and witnesses of crime (Walklate, 2012). However, this notion of 'rebalancing' was misplaced given that the adversarial system is set up with the perpetrator as a defendant against the State rather than the victim-survivor, and that *institutionally* the impact on the victim-survivor was considered irrelevant (Walklate, 2012).

While the implementation of the Code was and continues to be important, the specifics of the Code are not based in law, with any complaints being considered by individual criminal justice agencies (Hall, 2012). Essentially, victim-survivors of crime do not have a legal claim to rights except in specific circumstances (Walklate, 2012). Any unsatisfactory outcomes could be raised with an individual's MP who could then refer this on to the Parliamentary Commissioner for Administration for further investigation (Hall, 2012). However, where cases were escalated to this level, many were dismissed, citing that victims did not exhaust all complaint mechanisms available to them (Casey, 2008). At this time, a Victims and Witnesses Commissioner was also charged with monitoring the Victims' Code but victims of crime could not directly contact this individual with complaints (Home Office, 2006). Similar to Victims' Charters, the Code's ability to impose provisions was outside the remit of criminal justice processes. There were issues concerning the type of participation being allowed for victims of crime (Edwards, 2004). As per the Code, victims' opinions on the release of serious offenders were to be considered alongside parole board conditions placed on offenders' license and supervision (Hall, 2012). However, the Code tended to be occupied with service rights rather than the opinions of victims of crime and, as such, neglected victims' needs particularly relating to responses from the criminal justice system (Casey, 2008).

Domestic Homicide Reviews

Domestic Homicide Reviews (DHRs) were created under DVCVA and involve reviewing the circumstances in which a person has been killed due to violence, abuse or neglect from an intimate partner (Chantler et al., 2019; Home Office, 2016). Other countries have adopted the principles of DHRs using different terminology to describe them: e.g., Domestic Violence Fatality Review (DVFR) teams in the US and Domestic/Family Death Review panels/committees in Australia, New Zealand and Canada (Jones et al., 2024). These reviews became law in England and Wales with multi-agency conferences, referred to as Community Safety Partnerships (CSPs), being liable for creating crime reduction strategies at a local level (Chantler et al., 2019). DVFR in the US were established in 1990, with DHRs in England and Wales following two decades later (Pow et al., 2015; Jones et al., 2024). In April 2011, DHRs were made a requirement in Section 9 of the DVCVA, with a call for CSPs to undertake multi-agency reviews in cases of domestic homicide and produce a DHR in line with guidance from the Home Office (Home Office, 2016). In England and Wales, domestic homicide is a term that includes both intimate partner homicides and domestic homicides involving those aged 16 years and over (Home Office, 2016). This broader definition in England and Wales provides more scope than other countries, such as in Canada and the US where intimate partner homicides are only considered as part of DVFR (Dawson et al., 2017; Tolmie et al., 2017; Websdale, 2020). The review process includes acquiring written reports from agencies who engaged with the victim and/or perpetrator to explain the nature of contact, any assessments made relating to domestic violence/abuse, any support offered or referrals made to other agencies, and it is also necessary to speak with family and friends of the victim to obtain any additional information not known to agency professionals (Chantler et al., 2019). The rationale for DHRs is to identify lessons learnt to prevent future domestic homicides from occurring (Benbow et al., 2019).

However, due to each DHR being considered in its local constituency, it is difficult to consolidate and apply learning from further afield (Chantler et al., 2019). With that being said, some local areas have started to analyse groups of DHRs as a way of highlighting local learning. For example, the Home Office analysed 54 DHRs in 2013 and 40 DHRs in 2016 in a bid to highlight recommendations for best practice. Recommendations included better training for healthcare professionals, improvements to risk assessments, better provision for those with complex needs and better safeguarding practices especially in relation to children (Home Office, 2013, 2016). In 2014, an in-depth evaluation of 13 DHRs was conducted in the West Midlands, resulting in risk assessment, the use of Multi-Agency Risk Assessment Conferences (MARACs) in high-risk cases and information sharing being focused on in the analysis (Neville & Sanders-McDonagh, 2014). Similarly, 32 DHRs were analysed from England, highlighting contact with a GP, mental health, adult and child safeguarding, informal networks and risk assessments as central themes (Sharps-Jeffs & Kelly, 2016). More recently, media reports in conjunction with DHRs have been considered to identify risk, showing that 94% of cases involved the presence of stalking behaviour (Monckton-Smith et al., 2017). Jones et al. (2024) conducted similar research by examining DVFR/DHR recommendations, the impact of these recommendations and proposals for enhancing DVFR/DHR processes. As a result, they emphasised the importance of training and awareness, provision of services and inter-agency coordination, and recognising the impact of domestic homicides on children. However, as the notion of success can be conceptualised in different ways, it was difficult to evaluate successful outcomes for DHRs as they could fall outside of what is deemed a traditional successful outcome (Johnson & Stylianou, 2020; Jones et al., 2024). Furthermore, little training exists for implementing DVFR/DHR recommendations, meaning many are not reported as a priority (Jones et al., 2024).

Despite the positive implications of DHRs, they reportedly contain implementation inconsistencies, poor quality completion and have a lack of suitable services available for victims post-homicide (Boughton, 2021; Cadwallader & Kennedy, 2024; Chantler et al., 2019). Ethical considerations, specifically issues of anonymity, can be a cause for concern in terms of the production of DHRs, especially in view of insights gained (Jones et al., 2024). Furthermore, the quality of DHRs and the timeframes reviewed can differ significantly across the board (Chantler et al., 2019). In addition, case selection can be skewed whereby only one type of domestic homicide is reviewed, resulting in a lack of intersectionality (Dale et al., 2017). There also needs to be greater diversity in terms of older people, ethnic minorities and children; a finding echoed by a number of studies (Benbow et al., 2019; Bent-Goodley, 2013). Additionally, while DHRs were introduced under the DVCVA to make co-victims more visible, they are ineffectual when it comes to signposting or providing meaningful support for co-victims of intimate partner homicide, despite this being one of their main objectives (Boughton, 2021; Cadwallader & Kennedy, 2024; Chantler et al., 2019). A suggestion for a future alteration to DHRs is a change in the terminology to "domestic abuse fatality reviews" to ensure more inclusivity, especially where the victim has died by suicide in cases involving the presence of coercive control (Home Office, 2023).

Victims and Prisoners Bill 2015

The purpose of the *Victims and Prisoners Bill 2015* was to strengthen the rights of victims of crime, acknowledging a culture shift in terms of the way in which victims were viewed within the wider criminal justice system (Nickolls et al., 2023). It covered three overarching areas: victims of criminal conduct, victims of major incidents, and prisoners (*Victims and Prisoners Bill 2015*). This much anticipated bill was expected to provide accountability for victims in an attempt to improve their treatment by the criminal justice system, introduce an 'Independent Public Advocate' scheme to support victims at every stage of the criminal justice process, and make changes to parole system and parole board proceedings encouraging those with policing experience to sit on parole boards (Nickolls et al., 2023). There have been a number of criticisms of the bill, including the lack of engagement with the Victims' Code, thereby limiting the rights of victims (Victims' Commissioner, 2018, 2022); the expectation on victims to know their rights and act on them; and issues with the bill not going far enough to protect migrant victims (House of Commons Justice Committee, 2022).

In terms of this book, the most important amendment to the *Victims and Prisoners Bill* is related to the clause that explains what constitutes a 'victim' within the parameters of the law in England and Wales, expanding the current definition to include co-victims. This came with a caveat that more funding would likely be needed in order to meet the additional demands on services (Nickolls et al., 2023). As previous iterations did not include co-victims as victims of crime (House of Commons Justice Committee, 2022), this clause now acknowledges the impact on those bereaved by homicide and recognises them as legitimate victims within the remit of the law. The *Victims and Prisoners Bill* received royal assent in November 2024 making the bill an act of parliament.

Serious Crime Act 2015 *Amendment*

An amendment to the *Serious Crime Act 2015* was implemented to recognise and respond to those harms falling largely outside of the pre-existing framework for intimate partner abuse in England and Wales (Kelly & Westmarland, 2016; Munro et al., 2024; Strickland & Allen, 2017). The introduction of section 76 criminalised controlling or coercive behaviour in intimate or familial relationships (Munro et al., 2023; Strickland & Allen, 2017).

However, the statistics discussed earlier in this chapter (see 'Global Estimates') refer to 'any incident'; that a single incident of physical or psychological abuse equates to the same as a pattern of ongoing repeated abuse (Barlow et al., 2020; Boyle, 2018; Kelly & Westmarland, 2016; Myhill et al., 2022). This is further problematised by frontline police officer attitudes and understandings of coercive control (Barlow et al., 2020). Similarly, issues are often encountered at the prosecution stage, with victim withdrawal impacting report-to-charge ratios and attrition rates (Bettinson & Robson, 2020; Munro et al., 2024; Porter, 2020). With that being said, this change in legislation provided an acknowledgement that psychological and/or emotional abuse occurs within intimate and familial relationships and warrants a legitimate response.

Domestic Abuse Act 2021

The introduction of the *Domestic Abuse Act 2021* was a long-awaited change to law in England and Wales, seeking to create a statutory definition of domestic abuse which went beyond the physical elements of harm (Home Office, 2022). It also aimed to provide new civil responses to domestic abuse, including domestic abuse protection notices and protection orders; stop perpetrators from cross-examining their victims within civil and family court hearings; extend the remit of the coercive control offence to include post-separation; and create a new non-fatal strangulation offence, among others (Home Office, 2022).

The *Domestic Abuse Act 2021* includes a wider definition of intimate partner abuse, encompassing emotional, controlling/coercive and economic abuse, and has extended the offence to cover threats of 'revenge porn' (*Domestic Abuse Act 2021*). This expansion of the law shows increased understanding of modern intimate partner abuse, acknowledging issues of cyber/sexual abuse existing within intimate partner abuse, which has increased since the COVID-19 pandemic (Brudvig et al., 2020). However, it ignores the role of other forms of technology used to facilitate domestic abuse, such as smart home devices, banking applications or GPS locations used to stalk, gaslight or financially abuse loved ones, which are all prevalent forms of online harm (Brown et al.,

2018; Douglas et al., 2019; PenzeyMoog & Slakoff, 2021). It also includes new offences, which although common in intimate partner abuse, have not been considered offences until now: non-fatal strangulation (as mentioned earlier) and non-fatal suffocation (CPS, 2023). While these offences are considered as part of the *Domestic Abuse Act 2021*, they should be considered for all cases and not just those that are linked to intimate partner abuse. Nonetheless, the legislation does not define 'strangulation', 'strangles' or 'suffocation' so, again, this is open to interpretation (CPS, 2023).

Legal Responses to Online Harm

Since 2020, the UK government has attempted to respond to online harm using a number of different strategies including white and green papers, proposed legislation and acts of parliament. These responses have been outlined in the table below:

Table 2.1 UK Responses to Online Harm

Responses	*Overview*
Online Harms White Paper	Implementation of regulatory framework to discourage harmful behaviour overseen by an independent regulator.
Online Safety Bill	Establishment of statutory duties on user-to-user and search services (including illegal content) governed by Ofcom.
Online Safety Act	Introduction of a new regulatory framework which aims to make internet services safer in the UK.

Sources: Home Office, 2020, 2022; *Online Safety Act 2023*.

However, many of these legal remedies have been met with significant blowback and criticism. For example, the Online Harms White Paper did not address concerns relating to grey areas where content is considered harmful but legal, provided little detail in terms of the oversight of the regulator, and did not explore how it would fit with EU proposals following Brexit (Graydon, 2021; Martlew, 2019). Furthermore, it lacked rigor in terms of freedom of speech, placed faith in artificial intelligence for moderation and failed to provide a more concrete definition of harm (Graydon, 2021; Martlew, 2019). Similar conclusions were drawn from consultations regarding the Online Safety Bill especially in relation to what constitutes content and the problem of censorship (Chin-Rothmann, 2022; Popple, 2022; Sumption, 2022), with many suggesting that it would fail to provide meaningful safety online.

The subject of online safety continues to be criticised even with the introduction of the *Online Safety Act 2023*. The drawbacks of this legislation seemingly revolve around 'revenge pornography' or 'intimate image disclosure' where threats of or distribution of private sexual images to another person, without consent with the intention to cause harm, has been criminalised (Welsh, 2024). The sharing these images with the person featured in them has not been covered as yet. It has also not provided legal recourse for having these images removed from the online environment, which shows there is still a long way to go in terms of recognising and responding to online harms (Welsh, 2024).

Continuum Thinking and Intimate Partner Homicide

Given this book's feminist approach to co-victims of intimate partner abuse and homicide, it is important to establish a framework in which to situate the discussions relating to the following chapters (Chapters 3, 4 and 5). As such, this book draws on the notion of "continuum thinking" discussed by Boyle (2018) in which she makes use of Liz Kelly's (1988) work on the continuum of sexual violence and more recent research on the continuum of image-based sexual abuse (McGlynn et al., 2017). Kelly (1988) uses this conceptualisation of a continuum as a way to explore the range of sexual violence experienced by women in their lives, sometimes on multiple occasions. She places common forms of violence defined by men as acceptable (e.g., catcalling) on the same continuum as other forms of sexual violence (e.g., rape). Her continuum includes two component parts: first, it highlights that this continuum must involve a common character that underlies many different events; and second, it must also refer to a continuous series of events that progress on from one another and which cannot be differentiated. The common character described by Kelly includes abuse, intimidation, coercion, intrusion, threat and force men use to control women. These event(s) involving abuse or coercion cannot be clearly defined and there are no discrete categories into which men's behaviour can be placed.

Kelly's (1988) conceptualisation of a continuum was and continues to be revolutionary as it allows women to name and document the range of abuse they experience. This inclusive approach to sexual violence suggests that there is no straight line connecting the harmful experiences women have and that these experiences should not be considered within a hierarchy of harm. Instead, all experiences should be considered equally harmful as lots of women experience sexual violence on multiple occasions and those experiences considered more common (e.g., seeing sexual harassment as a bit of 'harmless fun') are also connected to other forms of harm which are criminalised (e.g., rape). Therefore, it is inappropriate to consider some forms of harm as more serious than others.

Similarly, McGlynn et al. (2017) argue that continuum thinking can also be conceptualised in relation to image-based sexual abuse. Firstly, she suggests that there is a myriad of practices which come under the umbrella term of image-based sexual abuse, and secondly that this type of abuse should be considered on a continuum with other types of sexual violence. Examples of these practices include all forms of non-consensual creation and/or distribution of private sexual images. McGlynn et al.'s (2017) rationale for replicating Liz Kelly's framework, within the remit of image-based sexual abuse, allows for both legislative and policy measures to be more comparable with the harms experienced by victim-survivors. It also has the potential to result in more effective approaches in terms of education and prevention of this type of harm (Hampton, 1998; McGlynn & Rackley, 2017; Salter & Crofts, 2015).

By the same token, this book reproduces Liz Kelly's continuum of sexual violence within the context of intimate partner homicide. With the aid of this framework, it helps us to better understand the harm experienced, the complexities of this harm, and also enables us to better inform policy and practice. It does this by utilising the continuum of online-offline harm which allows the harms that straddle both spaces to be recognised and documented within the same continuum (Munk & Kennedy, 2024). As such, existing offline harm risk factors associated with intimate partner homicide, such as coercive control, are discussed (Chapter 3). The chapter on emerging risk factors for intimate partner homicide, concerning online harm, then expands this remit (Chapter 4). It highlights that digital coercive control needs to be incorporated within the existing risk factor framework for intimate partner homicide. Only one study on intimate partner homicide has flagged this need, framing online harm as "homicide flags" (McLachlan & Harris, 2022: 629).

At this point, it is important to note that the events involving these risk factors cannot be separated as they amount to the full abusive experience, nor can they be placed into distinct categories as they constitute the 'web of abuse'. Events are not considered singular occurrences as often intimate partner abuse is a crime for which repeat victimisation is common (Barlow et al., 2018, 2019). In the same way that Kelly (1988) and Munk and Kennedy (2024) suggest that this connection is not linear, this could also be argued for intimate partner homicide as each abusive experience is unique to each victim but may share some commonalities. Furthermore, these risk factors should be considered equally serious as homicide is considered the final act. In subsequent chapters, the harms spanning the offline and online worlds are brought together to describe harms that overspill to the lives of co-victims of intimate partner homicide, particularly concerning victims' families. This unique perspective is discussed in Chapter 5, with Chapters 3 and 4 considering offline and online harms in more detail.

Conclusion

Researchers have previously discussed the subject of intimate partner abuse and homicide in great detail, particularly concerning the theoretical underpinnings of asymmetry and symmetry. This chapter does not seek to go over old ground but instead to situate these areas of focus within the larger discipline of victimology, locating the perspectives of co-victims. It provides a critical appraisal of the current prevalence of these respective areas and explores responses by the criminal justice system to both offline and online harms. Finally, it begins to unpack the approach of the following chapters by briefly discussing the continuum of online-offline harm.

References

Amir, M., 1971. *Patterns in Forcible Rape*. Chicago: University of Chicago Press.

Amour, M., 2003. Meaning making in the aftermath of homicide. *Death Studies*, 27 (6), pp. 519–540.

Andrews, M., 2002. Feminist research with non-feminist and anti-feminist women: Meeting the challenge. *Feminism and Psychology*, 12 (1), pp. 55–77.

Bacchus, L. J., Ranganathan, M., Watts, C. & Devries, K., 2018. Recent intimate partner violence against women and health: A systematic review and meta-analysis of cohort studies. *BMJ Open*, 8, doi: 10.1136/bmjopen-2017-019995.

Barlow, C., Walklate, S., Johnson, K., Humphreys, L. & Kirby, S., 2018. *Police Responses to Coercive Control* [online]. N8 Policing Research Partnership. Available at: https://documents.manchester.ac.uk/display.aspx?DocID=56477 [Accessed 24 March 2025].

Barlow, C., Johnson, K., Walklate, S. & Humphreys., 2020. Putting coercive control into practice: Problems and possibilities. *British Journal of Criminology*, 60 (1), pp. 160–179.

Benbow, S. M., Bhattacharyya, S. & Kingston, P., 2019. Older adults and violence: An analysis of domestic homicide reviews in England involving adults over 60 years of age. *Ageing and Society*, 39 (6), pp. 1097–1121.

Bent-Goodley, T. B., 2013. Domestic violence fatality reviews and the African American community. *Homicide Studies*, 17 (4), pp. 375–390.

Bettinson, V., 2019. Aligning partial defences to murder with the offence of coercive or controlling behaviour. *Journal of Criminal Law*, 83 (1), pp. 71–86.

Bettinson, V., & Robson, J., 2020. Prosecuting coercive control: Reforming storytelling in the courtroom. *Criminal Law Review*, pp. 1107–1126.

Bird, R., 1996. *Domestic Violence the New Law: Part IV of the Family Law Act 1996*. Bristol: Jordan Publishing.

Boughton, G. A., 2021. Investigating investigations: A critical evaluation of the England and Wales Domestic Homicide Review (DHR) process [online]. Ph.D. thesis, University of South Wales. Available at: https://pure.southwales.ac.uk/ws/portalfiles/portal/10052830/Final_PhD_Thesis_GraceBoughton_10_August_2022.pdf [Accessed 10 March 2025].

Box, S., 1983. *Power, Crime and Mystification*. London: Tavistock.

Boyle, K., 2018. What's in a name? Theorising the inter-relationships of gender and violence. *Feminist Theory*, 20(1), pp. 19–36.

Bradbury-Jones, C., & Taylor, J., 2013. Domestic abuse as a transgressive practice: Understanding nurses' responses through the lens of abjection. *Nursing Philosophy*, 14 (4), pp. 295–304.

Bradford, L., 2019. Hidden victims: The criminal justice experiences of homicide bereaved people in England and Wales [online]. Ph.D. thesis, The University of Sheffield. Available at: https://etheses.whiterose.ac.uk/27009/1/PhD%20L%20Bradford.pdf [Accessed 12 March 2024].

Bradford-Clarke, L., Davies, R. & Henley, A., 2022. When "ideal victim" meets "criminalised other': Criminal records and the denial of victimisation. *Probation Journal*, 69 (3), pp. 353–372.

Brooks-Hay, O. 2019. Doing the "right thing"? Understanding why rape victim-survivors report to the police. *Feminist Criminology*, 15 (2), pp. 174–195.

Brown, M. L., Reed, L. A. & Messing, J. T., 2018. Technology-based abuse: Intimate partner violence and the use of information communication technologies. In: Vickery, J. R., & Everbach, T., eds. *Mediating Misogyny: Gender, Technology, and Harassment*. Cham: Springer International Publishing, pp. 209–227.

Brudvig, I., Chair, C. & van der Wilk, A., 2020. *Covid-19 and Increasing Domestic Violence Against Women: The Pandemic of Online Gender-Based Violence* [online]. Washington, DC: World Wide Web Foundation. Available at: https://webfoundation.org/docs/2020/07/WWWF-Submission-COVID-19-and-the-increase-of-domestic-violence-against-women-1.pdf [Accessed 17 March 2025].

Burton, M., 2022. *Domestic Abuse, Victims and the Law*. Oxon: Routledge.

Cadwallader, M., & Kennedy, M. C., 2024. When cyberspace turns deadly: The significance of online harassment in intimate partner homicide. In: Munk, T., & Kennedy, M. C., eds. *Victimisation in the Digital Age: An Online-Offline Continuum Approach*. London: Routledge, pp. 151–168.

Cambridge Dictionary, 2025. Victim [online]. Available at: https://dictionary.cambridge.org/dictionary/english/victim [Accessed 19 January 2025].

Carrabine, E., Iganski, P., Lee, M., Plummer, K. & South, N., 2004. *Criminology: A Sociological Introduction*. Oxon: Routledge.

Casey, L., 2008. *Engaging Communities in Fighting Crime* [online]. London: Cabinet Office. Available at: https://www.safercommunitiesscotland.org/wp-content/uploads/engaging-communities-in-fighting-crime.pdf [Accessed 20 February 2024].

Casey, L., 2011. *Review into the Needs of Families Bereaved by Homicide* [online]. London: Victims' Commissioner. Available at: https://samm.org. /wp-content/uploads/2021/01/Review-needs-of-families-bereaved-by-homicide.pdf [Accessed 19 January 2025].

Chantler, K., Robbins, R., Baker, V., & Stanley, N., 2019. Learning from domestic homicide reviews in England and Wales. *Health & Social Care in the Community*, 28 (2), pp. 485–493.

Chin-Rothmann, C., 2022. *The United Kingdom's Online Safety Bill Exposes a Disinformation Divide* [online]. Washington, DC: Center for Strategic and International Studies. Available at: https://www.csis.org/analysis/united-kingdoms-online-safety-bill-exposes-disinformation-divide [Accessed 19 January 2025].

Christie, N., 1986. The ideal victim. In: Fattah, E. A., ed. *From Crime Policy to Victim Policy*. London: Palgrave Macmillan, pp. 17–30.

Clamp, K., 2022. *RJ and the Code of Practice for Victims of Crime: A Scoping Review of Service Provision in England and Wales* [online]. Nottingham: University of Nottingham. Available at: https://www.aarj.org.au/wp-content/uploads/2022/05/PCC-research-report-FINAL.pdf.

Crosbie-Burnett, M., & Klein, D. M., 2009. The fascinating story of family theories. In: Bray, J. H. & Stanton, M., eds. *The Wiley-Blackwell Handbook of Family Psychology*. Chichester, West Sussex: Wiley-Blackwell, pp. 37–52.

Crown Prosecution Service (CPS), 2023. *Strangulation and Suffocation* [online]. London: CPS. Available at: https://www.cps.gov.uk/legal-guidance/strangulation-and-suffocation#:~:text=This%20offence%20applies%20where%20strangulation,as%20impeded%20breathing%20or%20circulation [Accessed 17 March 2025].

Dale, M., Celaya, A. & Mayer, S., 2017. Ethical conundrums in the establishment and operation of domestic/family violence fatality reviews. In: Dawson, M., ed. *Domestic Homicides and Death Reviews: An International Perspective*. London: Palgrave Macmillan, pp. 229–256.

Daly, M., & Wilson, M., 1998. The evolutionary social psychology of family violence. In: Crawford, C., & Krebs, D., eds. *Handbook of Evolutionary Psychology: Ideas, Issues and Applications*. Mahwah, NJ: Lawrence Erlbaum, pp. 431–456.

Dawson, M., Shanaaz Mathews, S., Abrahams, N. & Campbell, J., 2017. Death reviews in the context of domestic homicide in low- to middle-income countries: South Africa as a case study. In: Dawson, M, ed. *Domestic Homicides and Death Reviews: An International Perspective*. London: Palgrave Macmillan, pp. 345–372.

Dignan, J., 2005. *Understanding Victims and Restorative Justice*. Buckinghamshire: Open University Press.

Dobash, R. P. & Dobash, R. E., 2004. Women's violence to men in intimate relationships: Working on a puzzle. *British Journal of Criminology*, 44 (3), pp. 324–349.

Domestic Abuse Act 2021 (c. 17).

Douglas, H., Harris, B. A. & Dragiewicz, M., 2019. Technology-facilitated domestic and family violence: Women's experiences. *British Journal of Criminology*, 59, pp. 551–570.

Dragiewicz, M., & Lindgren, Y., 2009. The gendered nature of domestic violence: Statistical data for lawyers considering equal protection analysis. *American University Journal of Gender, Social Policy & the Law*, 17 (2), pp. 229–268.

Dragiewicz, M., Woodlock, D., Salter, M. & Harris, B., 2022. "What's mum's password?": Australian mothers' perceptions of children's involvement in technology-facilitated coercive control. *Journal of Family Violence*, 37, pp. 137–149.

Duggan, M., 2018. Victim hierarchies in the Domestic Violence Disclosure Scheme. *International Review of Victimology*, 24 (2), pp. 199–217.

Edwards, I., 2004. An ambiguous participant: The crime victim and criminal justice decision-making. *The British Journal of Criminology*, 44 (6), pp. 967–982.

Edwards, S., 2006. More protection for victims of domestic violence? (The Domestic Violence, Crime and Victims Act 2004). *The Denning Law Journal*, 18 (1), pp. 243–260.

Family Law Act 1996 (c.33 & c.42)

Fattah, E. A., 1971. *La Victime est-elle coupable?* Montréal: Presses de l' Université de Montréal.

Fattah, E. A., 2000. Victimology: Past, present and future. *Criminologie*, 33 (1), pp. 17–46.

Ferguson, C., & McKinley, A., 2019. Detection avoidance and mis/unclassified, unsolved homicides in Australia. *Journal of Criminal Psychology*, 10 (2), pp. 113–122.

Ferrell, J., Hayward, K. & Young, J., 2008. *Cultural Criminology*. London: Sage.

Furedi, F., 1997/2002. *Culture of Fear: Risk Taking and the Morality of Low Expectation*. London: Cassell.

Furedi, F., 2013. *Moral Crusades in an Age of Mistrust*. London: Palgrave-Pivot.

García-Moreno, C., Jansen, H., Ellsberg, M., Heise, M. & Watts, C., 2005. *WHO Multi-country Study on Women's Health and Domestic Violence Against Women* [online]. Geneva: World Health Organization. Available at: chrome-extension://efaidnbmnnnibpcajpcglclefindmkaj/file:///C:/Users/morag/Downloads/924159358X_eng.pdf [Accessed 18 January 2025].

Graydon, F., 2021. *A Brief Critical Analysis of the Online Harms White Paper 2020* [online]. Nottingham: KCH Garden Square. Available at: https://kchgardensquare.co.uk/wp-content/uploads/2022/02/A-brief-critical-analysis-of-the-Online-Harms-White-Paper-2020.pdf [Accessed 19 January 2025].

Geis, G., 1973. Victimisation patterns in white collar crime. In: Drapkin, I., & Viano, E., eds. *Victimology: A New Focus*. Lexington, MA: D. C. Heath and Co., pp 86–106.

Gekoski, A., Adler, J. R. & Gray, J. M., 2013. Interviewing women bereaved by homicide: Reports of secondary victimisation by the criminal justice system. *International Review of Victimology*, 19 (3), pp. 307–329.

Graca, S., 2017. Domestic violence policy and legislation in the UK: A discussion of immigrant women's vulnerabilities. *European Journal of Current Legal Issues*, 22 (1), pp. 1–34.

Georgas, J., Berry, J. W., Van der Vijver, F. J. R., Kağitçıbaşi, C. & Poortinga, Y. H., 2006. *Families Across Cultures: A 30-Nation Psychological Study*. Cambridge: Cambridge University Press.

Gregory, A. C., Williamson, E., & Feder, G., 2017a. The impact on informal supporters of domestic violence survivors: A systematic literature review. *Trauma, Violence, & Abuse*, 18 (5), pp. 562–580.

Gregory, A., Feder, G., Taket, A., & Williamson, E., 2017b. Qualitative study to explore the health and well-being impacts on adults providing informal support to female domestic violence survivors. *BMJ Open*, 7, doi: doi: 10.1136/bmjopen-2016-014511.

Hagan, J., & Rymond-Richmond, W., 2009. *Darfur and the Crime of Genocide*. Cambridge: Cambridge University Press.

Hall, M., 2012. *Victims of Crime: Policy and Practice in Criminal Justice*. Oxon: Routledge.

Hall, M., 2017. Victims of crime: Culture, politics and criminal process in the 21st century. *Northern Ireland Legal Quarterly*, 68 (4), pp. 469–490.

Hampton, J., 1998. Punishment, feminism, and political identity: A case study in the expressive meaning of the law. *Canadian Journal of Law and Jurisprudence*, 11 (1), pp. 23–45.

Harris, A., 1997. Race and essentialism in feminist legal theory. In: Wing, A., ed. *Critical Race Feminism*. New York: New York University Press, pp. 11–18.

Harwin, N., & Barron, J., 2000. Domestic violence and social policy: Perspectives from Women's Aid. In: Hanmer, J., Itzin, C., Quaid, S., Wigglesworth, D., eds. *Home Truths About Domestic Violence: Feminist Influences on Policy and Practice: A Reader*. Oxon: Routledge, pp. 205–227.

Hayward, K. J., 2016. Cultural criminology: Script rewrites. *Theoretical Criminology*, 20 (3), pp. 297–321.

Hester, M., 2013. Who does what to whom? Gender and domestic violence perpetrators in English police records. *European Journal of Criminology*, 10, pp. 623–637.

Hindelang, M. J., Gottfredson, M. R. & Garofalo, J., 1978. *Victims of Personal Crime: An Empirical Foundation for a Theory of Personal Victimisation*. Cambridge, MA: Ballinger.

Holstein, J. A., & Miller, G., 1990. Rethinking victimization: An interactional approach to victimology. *Symbolic Interaction*, 13 (1), pp. 103–122.

Home Office, 2004. *The Domestic Violence, Crime and Victims Act 2004* [online]. London: Home Office. Available at: https://www.legislation.gov.uk/ukpga/2004/28/contents [Accessed 10 March 2025].

Home Office, 2006. *Rebalancing the Criminal Justice System in Favour of the Law Abiding Majority: Cutting Crime, Reducing Reoffending and Protecting the Public* [online]. London: Home Office. Available at: https://crimeline.co.uk/wp-content/uploads/2019/12/Rebalancing-the-CJS-in-favour-of-the-law-abiding-majority.pdf [Accessed 10 March 2025].

Home Office, 2013. *Domestic Homicide Reviews: Common Themes Identified as Lessons to be Learned* [online]. London: Home Office. Available at: https://data.parliament.uk/DepositedPapers/Files/DEP2013-1881/Domestic_Homicide_Review_-_Common_themes_v2__2_.pdf [Accessed 17 March 2025].

Home Office, 2016. *Multi-Agency Statutory Guidance for the Conduct of Domestic Homicide Reviews* [online]. London: Home Office. Available at: https://assets.publishing.service.gov.uk/government/uploads/system/uploads/attachment_data/file/575273/DHR-Statutory-Guidance-161206.pdf [Accessed 12 March 2025].

Home Office, 2020. *Online Harms White Paper: Closed Consultation* [online]. London: Home Office. Available at: https://www.gov.uk/government/consultations/online-harms-white-paper/online-harms-white-paper [Accessed 19 January 2025].

Home Office, 2022. *Policy Paper Online Safety Bill: Factsheet* [online]. London: Home Office. Available at: https://www.gov.uk/government/publications/online-safety-bill-supporting-documents/online-safety-bill-factsheet [Accessed 19 January 2025].

Home Office, 2023. *Domestic Homicide Review Legislation Consultation (Accessible Version)* [online]. London: Home Office. Available at: https://www.gov.uk/government/consultations/domestic-homicide-review-legislation-consultation/domestic-homicide-review-legislation-consultation-accessible-version [Accessed 12 March 2025].

Holt, A., 2021. *Family Criminology: An Introduction.* London: Palgrave Macmillan.

House of Commons Justice Committee, 2022. *Pre-legislative Scrutiny of the Draft Victims Bill: Second Report of Session 2022–23* [online]. London: House of Commons. Available at: https://committees.parliament.uk/publications/28831/documents/174248/default/ [Accessed 19 January 2025].

Jackson, C. L., Margolius, S. & Browning, S., 2022. The impact of intrafamilial homicide on the family system. *Journal of Family Violence*, 37, pp. 573–583.

Johnson, H., Eriksson, L., Mazerolle, P. & Wortley, R., 2019. Intimate femicide: The role of coercive control. *Feminist Criminology*, 14 (1), pp. 3–23.

Johnson, L., & Stylianou, A. M., 2020. Coordinated community responses to domestic violence: A systematic review of the literature. *Trauma Violence & Abuse*, 23 (2), pp. 506–522.

Johnson, M. P., 2006. Conflict and control: Gender symmetry and asymmetry in domestic violence. *Violence Against Women*, 12, pp. 1–16.

Jones, C., Bracewell, K., Clegg, A., Stanley, N. & Chantler, K., 2024. Domestic Homicide Review Committees' recommendations and impacts: A systematic review. *Homicide Studies*, 28 (1), pp. 78–98.

Kağitçıbaşi, Ç., 1990. Family and socialization in cross-cultural perspective: A model of change. In: Berman, J., ed. *Cross-cultural Perspectives: Nebraska Symposium on Motivation.* Lincoln, NE: Nebraska University Press, pp. 135–200.

Kağitçıbaşi, Ç., 1996. *Family and Human Development Across Cultures: A View from the Other Side.* Hillsdale, NJ: Lawrence Erlbaum.

Kauzlarich, D., Matthews, R. A. & Miller, W. J., 2001. Toward a victimology of state crime. Critical Criminology, 10, pp. 173–194.

Kelly, L., 1988. *Surviving Sexual Violence.* Cambridge: Polity.

Kelly, L., Burton, S. & Regan, L., 1996. Beyond victim or survivor: Sexual violence, identity and feminist theory and practice. In: Adkins, L., & Merchant, V., eds. *Sexualizing the Social: Power and the Organization of Sexuality.* Basingstoke: Palgrave Macmillan, pp. 77–101.

Kelly, L., & Westmarland, N., 2016. Naming and defining 'domestic violence': Lessons from research with violent men. *Feminist Review*, 112, pp. 113–127.

Kenney, J. S., 2004. Human agency revisited: The paradoxical experiences of victims of crime. *International Review of Victimology*, 11, pp. 225–257.

Kivisto, A. J., 2015. Male perpetrators of intimate partner homicide: A review and proposed typology. *Journal of the American Academy of Psychiatry and the Law*, 43, pp. 300–312.

Lamb, S., 1999. *New Versions of Victims.* New York: New York University Press.

Letschert, R. M., Haveman, R., de Brouwer, A. L. M. & Pemberton, A., 2011. *Victimological Approaches to International Crimes: Africa.* Cambridge: Intersentia.

Mama, A., 2000. Woman abuse in London's Black communities. In: Owusu, K., ed. *Black British Culture & Society*. Oxon: Routledge, pp. 89–110.

Martlew, N., 2019. *Online Harms White Paper: Seven Expert Perspectives* [online]. London: Digital Action. Available at: https://www.politico.eu/wp-content/uploads/2019/04/Seven-expert-perspectives-on-the-UK-online-harms-White-Paper-.pdf?utm_source=POLITICO.EU&utm_campaign=723cb52285-EMAIL_CAMPAIGN_2019_04_10_05_07&utm_medium=email&utm_term=0_10959edeb5-723cb52285-189780761#:~:text=There%20are%20also%20significant%20concerns%20raised%20by%20the%20White%20Paper%3A&text=There%20are%20serious%20and%20legitimate,speech%20principles%20would%20be%20ensured [Accessed 14 November 2022].

Mawby, R., & Walklate, S., 1994. *Critical Victimology*. London: Sage.

Mawby, R. I., 2016. Victim support in England and Wales: The end of an era? *International Review of Victimology*, 22 (3), pp. 203–221.

McGarry, R., & Walklate, S., 2011. The soldier as victim: Peering through the looking glass. *British Journal of Criminology*, 46 (6), pp. 900–917.

McGarry, R., & Walklate, S. 2015. *Victims: Trauma, Testimony and Justice*. Oxon: Routledge.

McGlynn, C., & Rackley, E., 2017. Image-based sexual abuse. *Oxford Journal of Legal Studies*, 37, pp. 1–17.

McGlynn, C., Rackley, E. & Houghton, R., 2017. Beyond 'revenge porn': The continuum of image-based sexual abuse. *Feminist Legal Studies*, 25, pp. 25–46.

McLachlan, F., & Harris, B., 2022. Intimate risks: Examining online and offline abuse, homicide flags, and femicide. *Victims & Offenders*, 17 (5), pp. 623–646.

Mendelsohn, B., 1956. The victimology. *Etudes Internationales de Psycho-Sociologie Criminelle*, 10, pp. 4–36.

Miers, D., 1989. Positivist victimology: A critique part 1. *International Review of Victimology*, 1 (1), pp. 1–29.

Miers, D., 2007. Looking beyond Great Britain: The development of criminal injuries. In: Walklate, S., ed. *The Handbook of Victims and Victimology*. Cullompton, Devon: Willan. pp. 337–362.

Ministry of Justice, 2020. *Code of Practice for Victims of Crime in England and Wales* [online]. London: Crown Copyright. Available at: https://assets.publishing.service.gov.uk/media/60620279d3bf7f5ceaca0d89/victims-code-2020.pdf [Accessed 12 March 2025].

Monckton Smith, J., 2012. *Murder, Gender and the Media: Narratives of Dangerous Love*. London: Palgrave Macmillan.

Monckton-Smith, J., Szymanska, K. & Haile, S., 2017. *Exploring the Relationship between Stalking and Homicide* [online]. Gloucestershire: Homicide Research Group University of Gloucestershire Centre for Learning and Innovation in Public Protection. In association with Suzy Lamplugh Trust. Available at: http://eprints.glos.ac.uk/4553/1/NSAW%20Report%2004.17%20-%20finalsmall.pdf [Accessed 12 March 2025].

Monckton Smith, J., Williams, A., & Mullane F., 2014. *Domestic Abuse, Homicide and Gender*. London: Palgrave Macmillan.

Munk, T., & Kennedy, M., 2024. *Victimisation in the Digital Age: An Online/Offline Continuum Approach*. Oxon: Routledge.

Munro, V. E., Bettinson, V. & Burton, M., 2024. Coercion, control and criminal responsibility: Exploring professional responses to offending and suicidality in the context of domestically abusive relationships. *Social & Legal Studies*, 33 (3), pp. 392–419.

Murdock, G. P., 1949. *Social Structure*. New York: Free Press.

Musgrove, A., & Groves, N., 2007. The Domestic Violence, Crime and Victims Act 2004: Relevant or 'removed' legislation? *Journal of Social Welfare & Family Law*, 29 (3–4), pp. 233–244.

Myhill, A., 2015. Measuring coercive control: What can we learn from national population surveys? *Violence Against Women*, 21 (3), pp. 355–375.

Myhill, A., 2017. Measuring domestic violence: Context is everything. *Journal of Gender Based Violence*, 1 (1), pp. 33–44.

Myhill, A., Johnson, K., McNeill, A., Critchfield, E. & Westmarland, N., 2022. 'A genuine one usually sticks out a mile': Policing coercive control in England and Wales. *Policing & Society*, 33 (4), pp. 398–413.

Mythen, G., & McGowen, W. 2017. Cultural victimology revisited: Synergies of risk, fear and resilience. In: Walklate, S., ed. *Handbook of Victims and Victimology*. Oxon: Routledge, pp. 364–378.

Neville, L., & Sanders-McDonagh, E., 2014. *Preventing Domestic Violence and Abuse: Common Themes and Lessons Learned from West Midlands' DHRs* [online]. London: Middlesex University London. Available at: https://www.westmidlands-pcc.gov.uk/wp-content/uploads/2019/05/SPCB-140911-Domestic-Homicide-Reviews-Research-Appendix-1.pdf [Accessed 17 March 2025].

Nickolls, L., Rowland, L., Cowie, G. & Dawson, J., 2023. *Research Briefing: The Victims and Prisoners Bill* [online]. London: House of Commons Library. Available at: https://researchbriefings.files.parliament.uk/documents/CBP-9792/CBP-9792.pdf [Accessed 19 January 2025].

O'Brien, M., 2005. What is cultural about cultural criminology? *British Journal of Criminology*, 55, pp. 599–612.

Office for National Statistics (ONS), 2024. *Domestic Abuse Victim Characteristics, England and Wales: Year Ending March 2024* [online]. London: ONS Centre for Crime and Justice. Available at: https://www.ons.gov.uk/peoplepopulationandcommunity/crimeandjustice/articles/domesticabusevictimcharacteristicsenglandandwales/yearendingmarch2024 [Accessed 18 January 2018].

Online Safety Act 2023 (c. 50)

Pain, R., 2014. Everyday terrorism: Connecting domestic violence and global terrorism. *Progress in Human Geography*, 38 (4), pp. 531–550.

Pasternak, B. E., Ember, C. R. & Ember, M., 1976. On the conditions favoring extended family households. *Journal of Anthropological Research*, 32, pp. 109–123.

PenzeyMoog, E., & Slakoff, D. C., 2021. As technology evolves, so does domestic violence: Modern-day tech abuse and possible solutions. In: Bailey, J., Flynn, A. & Henry, N., eds. *The Emerald International Handbook of Technology-Facilitated Violence and Abuse*. Leeds: Emerald Publishing Limited, pp. 643–662.

Pequegnat, W., & Bray, J. H., 1997. Families and HIV/AIDS: Introduction to the special section. *Journal of Family Psychology*, 11 (1), pp. 3–10.

Petrosky, E., Blair, J. M., Betz, C. J., Fowler, K. A., Jack, S. & Lyons, B. H., 2017. Racial and ethnic differences in homicides of adult women and the role of intimate partner violence – United States, 2003–2014. *MMWR Morbidity and Mortality Weekly Report*, 66 (28), pp. 741–746.

Popenoe, D., 1988. *Disturbing the Nest: Family Change and Decline in Modern Societies*. Chicago, IL: Aldine.

Popple, L., 2022. *Online Safety Bill – Are You Caught?*London: TaylorWessing. Available at: https://www.taylorwessing.com/en/interface/2022/the-online-safety-bill—the-uks-answer-to-addressing-online-harms/online-safety-bill-are-you-caught [Accessed 19 January 2025].

Porter, A., 2020. *Prosecuting Domestic Abuse in Neoliberal Times: Amplifying the Survivor's Voice*. London: Palgrave Macmillan.

Pow, A. M., Murray, C. E., Flasch, P., Doom, E. & Snyder, M., 2015. Learning from experience: A content analysis of domestic violence fatality review team reports. *Partner Abuse*, 6 (2), pp. 197–216.

Quinney, R., 1972. Who is the victim? *Criminology*, 10 (3), pp. 309–329.

Rafter, N., & Walklate, S., 2012. Genocide and the dynamics of victimization: Some observations on Armenia. *European Journal of Criminology*, 9(5), pp. 514–526.

Reed, M. D., & Caraballo, K., 2022. Voice of the victims: Accounts of secondary victimization with the court system among homicide co-victims. *Journal of Interpersonal Violence*, 37 (13–14), NP10832–NP10861.

Rogers, M., 2020. Exploring the domestic abuse narratives of trans and non-binary people and the role of cisgenderism in identity abuse, misgendering and pathologizing. *Violence Against Women*, 27 (12–13), pp. 2187–2207.

Rock, P., 1994. *Victimology*. Aldershot: Dartmouth.

Rock, P., 1998. Murders, victims and 'survivors': The social construction of deviance . *The British Journal of Criminology*, 38 (2), pp. 185–200.

Rock, P., 2002. On becoming a victim. In: Hoyle, C., & Young, R., eds. *New Visions of Crime Victims*. Oxford: Hart. pp. 1–22.

Rogers, M. M., Fisher, C., Ali, P., Allmark, P. & Fontes, L., 2023. Technology-facilitated abuse in intimate relationships: A scoping review. *Trauma, Violence, & Abuse*, 24 (4), pp. 2210–2226.

Rothe, D., & Kauzlarich, D., 2014. *Towards a Victimology of State Crime*. 1st ed.Oxon: Routledge.

Salter, M., & Crofts, T., 2015. Responding to revenge porn: Challenging online legal impunity. In: Comella, L., & Tarrant, S., eds. *New Views on Pornography: Sexuality, Politics and the Law*. Westport: Praeger Publishers, pp. 233–255.

Sardinha, L., Maheu-Giroux, M., Stöckl, H., Meyer, S. R. & García-Moreno, C., 2022. Global, regional, and national prevalence estimates of physical or sexual, or both, intimate partner violence against women in 2018. *The Lancet*, 399, pp. 803–813.

Scarr, L., & Kennedy, M., 2023. 'They didn't want to upset the client': Stalking in hands-on occupations. In: Mellins, M., Wheatley, R. & Flowers, C., eds. *Young People, Stalking Awareness and Domestic Abuse*. London: Palgrave Macmillan, pp. 201–223.

Sharp-Jeffs, N., & Kelly, L., 2016. *Domestic Homicide Review (DHR): Case Analysis* [online]. London: Standing Together Against Domestic Violence & London Metropolitan University. Available at: https://repository.londonmet.ac.uk/1477/1/STADV_DHR_Report_Final.pdf [Accessed 17 March 2025].

Smith, S. G., Chen, J., Basile, K. C., Gilbert, L. K., Merrick, M. T., Patel, N., Walling, M. & Jain, A., 2017. *The National Intimate Partner And Sexual Violence Survey (NISVS): 2010–2012 State Report* [online]. Atlanta, GA: National Center for Injury Prevention and Control. Available at: https://stacks.cdc.gov/view/cdc/46305 [Accessed 17 January 2025].

Spalek, B., 2006. *Crime Victims: Theory, Policy and Practice*. London: Palgrave Macmillan.

Spencer, C. M., 2018. A meta-analysis of risk factors for intimate partner homicide: Examining male perpetration and female victimization [online]. Ph.D. thesis, Kansas State University. Available at: https://krex.k-state.edu/server/api/core/bitstreams/dbd914ee-c187-4cde-8f6f-73d9775e0cfc/content [Accessed 17 March 2025].

Spencer, C. M., & Stith, S. M., 2020. Risk factors for male perpetration and female victimization of intimate partner homicide: A meta-analysis. *Trauma, Violence & Abuse*, 21 (3), pp. 527–540.

Spencer, D., 2014. Corporeal realism and victimology. *International Review of Victimology*, 21 (1), pp. 31–44.

Stark, E., 2007. *Coercive Control: How Men Entrap Women in Personal Life*. New York: Oxford University Press.

Stark, E., 2009. Rethinking coercive control. *Violence Against Women*, 15 (12), pp. 1509–1525.

Stark, E., 2023. *Coercive Control: How Men Entrap Women in Personal Life*. 2nd ed. New York: Oxford University Press.

Stöckl, H., Devries, K., Rotstein, A., Abrahams, M., Campbell, J., Watts, C. & Garcia Moreno, C., 2013. The global prevalence of intimate partner homicide: A systematic review. *The Lancet*, 382, pp. 859–865.

Strickland, P., & Allen, G., 2017. *Domestic Violence in England and Wales, Briefing Paper Number 6337* [online]. London: House of Commons Library. Available at: http://researchbriefings.files.parliament.uk/documents/SN06337/SN06337.pdf [Accessed 19 January 2025].

Strobl, R., 2010. Becoming a victim. In: Shoham, S. G., Knepper, P. & Kett, M., eds. *International Handbook of Victimology*, Boca Raton, FL: CRC Press, pp. 1–26.

Sumption, J., 2022. The hidden harms in the Online Safety Bill. *The Spectator* [online], 20 August. Available at: https://www.spectator.co.uk/article/the-hidden-harms-in-the-online-safety-bill/ [Accessed 19 January 2025].

Swanson, S., Nygård, R. H. & Saus, M., 2022. Native American social work – Including family and community. *Journal of Social Work*, 22 (3), pp. 615–636.

Tapley, J., & Davies, P. 2020. *Victimology: Research, Policy and Activism*. Switzerland: Palgrave Macmillan.

Tolmie, J., Wilson, D. & Smith, R., 2017. New Zealand. In: Dawson, M., ed. *Domestic Homicides and Death Reviews: An International Perspective*. London: Palgrave Macmillan, pp. 159–198.

Van Wijk, P., 2013. Who is the "little old lady" of international crimes? Nils Christie's concept of the ideal victim re-interpreted. *International Review of Victimology*, 19 (2), pp. 159–179.

Victims and Prisoners Bill 2015.

Victims' Commissioner, 2018. *2017/2018 Annual Report: Victims' Commissioner for England and Wales* [online]. London: Victims' Commissioner. Available at: https://cloud-platform-e218f50a4812967ba1215eaecede923f.s3.amazonaws.com/uploads/sites/6/2021/12/VC-Annual-Report-2017-18.pdf [Accessed 19 January 2025].

Victims' Commissioner, 2022. *2021/22 Annual Report Dame Vera Baird QC Victims' Commissioner for England and Wales* [online]. London: Crown Copyright. Available at: https://cloud-platform-e218f50a4812967ba1215eaecede923f.s3.amazonaws.com/uploads/sites/6/2022/06/MOJ7216_Victims-commisioner-Annual-report_AW-WEB.pdf [Accessed 19 January 2025].

Von Hentig, H., 1940/41. Remarks on the interaction of perpetrator and victim. *Journal of Criminal Law and Criminology*, 31, pp. 303–309.

Walby, S., 2009. *The Cost Of Domestic Violence: Up-Date 2009* [online]. Lancaster: Lancaster University. Available at: https://openaccess.city.ac.uk/id/eprint/21695/ [Accessed 18 January 2025].

Walby, S., & Allen, J., 2004. *Domestic Violence, Sexual Assault and Stalking: Findings from the British Crime Survey. Home Office Research Study 276*. London: Home Office.

Walby, S., & Towers, J., 2017. Measuring violence to end violence: Mainstreaming gender. *Journal of Gender-Based Violence*, 1 (1), pp. 11–31.

Walklate, S., 1990. Researching victims of crime; critical victimology. *Social Justice*, 17, pp. 25–42.

Walklate, S., 2001. *Gender, Crime and Criminal Justice*. Cullompton, Devon: Willan.

Walklate, S., 2007. *Imagining the Victim of Crime*. Buckinghamshire: Open University Press.

Walklate, S., 2011. Reframing criminal victimization: Finding a place for vulnerability and resilience. *Theoretical Criminology*, 15(2), pp. 179–194.

Walklate, S., 2012. Courting compassion: Victims, policy and the question of justice. *The Howard Journal of Criminal Justice*, 51 (2), pp. 109–121.

Walklate, S., 2014. Sexual violence against women: Still a controversial issue for victimology? *Victimology: An International Review*, 20 (1), pp. 71–84.

Walklate, S., Mythen, G. & McGarry, R., 2011. Witnessing Wootton Bassett: An exploration in cultural victimology. *Crime, Media, Culture*, 7(2), pp. 149–165.

Websdale, N., 2020. Domestic violence fatality review: The state of the art. In: Geffner, R., White, J. W., Hamberger, L. K., Rosenbaum, A., Vaughan-Eden, V. & Vieth, V. I., eds. *Handbook of Interpersonal Violence across the Lifespan*. London: Springer International Publishing, pp. 1–23.

Welsh, K., 2024. The Online Safety Act 2023: A new dawn for regulating image-based domestic abuse? In: Munk, T., & Kennedy, M. C., eds. *Victimisation in the Digital Age: An Online-Offline Continuum Approach*. Oxon: Routledge, pp. 121–136.

Wertham, F., 1949. *The Show of Violence*. New York: Doubleday.

Wolfgang, M. E., 1958. *Patterns in Criminal Homicide*. Philadelphia: University of Pennsylvania Press.

3 Offline Harm

Existing Risk Factors in the Web of Abuse

Introduction

This chapter provides a detailed account of risk factors associated with intimate partner homicide as considered by victims' families'. While many of these risk factors are already well-established in the literature and in empirical research, what sets this chapter apart from other discussions of intimate partner homicide is that these risk factors have been identified by co-victims. Given they often have a front row seat to the abuse experienced by their loved ones, this puts them in a unique position to identify these risk factors indiscriminately. As outlined in Chapter 1, this chapter only discusses risk factors identified by co-victims and therefore cannot cover all risk factors for intimate partner homicide. The dialogue in this chapter is coupled with case studies from empirical qualitative research to inform the observations from co-victims and support their narratives.

Chapter 2 makes reference to a theoretical framework called "continuum thinking" and explains its origins. This chapter seeks to reaffirm this approach and provide a more detailed account in relation to offline harm. The continuum of online-offline harm, a new concept, was outlined in Munk and Kennedy's (2024) edited collection which draws on a range of victimisation. It postulates that the offline and online worlds cannot be separated as they are part of the same continuum. Gosse (2021) challenges the binary constructs of 'offline' and 'online', suggesting that they are problematic as our interactions with the different worlds are more complex than this. Criminologists continue to place harm into categories which is unhelpful as it suggests that some forms are *more real* than others and, as such, are considered more serious than others. Jurgenson (2011: para. 2) describes this *real* and *less real* binary as "digital dualism", whereby the offline and online worlds are perceived differently. These conflicting views can, ultimately, impact how the public and media construct harm, which can have significant consequences for victim-survivors (McGlynn et al., 2021; McLachlan & Harris, 2022).

As such, this chapter forms the basis for the continuum of online-offline harm by first discussing risk factors for intimate partner homicide. It begins with offline harm risk factors as these were identified long before the emergence

DOI: 10.4324/9781003464488-3

of the internet and mobile technologies. The use of the term 'offline' in this chapter simply differentiates physical and in-person harm with that of 'online' harm, utilising linguistics to describe and document the harms falling into this area of focus. However, this does not imply they are more important or more harmful than those presented in the online environment. This is line in with perspectives relating to continuum thinking which do not seek to place either form of harm in a hierarchy (Kelly, 1988; Munk & Kennedy, 2024). Instead, they are placed on the same continuum.

Precursors to Intimate Partner Homicide

Jealousy and Envy

The motivations for coercive control and intimate partner homicide have been extensively researched over the past 40 years, with male jealousy being a central tenet in the justification for fatal abuse (Aloyce et al., 2023; Wilson & Daly, 1993; Martinez, 2015; Vatnar et al., 2017). Infidelity, or presumed infidelity, has been considered a key motivator for abuse where male jealousy provides the context for such abuse (Aldridge & Browne, 2003; Enander et al., 2021; Kivisto, 2015; Stark, 2007; Wilson & Daly, 1992). This rationale has continued to ensure violence against women is justified, endured and normalised within society (García-Moreno, 2013; Ingala-Smith, 2018). Furthermore, jealousy is often underpinned by other factors, such as a sense of ownership and a desire for exclusive control over the victim (Aldridge and Browne, 2003; Stark, 2007; Wilson & Daly, 1992). On the whole, jealousy contributes to around 33% of intimate partner homicides (Martinez, 2015). Romantic or sexual jealousy can be considered as:

> ... a complex psychological system whose functioning is inferred from observable combinations of circumstance and response – a system that is activated by a perceived threat that a third party might usurp one's place in a sexual relationship and that generates a diversity of circumstantially contingent responses aimed at countering the threat.
>
> (Wilson & Daly, 1992: 303)

However, it must be noted that defining the concept of jealousy is difficult as it cannot be expressed as solely internal or external (Wilson & Daly, 1992). Kivisto (2015) echoes these sentiments, suggesting that there is still a lack of clarity in terms of definitions for jealousy. Similarly, the ways in which jealousy is expressed can be contingent on personality, relational features and cultural context (Aloyce et al., 2022; Buss, 2013). Guerrero et al. (2005: 233) updates this definition by suggesting that romantic jealousy can be characterised by:

> ... a multifaceted set of affective, behavioral, and cognitive responses that occurs when the existence and/or quality of a person's primary relationship is threatened by a third party.

With that being said, Kivisto (2015) believes that jealousy and envy are factors that may be present in cases of intimate partner homicide but the area of envy has received little attention (Kivisto, 2015). Richards (2000) assesses the difference between jealousy and envy, stating that jealousy encompasses a fear of losing an item or person to another whereas envy is a feeling towards another who already possesses such item or person. Furthermore, envy reflects the impossibility of possessing that item or person. Klein (1997) suggests that the envious person displaces their focus to the item or person they wish to possess, thereby directing negative, harmful feelings towards said desired item or person. This results in an urge to destroy or spoil that item or person (Debbane, 2011; Kivisto, 2015; Klein, 1997). This is described aptly by Bion (1992: 102) who explains that:

> Envy contributes to the belief that external objects are the patient's thoughts. Since he cannot admit dependence on an external object, he claims (in order ultimately to escape feeling envy) that he is, like the breast that feeds itself, the producer as well as the consumer of that on which he depends for this life.

However, Klein (1997) has been heavily criticised for insufficient conceptual clarity. Sometimes she describes envy as a feeling and, in other sentiments, she considers it an impulse (Debbane, 2011; Feldman & de Paola, 1994). This discussion appears to be broadly simplified, forgoing the nuanced nature of this feeling. Similarly, both Bion and Klein use envy and destructiveness in the same sentences in their summations, showing a lack of distinction between these two terms. Furthermore, Klein's work is said to lack comprehensive rigour in the metapsychology field (Debbane, 2011). It is, therefore, clear that envy is a complex psychological phenomenon which is still not fully understood.

A Case of Familial Jealousy

Fergus is the brother of 47-year-old Jackie who was murdered by her husband, Alastair, in 2003. Her 17-year-old son Wallis was also killed during his attempt to protect his mother, with Alastair taking his own life after killing his wife and son. Their daughter survived as she was attending university at the time. Fergus reflected on his sister's kind and thoughtful nature:

> I remember Jackie thinking what I need is for the plane to crash and for nobody to be hurt except Alastair. I love that story because of [how] lovely and kind it is, nobody gets hurt except Alastair in a guise like an act of God or an accident. For me that kind of sums up the difference between normal people and bad people, she's playing by the Queensberry rules hoping an accident will take him out. He's not, he's just choosing to murder to get his way, Jackie's hoping for a bit of luck to get her way, is

that a lovely? It's lovely, for me that just defines kindness and normality although, of course, it's useless in the face of a murderer ...

(Fergus, Brother)

In the 14 months leading up to the murder, from September 2002 onwards, Jackie had asked Alastair for a divorce which he refused to grant. Between this time and the day Jackie was murdered, Alastair sent numerous death threats to Jackie and her family by way of letters, he emptied the couple's joint bank account, cancelled her healthcare with his firm and glued the locks at the couple's shared house. Fergus also remarked that Alastair:

> ... had hoped we [himself, Jackie and the two children] could produce a MacDonald type family [close-knit family], he was very jealous of the relationship Jackie had with her sibling, family and mum ...

In this case, there is clear evidence of familial jealousy from Alastair, which has not previously been considered in the context of intimate partner homicide. From Fergus's perspective, Alastair was jealous of Jackie's relationship with her family and, as such, wanted to model his family on its 'MacDonald-ness'. As Alastair admired the relationship that Jackie had with her family and how she interacted with them, he wanted to reproduce or foster a similar relationship with his wife and children. As demonstrated in the section above, there are strong links to jealousy in the literature (Aloyce et al., 2023; Campbell et al., 2007; Martinez, 2015; Vatnar et al., 2017; Wilson & Daly, 1993). However, these links do not explain whom jealousy is directed to or in what context this type of jealousy arises. It is reasonable to suggest that jealousy is often aimed at the victim but this can extend and overspill to others.

Table 3.1 Different Contexts for Jealousy

Jealousy Context	*Characteristics of Jealousy*
Familial Jealousy	Centres on the perpetrator's obsession with the relationship the victim has with her family (i.e., parents and siblings) and his attempt to model her family on his own.
Economic Jealousy	Focuses on the perpetrator's inability to provide for the victim and the abuse is directed at the victim as punishment for career success.
Sexual Jealousy*	Concentrates on the perpetrator's feelings of sexual entitlement towards the victim where he sees the victim as his property irrespective of their relationship status.

Sources: Aldridge & Browne, 2003; Campbell et al., 2007; Wilson & Daly, 1992.

*Literature and empirical research considering jealousy almost always refers to sexual jealousy under the umbrella term of jealousy.

Proprietariness or Proprietary Behaviours

Wilson and Daly (1992) used the term "proprietariness" to describe an evolutionary psychological mechanism, in which, men assert their right to women's sexuality and reproductive capacity. As such, it is considered a "cultural artifact" rather than a "masculine psychological adaption" (Wilson & Daly, 1993: 278). This evolutionary logic goes further by having other implications, such as a sense of *right* or *entitlement* over people, particularly women. Martinez (2015) explains proprietariness as a set of beliefs and values ascribed to a person's partner where they are viewed as a type of property. This goes hand in hand with entitlement, which is either a result of proprietariness (or proprietary behaviours) or co-exists with proprietariness (Bouffard, 2010; Martinez, 2015).

Moreover, proprietariness is also linked to sexual jealousy given its origins as an evolved aspect of human male psychology (Wilson & Daly, 1993). However, the term proprietariness describes a more encompassing mindset than jealousy (Serran & Firestone, 2004). This mindset has implications for males when there is competition for sexual mates, and emerges in situations where there is a strong likelihood that men will lose their sole rights over a female sexual partner (e.g., as a result of assumed infidelity or actual infidelity) (Graham et al., 2022). As such, intimate partner homicide is a consequence of male desire to have control over women, including their reproductive capacity, in addition to a fear of desertion (e.g., fear of their female sexual partner having a child with another man) (Graham et al., 2022; Serran & Firestone, 2004). Others agree with this conceptualisation, highlighting that male sexual proprietariness is a key factor in male-perpetrated intimate partner homicide towards female intimate partners (Eriksson & Mazerolle, 2013; Johnson, 2012).

However, other evolutionary explanations have asserted that intimate partner homicide is a byproduct or "slip-up" of intimate partner abuse where the death of a female sexual partner is a mistake occurring as a result of non-fatal controlling behaviour (Kaighobadi et al., 2009). Kaighobadi et al. (2009) offer another alternative explanation, namely the homicide adaptation hypothesis, which suggests that intimate partner homicide ensures successful male reproduction when there is a suspicion of female infidelity. This hypothesis provides a rationale for homicide by suggesting it is a response to issues related to groups of individuals living together. Intimate partner homicide is, therefore, an evolved adaption where men may benefit from killing their partner if their partner has engaged in sexual contact with another, where this union may have resulted in a child which is not genetically theirs, or where the cost of the infidelity impacts their reputation (Holub & Barbaro, 2018). Similar to feminist theories, evolutionary perspectives acknowledge the role of gender in intimate partner homicide where male dominance and control are considered key drivers for fatal abuse (Graham et al., 2022). They also take into account micro- or individual-level elements, such as biology or psychology, which may contribute to intimate partner homicide perpetration.

Yet, they also fail to appreciate other meso- or macro-level factors, such as peer relationships, poverty or oppression (Graham et al., 2022). Similarly, evolutionary theories overlook other intersections, such as race, class and sexuality, with their primary focus being on male-perpetrated abuse towards female partners in heterosexual relationships. Moreover, there is little further discussion on why intimate partner homicide occurs beyond suspected or actual infidelity (Graham et al., 2022). Johnson (2012) also suggests that evolutionary frameworks have the potential to justify female oppression and intimate partner homicide as both the *homicide adaptation hypothesis* and concept of *proprietariness* are framed as adaptive behaviours.

The Fast and the Furious Case

Tam and Miari are the parents of 17-year-old Blair who was murdered by an acquaintance, Jackson, in 2013. Blair's parents felt they had a close relationship with their daughter, with Tam reflecting on this relationship by stating:

> ... as far as I'm concerned when she was here she was a model daughter.
>
> (Tam, Father)

Jackson introduced himself to Blair around 14 months prior to killing her, after being hired at a garage a short walk from her family home. While Jackson had asked Blair out on several occasions, she had made it clear that she was not interested in him in a romantic way, instead describing him to her father as a brotherly figure:

> ... there's a platonic friendship from Blair's side and from his side it seems that he did want a relationship with Blair but we'll never know if he wanted a real relationship and he murdered her because she got another boyfriend ...
>
> (Tam, Father)

Tam went on to identify his daughter as a motherly figure as she:

> ... looked after him and mothered him as he would often stand to one side [in social situations] and look a bit left out and everything and Blair would go "oh come on Jackson join in" and stuff like this.

However, this persistence to date Blair continued and Blair's father felt it reached a point of no return. After an invitation to see a film with Jackson, Blair refused due to prearranged plans with her boyfriend. Tam believed that the response to this encounter was the catalyst for his daughter's murder as Blair had prioritised her boyfriend over Jackson and he could no longer stand aside in her life:

> They would socialise together but he would still send Blair texts saying "do you want to go to the pictures?" ... and one of the last ones said "do you wanna come and watch Fast and Furious 7?" And Blair had texted back and said "I'd have loved to come with you but I'm going with Matt [boyfriend] tonight". Apparently, that was the one that tipped him over the edge. Apparently, that was the one that really set him off ...

In this case, the victim's father provides a narrative which can be linked to proprietary behaviour and this sense of entitlement, particularly sexual entitlement, over the victim. While the perpetrator and victim were not sexual intimates but acquaintances, this still played an important role in the homicide. Some suggestions have been made relating to this idea that often lethal violence occurs in relationships that were initially formed on the basis of some positive attachment and larger gendered notions of possession (Polk, 1994; Stark, 2007, 2023). This is underpinned by historical discourses which see women as the property of men (Franzway et al., 2019). Stark (2007, 2023) suggests violent men's jealousy turns women into possessions, thereby diminishing a woman's sense of personhood. Such essentialist masculinity discourses argue men are entitled to sex (Gavey, 2003). In this case, the perpetrator felt like he owned the victim or had a right to her, irrespective of them not being in a relationship. The information not outlined here is that after murdering Blair, he took her body to the cinema to watch the *Fast and Furious* 7 film in order to have the date he felt he was owed. This shows that jealousy and envy, coupled with proprietariness, are a cause for concern when it comes to fatal abuse.

Previous History of Abuse

As mentioned earlier, the motivations or rationale for intimate partner homicide are informed by jealousy, envy and proprietariness, which are psychological phenomena ingrained within the male psyche. However, there is also a well-established link between prior abusive behaviours and future fatally abusive behaviours (Matias et al., 2020; Spencer, 2018; Spencer & Stith, 2020). From a general perspective, previous offending of any type is a predictor of future offending (Andrews & Bonta, 2006; Dobash et al., 2009). In terms of individuals who commit intimate partner homicide, studies conducted in Canada, Sweden, the United States and the United Kingdom suggest a link between previous convictions (of any crime type) and intimate partner homicide (Dawson & Gartner, 1998; Dobash et al., 2004; Dobash et al., 2009; Grann & Wedin, 2002; Moracco et al., 1998). More specifically, research has shown that perpetrators of intimate partner homicide are likely to have abused previous partners or been involved in other criminal activity, with arrests for either being considered potential risk factors (Campbell et al., 2003, 2007; Daly & Wilson, 1998; Jayasuriya et al., 2011; Kivisto, 2015; Monckton Smith et al., 2014; Spencer, 2018; Spencer & Stith, 2020; Vatnar et al., 2017).

Campbell and colleagues (2003, 2007) stated that a history of intimate partner abuse is apparent in the majority of intimate partner homicide cases, which equates to approximately 67–75% of victims killed by their partners. This correlates with findings from other studies in North America and the United Kingdom (Campbell & Glass, 2009; Nicolaidis et al., 2003). However, Kivisto (2015) suggests that the likelihood of previous partner abuse varies considerably, with estimates being anywhere between 20% and 70%. Similar conclusions have been drawn by other researchers (Aldridge & Browne, 2003; Dobash et al., 2009; Enander et al., 2021; Spencer et al., 2022; Vatnar et al., 2017). With that being said, Kivisto (2015) has urged that figures relating to prior partner abuse are treated with caution and that they need to be considered on a case-by-case basis, as estimates are difficult to establish due to the samples used in previous studies. For example, Dutton and Kerry (1999) suggested that 75% of incarcerated men convicted of intimate partner homicide in their sample admitted to intimate partner abuse or had evidence of this in their institutional record. Belfrage and Rying (2004) reported slightly lower figures in their sample, with 36% of psychiatric patients in Sweden having a previous history of intimate partner abuse. This clearly shows that there are a number of contributing factors to take into consideration when it comes to estimates concerning whether or not previous intimate partner abuse is a risk factor for future intimate partner homicide. Nevertheless, there is an important link in terms of the escalation of abuse between intimate partner abuse and homicide (Dobash et al., 2009; Vatnar et al., 2017).

In addition to a previous history of abuse towards the victim or other former partners, the literature shows that perpetrators' involvement in other criminal offences could also be considered a risk factor for intimate partner homicide from a national and international perspective. For example, previous research has indicated a link between intimate partner homicide and having direct access to a gun or weapon, and/or having firearms offences (Dobash et al., 2009; Matias et al., 2020; Moreschi et al., 2016; Pereira et al., 2013; Spencer, 2018; Toprak & Ersoy, 2017); robbery (Dobash et al., 2009; Moreschi et al., 2016); non-fatal strangulation (Dobash et al., 2009; Dobash & Dobash, 2011; Campbell et al., 2007; Matias et al., 2020; Spencer, 2018; Spencer & Stith, 2020); threatening behaviours towards the victim (Matias et al., 2020; Moreschi et al., 2016; Pereira et al., 2013; Spencer, 2018); and stalking (Matias et al., 2020; Spencer, 2018; Spencer & Stith, 2020).

The Perpetrator with a Catalogue of Convictions

Niall and Mia are the parents of Hilda, who was murdered by her ex-partner, Mac, in 2014. After a short four-month relationship, Niall explained that Mac became obsessed with his daughter and was constantly phoning and messaging her. For the most part, Niall and Mia were unaware of the extent of the abuse and couldn't understand why, after leaving the area to work on a cruise ship, which was her dream job, their daughter told them she wanted to come home after only a few weeks. Naill described Hilda as:

> ... a determined character and individual that once she set her mind on something she would persevere and follow it through ... she was quite strong and she usually handled most of the stuff herself and she didn't need a lot of help from them [her parents] ... she had the gift of the gab, she had all sorts of confidence, she was veracious, she was outgoing, she had a big circle of friends ...

Hilda was, therefore, in a position to either deal with issues herself or seek counsel from friends. While Niall and Mia characterised their relationship with Hilda as fairly close, they felt she kept to herself to protect them from the perpetrator. However, as Hilda was only 20 years old, her parents felt she was a little naïve by saying that she could:

> ... turn him [perpetrator] around or I can ... I can't remember the phrase she used now ... I can sort him out or something, I can make him better.
>
> (Niall, Father)

After Hilda's death, Niall and Mia learnt that Mac had a previous history of abusing women and was also involved in other criminal activities relating to violence, driving infractions, and had previously been imprisoned:

> ... he was arrested 23 times in the previous six years ... escalating violence. He'd previously abused two other partners prior to Hilda, both were on the domestic violence register. One of them had been into hospital but neither of them would press charges, he poured petrol through one of their letterboxes, so he was well known to the authorities and the police and all this information was out there, but they didn't put any of it together. He was out on bail when he killed Hilda with taking without consent, grievous body harm, driving without insurance, driving without a licence so he was a bad boy with a catalogue of convictions. He'd been in prison apparently ... and this was before he had met Hilda, but I don't know much about that and, yes, he had a massive checkered history and he was on a course of self-destruction or to destruct someone else. He had previously abused his mum as well ... he comes from a family certainly on his dad's side that are career criminals ...
>
> (Niall, Father)

This case shows clear links to prior offending behaviour, some of which relates to domestic abuse in addition to other infractions (Andrews & Bonta, 2006; Dobash et al., 2009; Matias et al., 2020; Spencer, 2018; Spencer & Stith, 2020). While this is in regards to only one specific case, it highlights the range of offences perpetrators of intimate partner homicide may commit. It also shows for Mac that there was a clear pathway from more minor offences which then escalated to murder. This supports existing literature on the assertion that a previous history of abuse can be considered a contributing factor for intimate partner homicide.

Documenting the 'Web of Abuse'

As discussed previously, the precursors to intimate partner homicide include jealousy, envy and proprietary behaviours, with a previous history of general and/or partner abuse being risk factors for future lethal behaviours. There is also an acknowledgement that there is an increased risk of homicide when potential or actual separation occurs (Campbell et al., 2003, 2007; Spencer, 2018; Spencer & Stith, 2020; Wilson & Daly, 1993). All co-victims interviewed reported their loved ones as being separated from the perpetrator at the time of their death. However, this is not discussed any further in this book as it was not a factor overtly discussed by co-victims. Instead, it was an established fact. While the previous section considered previous intimate partner abuse more generally, this part outlines specific forms of intimate partner abuse which are deemed risk factors for intimate partner homicide. This includes a detailed discussion of coercive control underpinned by the 'web of abuse'.

This construction of the web of abuse was referred to as the "web of violence" in its early iteration, and was considered in relation to animal cruelty (Solot, 1997: 257). Others have considered this the "tangled web of abuse" (Faver & Strand, 2003: 238), more simply "a web of abuse" (Kirkwood, 1993; Pitman, 2010), a "web of entrapment" (Morris, 2009: 417), or a "web model of domestic violence and abuse" (Chowdhury & Winder, 2022: 1). However, although reference was made to emotional abuse in Kirkwood's (1993) consideration of the web of abuse, there is no explanation as to what is at the centre of the web or how it links to the effects of power and control in other areas of the victim's relationship, whether that be pre- or post-separation (Pitman, 2010). Pitman (2010) also suggests that if emotional abuse can be plotted on a web, then other forms of abuse may be similarly conceptualised.

In Solot's (1997) discussion, he suggested that academics like to build walls by categorising forms of abuse. Kelly (1988) also alluded to this in her early work on sexual violence. However, as with any walls built, they obstruct our view, thereby halting our ability to see the full picture of abuse, and they also prevent us from making use of each other's tools or methods for researching such abuse (Solot, 1997). Solot (1997: 257) also made reference to the "landscape of violence", in which he suggested there was a familiarity with violence, or indeed abuse itself, regardless of the type perpetrated, the potential victims affected or the preventive measures offered. Still, the research discourse, language and methodologies used to unpack abuse are radically different despite being a part of this larger web of abuse. Solot (1997) explored the interconnected nature of the web of abuse by explaining that each facet of the abuse is connected to others, with some aspects being intertwined multiple times. Faver and Strand (2008) went further by suggesting that the web of abuse is omnidirectional, meaning that abuse can be perpetrated beyond the victim. Similar discussions have been encountered in other scholarly work (Kirkwood, 1993; Morris, 2009; Pitman, 2010; Chowdhury & Winder, 2022).

The Anatomy of Coercive Control

Stark's (2007, 2023) work on coercive control has been well documented and influential in intimate partner abuse and homicide research and legislation for decades. While many scholars view intimate partner abuse through the lens of Stark's (2007, 2023) concept of coercive control, the understandings behind this concept have existed for some time (Dobash & Dobash, 1980; Follingstad & De Hart, 2000; Marshall, 1992a, 1992b; Pence & Paymar, 1993; Schechter, 1982; Stark, 2023; Tolman, 1989; Walker 1984). Coercive control can be defined as:

> an act or pattern of acts of assault, threats, humiliation and intimidation or other abuse that is used to harm, punish, or frighten their victim.
>
> (Monckton Smith et al., 2014: 30)

Coercive control involves a plethora of behaviours which seek to exploit a partner's capabilities and resources for personal gain and gratification. It removes the victim's autonomy and means to escape and regulates their behaviour so it conforms to traditional gender norms (Stark, 2007). It has been described as both a civil rights issue and a criminal justice issue (Stark, 2007, 2023). Stark (2013) maintains that coercive control is the most accurate predictor for homicide by a ratio of 9:1. Two influential pieces of legislation, namely the *Serious Crime Act 2015* and the *Domestic Abuse Act 2021*, have incorporated controlling and coercive behaviour into statute to allow for the prosecution of such behaviours. This is discussed in more detail in Chapter 2. Arguably, there was an urgent need for new law to reflect the patterns of coercion and control evidenced in research and personal testimony from victim-survivors who have experienced repeat victimisation (Stark & Hester, 2018). Reevaluating current provision was necessary as the criminal justice response to intimate partner abuse at the time was too narrow to support women's far-reaching and complex calls for help. In addition, there were high attrition rates for repeat offenders and an increase in women reporting violent crimes, which has been steadily increasing since 2009 (Stark & Hester, 2018).

According to Stark (2007, 2023), there are four overlapping and interlinking dynamics constituting the anatomy of coercive control, including the presence or absence of violence, intimidation, isolation and control (Kennedy, 2022). A thorough discussion of these elements follows, beginning with the coercive control and physical injury, then coercive control and intimidating behaviour, coercive control and isolation, and finally the 'control' in coercive control.

Coercive Control and Physical Injury

First, coercive control can occur in the presence or absence of physical abuse. In cases where physical abuse is used within the context of coercive control, there are arguably three ways in which this can be perpetrated: (i) physical assaults, (ii) physical neglect, (iii) sexual violence/sexual coercion. Interestingly, Little (2023: 19) considers the body as a "site of violence", describing physical intimate partner abuse as "intimate war" where injury and pain experienced by the body are literal embodied experiences of intimate partner abuse. Similar comparisons can be drawn to military warfare and the experiences of soldiers in global conflicts (Little, 2023). In contrast, Stark (2007) suggests that where physical abuse is present, the overriding aim for the perpetrator is dominance. This prevents the victim from escaping, puts an end to conflict, and allows the perpetrator to exert male privilege over resources and the victim's agency (Crossman & Hardesty, 2018; Douglas et al., 2019; Kennedy, 2022; Stark, 2007, 2023; Walby & Towers, 2018; Woodlock, 2017). Examples of physical abuse can include hitting, choking, shaking, biting, shoving, grabbing, slapping, burning, scratching, hair pulling and other controlled or impulsive attacks on the victim (Devries et al., 2013; Kennedy, 2022; Spencer et al., 2022; Stewart et al., 2021). Some of these attacks may be perceived to be more or less serious than others. However, Stark (2007, 2009) maintains that it is not the severity of the physical attacks which is important. Instead, the prominent feature in cases of coercive control is the cumulative harm, which persists in combination with other types of harm.

HIDDEN INJURY

Furthermore, physical attacks may be directed to a particular part of the body which is not visible to others, so that any resulting cuts and bruises can be concealed (Hellman & Hurley, 2023; Sanderson, 2008). Other forms of physical abuse may leave no evidence of physical injury, such as administering ice-cold baths or asphyxiation (Sanderson, 2008). Data from the National Trauma Data Bank for 2007–2014 suggests that both visible and hidden injuries need to be considered by healthcare providers in cases of intimate partner abuse (Porter et al., 2019). This is due to the incidence and long-term implications of both visible and hidden injuries. As reported by Porter et al. (2019), 30% of the women sampled, with an average age of 37.5 years, presented with fractures to their vertebrae, torso (including the chest, abdomen, pelvis and back), and ribs. Facial fractures were more widespread in women aged 18–39 years, and those aged 60 and over were more likely to have fractures to their ribs or thigh bones (Porter et al., 2019). Often the assumption is that intimate partner abuse victim-survivors will have visible injuries appearing on their face, but many perpetrators will injure partners in hidden places on the body so injuries are easier to conceal under clothing (Hellman & Hurley, 2023).

NEGLECT AND SEXUAL ABUSE

Other ways in which physical abuse can be used as a means of control and coercion are through physical neglect and sexual abuse. For example, perpetrators may refuse victims their basic needs such as food or shelter (Brandhorst & Clark, 2022; Frost et al., 2023; Lentz, 2018). This can be particularly common in elder abuse (Knight & Hester, 2016). Physical neglect can also be coupled with sexual coercion. Thiel de Bocanegra et al. (2010) reported that 66% of their sample of women from domestic violence shelters were forced to have sex with partners. Of these women, some were threatened with food restrictions if they did not comply with their partner's sexual expectations. In addition, food insecurity can also be a consequence of perpetrators withholding money or resources to pay for food expenses (Brandhorst & Clark, 2022; Frost et al., 2023; Lentz, 2018; Rahman et al., 2013). This is arguably more precarious in countries where families are living in poverty or living on the edge of poverty. Withholding food can be combined with patriarchal social practices and power, and can be used as an extension of physical abuse with long-term nutritional consequences (Lentz, 2018).

As previously mentioned, sexual abuse or coercion may also be a tactic used by perpetrators. In these instances, perpetrators may force the victim to engage in sexual contact with them, which is degrading, or may withdraw or refuse sex as a way of isolating them further (Kennedy, 2022; Mitchell & Raghavan, 2019; Raghavan et al., 2014; Rees et al., 2006; Stark, 2007, 2012, 2017, 2018). They may also use rape or sexual coercion to dominate their partners even after they have separated (Rees et al., 2006; Stark, 2007, 2017, 2018). Often as the control progresses within an abusive relationship, the failure to comply with men's wishes tends to reduce so that ultimately women feel that the physical and/or sexual abuse they suffer is happening for nothing (Mršević & Hughes, 1997).

Marshall and Holtzworth-Munroe (2002) suggested that those who perpetrated psychological aggression were more likely to use abusive tactics that were less visible and more likely to be overlooked, including sexual coercion. DeGue et al. (2010) reported that perpetrators of sexual coercion, rather than sexual assault, tended to use sexual coercion with the intention of controlling their partner. In comparison, those who perpetrated sexual assault did so in the moment without considering how their behaviour impacted others. Logan et al. (2007) examined the similarities and differences in sexual coercion and degradation of women experiencing abuse. The findings were split into two groups: forced sex and no forced sex. Where the perpetrator had verbally pressured their partner, over 90% of the forced sex group reported being pressured into sex which made them feel uncomfortable, with 28% of the no forced sex group reporting this (Logan et al., 2007). Furthermore, 81% of the forced sex group disclosed their partners' demeaning sexual practices towards them, with 29% of the no forced sex group also describing these. Logan et al.'s (2007: 79) study identified sex as another means of control, whereby partners could express "ownership" over their significant others. This links back to previous discussions on jealousy, envy and proprietary behaviours, which are factors that underpin controlling and coercive behaviours. Refusal of sex by wives or partners has also been identified as a factor in intimate partner abuse and homicide (Adinkrah, 2017). This is often associated with infidelity, whereby refusal to have sex with husbands or partners may indicate an affair. However, this research is specific to married couples in Ghana so may not be comparable to other parts of the world.

WITHDRAWAL OF SEX OR INTIMACY

Conversely, some perpetrators withhold affection as part of their abusive tactics. This has been identified as a passive medium of control which can be most commonly associated with emotional or psychological abuse (Lammers, 2002; Lammers et al., 2005; Sharma, 2023). In doing so, the perpetrators of this form of abuse may refuse or withdraw sex or intimacy in order to pressure victims to submit to them or as a means of punishment (Lammers, 2002, Lammers et al., 2005; Sharma, 2023). This often occurs in conjunction with victims not adhering to gendered expectations and can have significant consequences for victims in terms of their identity. Furthermore, it can lead to feelings of confusion, loneliness, low self-esteem, anger, guilt and despair (Lammers, 2002, Lammers et al., 2005). Interestingly, others have investigated withholding sex in the context of forgiveness, framing this behaviour as revenge (McNulty, 2020). However, refusing or withdrawing sex or intimacy has not received a lot of attention amongst scholars. Instead, much of the research discourse focuses on victims refusing to engage in sexual activity or being forced to engage in sexual activity which is degrading or makes them feel uncomfortable.

Coercive Control and Intimidating Behaviour

Intimidation is considered the second key element in the technology of coercive control (Kennedy, 2022; Stark, 2007, 2012, 2023). As such, this tool of coercion is used by perpetrators to frighten, to engender secrecy, to encourage dependence and compliance, and to enable the victim's loyalty (Karakurt & Silver, 2013; Kennedy, 2022; Salari & LeFevre Sillito, 2016; Stark, 2007, 2023). This can result in shame (Stark, 2007, 2023). Arguably, there are three ways in which the perpetrator can intimidate the victim. These include the use of active or passive threats, surveillance and degradation (Kennedy, 2022; Stark, 2007, 2023). The use of effective intimidation in controlling relationships is reliant on the victim's experiences with previous partners. Her experiences provide a basis for future behaviour in terms of how a partner is likely to act, what she thinks he will do and what he is prepared to do (Stark, 2023).

In literature relating to rape and sexual abuse, this has been referred to as the "female fear" (Gordon & Riger, 1991: 4). It was later developed into the "shadow of sexual assault" thesis which suggests that the fear of rape women experience becomes a "master offense" (Ferraro, 1996: 667–669), increasing fear of all other crimes (Riger & Gordon, 1981; Vera-Gray, 2018). As rape is an offence mainly affecting women, this perpetual fear casts shadows on other crimes whereby women victimised by acquisitive crimes (e.g., robbery) can simultaneously fear the possibility of rape (Ferraro, 1996; Vera-Gray, 2018). However, the previous work discussed is specific to rape and sexual assault rather than intimate partner abuse and homicide. That being said, this discourse highlights an innate disparity that women face in public spaces which can make them more vulnerable in their personal lives (Stark, 2023). As Stark (2007, 2023) mentions, the structural gender inequalities that women experience reduce their capacity to resist psychological power from perpetrators.

ACTIVE AND PASSIVE THREATS

Threats are another medium to intimidate victims of intimate partner abuse and homicide, with clear reference to the use of threats being outlined in previous literature and empirical study (Boonzaier & de la Rey, 2004; Campbell et al., 2007; Cavanagh et al., 2001; Dutton & Goodman, 2005; James & Farnham, 2003; Liem & Roberts, 2009; Monckton Smith et al., 2014; Pain, 2014; Stark, 2007, 2012, 2023; Tyner, 2012; Walby & Towers, 2018). Broadly speaking, threats can be categorised in two ways: active or passive. Active threats tend to be more direct, such as threats to harm (including non-fatal strangulation and acid attacks) and threats to kill (Pain et al., 2014; Stark, 2007, 2023; Stewart et al., 2021; Tyner, 2012; Walby & Towers, 2018). However, passive threats are more indirect, including the use of the silent treatment, refusing to speak to children or refusing sexual advances or intimacy (Kennedy, 2022; Lammers, 2002; Lammers et al., 2005; Sharma, 2023).

While the literature is limited in its approach to discussing threats as active or passive in relation to perpetrators, Bostock et al. (2009) and Bahrami et al. (2015) have considered this in terms of the strategies victim-survivors use to manage victimisation in abusive relationships. In older literature, Copelon (1994) draws synergies between elements of torture and domestic abuse, citing active or passive forms of torture prisoners are subjected to and how these are often seen in cases of domestic abuse. In addition, threats can extend to children in the household where the perpetrator threatens to remove or relocate children, but this can also go beyond the immediate family to the victim's extended family, friends and pets (Monckton Smith et al., 2014; Stark, 2007, 2023).

While the distinction between active and passive threats, linguistically and practically, is important in terms of the nature of victimisation, the most significant consequence for victims is the impact threats can have on their autonomy. Moreover, it is important to note that physical violence is not always necessary for compliance. Instead, it is the fear created by threats that causes the most harm in cases of coercive control (Monckton Smith et al., 2014; Pain, 2014; Stark, 2007, 2023).

Table 3.2 Examples of Active and Passive Threats

Threat Type	*Example of Threat*
Active Threat	Threats of harm to others and/or self*
	Threats of harm with a weapon*
	Threats of sexual abuse
	Threats of acid attack*
	Threats to kill*
	Threats to share intimate or sexually explicit images or videos
	Threats of outing (incl. HIV status)
	Threats to leave
	Threats to take own life
	Threats of forced marriage
	Threats of criminal damage
	Threats to remove children from victim
Passive Threat	Use of silent treatment *
	Refusal to engage in intimacy of any kind and/or sexual activity
	Withdrawal of intimacy of any kind and/or sexual activity
	Withholding intimacy of any kind and/or sexual activity

Sources: Campbell et al., 2007; Cavanagh et al., 2001; James & Farnham, 2003; Liem & Roberts, 2009; Monckton Smith et al., 2014; Pain, 2014; Stark, 2007, 2023; Stewart et al., 2021; Walby & Towers, 2018.

*Aimed at the victim, children (incl. foetus), pets and/or other extended family, friends or co-workers

THE USE OF GASLIGHTING

Gaslighting is another means of manipulation and control used to intimidate the victim in abusive relationships (Abramson, 2014; Dutton, 2007; Hayes & Jeffries, 2016; Petric, 2018; Rietdijk, 2018; Sweet, 2019). According to Sweet (2019: 851), gaslighting is "a type of psychological abuse aimed at making victims seem or feel 'crazy,' creating a 'surreal' interpersonal environment". This type of abuse has also been described as 'crazy-making' (Abramson, 2014; Hayes & Jeffries, 2016). It specifically targets a victim's judgments, perceptions and their view of reality, the purpose being for the victim to submit to the perpetrator's will, thereby surrendering her own sense of self, autonomy and agency (Dorpat, 1994, 1996). It can be carried out both consciously or unconsciously (Bhatti et al., 2023; Dorpat, 1996). Gaslighting can operate in a number of different ways. Perpetrators may threaten their partners by telling them deliberate lies or embarrassing them in public, or they may lie and assert that abuse has not taken place, suggesting to the victim that it's all 'in their head'. The motivation for gaslighting is to remind the victim that her safety may be compromised if she attempts confrontation or fails to accept the perpetrator's version of events, no matter how outrageous they are (Stark, 2007, 2023). In the same way coercive control more generally has been compared to the oppression of prisoners of war, gaslighting follows the same manipulative tactics used in these settings (Dorpat, 1996). It has also been used as part of the brainwashing and indoctrination methods adopted by cults and by fascist and communist regimes (Dorpat, 1996). Gaslighting has even been discussed in the context of politics, with President of the United States, Donald Trump being accused of gaslighting America during his first presidential administration (Leve, 2017; Sweet, 2019).

Until recently, gaslighting has been considered almost entirely by psychologists, but Sweet (2019) argues that this phenomenon is important to sociological inquiry given its roots in social and institutional inequality, as well as the structural vulnerabilities inherent in gendered forms of abuse. Similarly, the existing psychological discourse tends to exclude context (Sweet, 2019). Research spanning decades has shown the importance of social context in abuse with the two being intrinsically interconnected (Stark, 2010; Sweet, 2019). Older literature pertaining to gaslighting appears to overlook the social characteristics which enable the exertion of power (Stern, 2007, 2018). It must be noted that the effectiveness of gaslighting can be tied to social characteristics such as gender, race, nationality, sexuality and class (Sweet, 2019). Perpetrators who utilise gender-based stereotypes, structural inequalities and institutional vulnerabilities in intimate relationships further the effects of gaslighting, particularly in situations where power is unequal in relationships (Sweet, 2019). Sweet (2019) argues that women's lack of cultural, economic and political capital makes them more susceptible to gaslighting as men do not have these structural barriers to contend with. As such, she believes gaslighting is a gendered social phenomenon, thereby drawing similar assumptions to Stark (2007, 2023) in terms of coercive control's wider exploitation of gender and sexuality. Moreover, Sweet (2019: 852) suggests that gaslighting differentiates from other forms of abuse as it is characterised by "feminized irrationality".

Interestingly, gaslighting is not considered a distinct form of psychological abuse and is often discussed in relation to coercive control or intimate terrorism (Johnson, 2006, 2008; Stark, 2007; Sweet, 2019). Sweet (2019) suggests this is a massive oversight given the importance of dissecting the different forms of abuse in order to better understand the sociocultural context in which gaslighting occurs and its effectiveness thereafter (Johnson, 2008; Myhill, 2015; Stark, 2010). This book supports this to some extent and explains this further in relation to online harm in Chapter 5. In 2014, the National Domestic Abuse Hotline surveyed 2,500 callers, asking them about their experiences of coercive control. Of the adult women who agreed to participate in the survey, 73.8% reported their partner exhibiting behaviours akin to gaslighting and 50% disclosed gaslighting being used as a barrier to accessing support (Warshaw et al., 2014). While these figures – albeit outdated – provide some insight into the prevalence of gaslighting, they overlook our understanding of "abusive acts by their ability to coerce" (Sweet, 2019: 854). The importance of this lies in the gendered nature of gaslighting where fear plays a major part in women's ability to resist and respond to abusive tactics (Anderson, 2005; Ross, 2012; Sweet, 2019).

SURVEILLANCE AND MONITORING BEHAVIOUR

Another intimidation tactic used by perpetrators is surveillance (Dutton & Goodman, 2005; Stark, 2007, 2012, 2023). The purpose of surveillance is to monitor victims, collecting information often without their knowledge or consent. Surveillance and monitoring behaviour impacts the victim's sense of privacy (Stark, 2007, 2023). Arguably, this facet of coercive control lies on a continuum with surveillance involving either direct or indirect monitoring behaviours (Logan & Walker, 2009; Stark, 2007, 2023). Direct monitoring behaviours may include perpetrators overtly following the victim whereas indirect monitoring behaviours may involve perpetrators enlisting the aid of a 'spy' who will follow the victim and report back on their activities (Dutton & Goodman, 2005; Johnson, 2008; MacMillan, 2022; Tahna et al., 2010). The information gained from surveillance can be used to embarrass or control the victim at a later point (Stark, 2023). Perpetrator motivation in these instances is to demonstrate omnipresence and omnipotence (Fraser et al., 2010; George & Harris, 2014; Harris & Woodlock, 2019; MacMillan, 2022; Monckton Smith et al., 2014; Stark, 2007, 2012, 2023; Woodlock, 2017).

French and Raven's (1959) theory of social power suggests that coercion cannot occur without surveillance, or at the very least, without the victim believing they are being monitored. Three additional factors need to be considered as part of the theory of social power: (i) "setting the stage" where the perpetrator shows his ability to coerce, (ii) the perpetrator needs to acquire information on the victim to know whether or not they need to impose conditions for noncompliance, and (iii) compliance and resistance are both outcomes to coercion (Dutton & Goodman, 2005: 745; Raven, 1993). This links with the discussion on active and passive threats earlier. As threats are reliant on noncompliance, surveillance is utilised as a means of seeing whether compliance has been achieved or not (Dutton & Goodman, 2005). However, it must be noted that Dutton and Goodman's (2005) research was based on clinical experience and domestic violence experts rather than victim-survivor accounts (Sharp-Jeffs et al., 2018).

Similar to other facets of coercive control discussed previously, the perpetration of surveillance or monitoring behaviour can be extensive but also unique to each individual experience of abuse (Monckton Smith et al., 2014; Stark, 2007, 2023). As such, there is no roadmap for abuse. Each victim's experience is very personal to them. For those victims who are constantly monitored, their social circle can become very small. They may choose to isolate themselves from both formal or informal support structures, stop communicating with others altogether, or stop doing part or all of their daily activities (MacMillan, 2022; Stark, 2007, 2023). Bowstead (2011) draws parallels with the work of Foucault in terms of the impact of surveillance on women in abusive relationships. She suggests that women internalise the gaze of surveillance in the same way prisoners do, thereby regulating their behaviour as a result. As argued by Foucault (1991: 201), "surveillance is permanent in its effects, even if it is discontinuous in its action", showing that even after monitoring behaviours have subsided, the effect remains unchanged and long-term.

STALKING

Stalking is one of the most common behaviours attributed to coercive control. Within the literature, it has been suggested that both behaviours are often present at the same time (Norris et al., 2011; Monckton Smith et al., 2017). Definitions of stalking have varied in the literature due to researchers and clinicians failing to come to a consensus (Scarr & Kennedy, 2023). The Suzy Lamplugh Trust provides a more comprehensive definition explaining stalking as:

> a pattern of fixated and obsessive behaviours which is repeated, persistent, intrusive and causes fear of violence or engenders alarm and distress in the victim.
>
> (Suzy Lamplugh Trust, 2021: 1)

Others have considered stalking as unwanted, persistent behaviour which induces fear (Canter & Ioannou, 2004; Logan & Walker, 2009; Melton, 2007; Mullen et al., 2009; Woodlock, 2017). Stalking behaviours can include watching, following, spying, repeated unwanted contact, threats of harm or suicide, property damage, and spreading rumours in both personal and professional settings (Bracewell et al., 2020; Brady & Nobles, 2017; Scarr & Kennedy, 2023). Comparable to surveillance and monitoring behaviour, perpetrators may employ particular stalking tactics which are individual to the victim, or behaviours that only the victim would understand as stalking. Context and intent are incredibly important in terms of stalking as some behaviours can be considered harmless and legal without taking into account the bigger picture (Brady & Nobles, 2017; Scarr & Kennedy, 2023; Stark, 2007, 2023).

Stark (2023) suggests that stalking within the context of intimate relationships is a more serious offence than 'stranger' stalking, given the personal connection between the perpetrator and victim. However, 'stranger' stalking is often more readily identified as stalking and is usually taken more seriously (Monckton Smith et al., 2017; Scott et al., 2010; Scott, 2020). Stalking continues to be considered a gendered crime, with women being overrepresented as victims and men being overrepresented as perpetrators (Stark, 2007, 2023). This is further emphasised by estimates of stalking behaviour. For instance, there were 17,230 incidents of stalking recorded as part of the crime survey for England and Wales as of March 2023, with 9,104 being reported by women and 8,126 reported by men (ONS, 2023). However, these estimates need to be treated with caution due to a survey error which led to some participant data being lost between October 2022 and January 2023. Similarly, many victims of stalking may not report the crime, especially in intimate relationships, for a number of reasons, such as fear of not being believed or inadequate support from formal support services (Scarr & Kennedy, 2023).

Stalking has been the subject of empirical inquiry since as far back as 1988 with perpetrators who engage in stalking behaviours being considered the most dangerous (Monckton Smith et al., 2017). Interest in stalking has continued into the 21st century due to its links to violence and abuse, coercive control, and homicide (James & Farnham, 2003; Meloy, 1996; McFarlane et al., 1999; Southworth et al., 2007). Research has shown that stalking occurred in 68% of cases 12 months before attempted or actual homicide was perpetrated against the victim (McFarlane et al., 2002; Monckton Smith et al., 2014, 2017). It is therefore considered a major risk factor for violence and homicide (Kennedy, 2022; Monckton Smith et al., 2017; Scott et al., 2010; Stark, 2007, 2023). Given the link between stalking and fatal violence, Richards (2016) has gone so far as to describe it as "murder in slow motion".

The Art of Drive-Bys and Stakeouts

Nelson is the brother of 24-year-old Amber who was murdered by her ex-partner, Thornton, in 2016. Nelson explained that Amber and Thornton had only been seeing each other for around six months before she was murdered. Thornton's possessive nature had developed into stalking which Amber reported to the police on several occasions. Nelson also explained that he and his family were unaware of some of the incidents of stalking until after Amber was murdered:

> … The stalking itself obviously started fairly … well to be honest it started during the relationship so there was more it was "where are you?" And there was also stuff we learnt later on, you know, so asking her work colleagues to confirm where she is so "send me a picture of where you are and what you are wearing", you know what I mean, its controlling and is actually stalking but during the relationship and then that obviously continued after they broke up it was just a control thing I think and then the rest and got worse and worse …

Nelson described occasions where stalking was perpetrated in the form of drive-bys and stakeouts. The is particularly important as the perpetrator did not live locally, driving hours to spy on the victim:

> He did stake out her place a few times. It was a long drive but he [drove] all the way down two days before he killed her, he drove all the way down, was taking pictures of the windows and entry points of the house and stuff and that's what we know of because they [police] found photos on his phone but yeah but I think it's a couple of hour drive he's from up from Elgin to down to North Berwick …

This case highlights how stalking can be perpetrated within an abusive relationship post-separation. It shows this possessive need to control the victim, and where intimacy cannot be sought, perpetrators can find alternative routes to show their determination for contact and control. Drive-bys are one method of surveillance which can still maintain control over victims without physical presence as victims are often acutely aware of being watched (Canter & Ioannou, 2004). This provides an alternative perspective on stalking which can also be linked to jealousy, envy and proprietariness discussed earlier in this chapter. It corroborates other accounts of stalking within the literature which frame this form of harm as a risk factor for intimate partner homicide.

MICROREGULATION

As described by Stark (2007, 2023), microregulation is another way in which perpetrators intimidate victims. In relationships characterised by coercive control, perpetrators view separateness from the victim as detrimental to their relationship (Crossman & Hardesty, 2018; Stark, 2007, 2023; Tolman, 1989). This unique behaviour is part of the anatomy of coercive control (Stark, 2007, 2023). Perpetrators who engage in microregulation do so to control every part of the victim's daily life, regardless of how meaningless the activities are (Stark, 2007, 2023). The purpose of such behaviour is to introduce fear, remove the victim's autonomy and test loyalty (Dobash & Dobash, 1980; Pain, 2014; Stark, 2007, 2023). This fear is instilled in the most superficial decisions women make, eventually making the choice itself frightening. At times, this microregulation may move from the home environment to being more portable, whereby perpetrators may use 'check-ins' to intimidate the victim (Stark, 2007, 2023). Microregulation coupled with microsurveillance heightens the vehemence of the abuse in a way that no other form of oppression does (Stark, 2023). This is where digital coercive control can be utilised to extend the abuse further. A more in-depth discussion of digital coercive control will appear in Chapter 4.

The consequences of microregulation are serious. Some victims push back against the pervasive scrutiny while others become more and more isolated from support (Harris & Woodlock, 2019; Raghavan et al., 2019; Stark, 2023). For those victims who attempt to rebel against microregulation, they find ways to reassert their autonomy by meeting the perpetrator's demands on their terms (Stark, 2023). For example, they may call home from a withheld number so the perpetrator is unaware of their location. However, restriction of this kind can also lead women to limit contact with informal social support such as family and friends (Stark, 2023; Viñas-Racionero et al., 2023).

Often the prevalence of microregulation is not directly measured or recorded in empirical research, with other facets of coercive control taking priority. However, Viñas-Racionero et al.'s (2023) study on Spanish femicide cases does provide a partial picture of victims' experiences of microregulation from interviews with victims and perpetrators' social circles. From the sample of 150 femicides (2006–2016), they found microregulation was present in 75% of cases. In 16% of these cases, microregulation and restriction was situational rather than pervasive where these behaviours were a result of persistent conflict, especially in instances where trust was broken. This is consistent with much older research by Tolman (1989) where 85% of American women in his study reported their partner monitoring their time.

DEGRADATION AND SHAMING

Degradation and shaming are also aspects of coercive control. On the one hand, degradation seeks to obliterate the victim's self-respect whereas shaming is used to enable the victim's compliance (Logan et al., 2007; Stark, 2007, 2012, 2023). Self-respect is particularly important in ascertaining a person's worth and, ultimately, impacts their personhood. Without it, people have nothing to strive for (Rawls, 1971; Stark, 2023). In degradation, constant remarks and name-calling by perpetrators can have a negative effect on a victim's personhood (Logan et al., 2007; Stark, 2007, 2012, 2023). As mentioned earlier, victims of coercive control are largely isolated from their social circle so approval and judgment from perpetrators are extremely important to them. In these circumstances, victims often have little to no capacity for positive self-talk (Stark, 2007, 2023). Given the gendered nature of coercive control, it is unsurprising that male perpetrators target areas linked to female gender identity. These are usually areas victims are already uncomfortable with such as their looks or weight (Stark, 2007, 2023).

Shaming differs from degradation as it tends to involve branding the victim as a way of demonstrating ownership (Johnson et al., 2019; Stark, 2007, 2012, 2023). This type of behaviour also leaves the victim open to abuse from others. As perpetrator's branding is visible to others, it shows the that the victim is the perpetrator's property but also that she is vulnerable to further victimisation. Branding can include tattoos, bite marks, piercings or burns (Stark, 2007, 2023). Suicide attempts have been linked to branding due to the underlying reminders of ownership (Stark, 2007, 2023). While branding has been discussed in the literature to some extent, research concerning this aspect of coercive control is limited and warrants further exploration.

Further shaming rituals can include activities relating to the partner's sexual or basic bodily functions (Stark, 2007, 2023). This has been discussed earlier in the section on "Neglect and Sexual Abuse". Similarly, they may involve the partner complying with a set of distinct rules. Other forms of shaming may encompass the victim being coerced into committing criminal activities (Barlow, 2016; Stark, 2007, 2023; Weare & Barlow, 2019). As with degradation, shaming also has isolating properties.

Coercive Control and Isolation

The third component involved in coercive control is isolation (Myhill & Hohl, 2016; Stark, 2007, 2023). This component aims to stop the victim disclosing abuse, enables dependence, demonstrates exclusive possession of the victim and prevents them from seeking help or support (Arnold, 2009; Rose et al., 2011; Stark, 2007, 2012, 2023). It is also important to note that isolation can operate at two different levels. Victims are often isolated *from* informal and formal support, but they are also isolated *at* particular events or places where they are expected to engage with others (Stark, 2023). For example, victims may be isolated at their workplace or at family events. Similarly, isolation can work on both a physical and emotional level until total control is achieved (Baldwin et al., 2015; Duron et al., 2021). In physical isolation, perpetrators control information movement by limiting victims' contact with the outside world. This can include physical isolation by moving the victim to a remote geographic area (Duron et al., 2021). Emotional isolation enables the perpetrator to create psychological space between the victim and their support network in order to inhabit it. This can be achieved by monopolising the victim's attention or by lying and manipulating the victim's reality (Duron et al., 2021). However, isolation differs significantly within each relationship. This behaviour can negatively impact victims' identities and selfhood thereby preventing their independence (Stark, 2007, 2023). As isolation increases within the relationship, the victim's social network diminishes meaning her only source of validation is the perpetrator (Dutton & Goodman, 2005; Stark, 2007, 2023). As such, many women in this position can become isolated from family, friends, work and help.

The support explored by women in relationships characterised by coercive control can differ depending on what they need and who is approached. Social support can be divided into two broad types: emotional and instrumental (Hasbullah et al., 2016; Liang et al., 2005; Rose et al., 2000). While support is multifaceted, the main focus of social support is to help victims better understand and cope with abuse (Rose et al., 2000). It provides a different perspective on the abuse, framing it in a way that shows them they are not at fault for their experiences; it potentially changes their environment by giving them the necessary physical tools (e.g., money, housing) to separate themselves from abuse; and it helps victims to manage emotions related to their abuse. It also validates the abuse victims are experiencing and offers reassurance which enables them to identify it (Rose et al., 2000). Ultimately, social support aids women's mental health, personhood and self-esteem, which is vital to them coping and potentially leaving abusive relationships (Hasbullah et al., 2016; Latta & Goodman, 2011; Liang et al., 2005; Rose et al., 2000). The sources of the aforementioned support can be separated into informal and formal support outlined further below.

ISOLATION FROM INFORMAL SUPPORT

Informal support can include a number of people in the victim's life such as immediate and extended family, friends, work colleagues, neighbours and others the victim may confide in (Goodman & Smyth, 2011; Latta & Goodman, 2011; Liang et al., 2005; Rose et al., 2000; Trotter & Allen, 2009; Stark, 2007, 2023). Emotional support is often sought from female family members or friends (Liang et al., 2005; Rose et al., 2000). However, this support is not always positive with women being dissatisfied with the advice offered, being pressured to leave the perpetrator before they are ready to do so or commenting on a lack of understanding from those they confide in (Goodman & Smyth, 2011; Trotter & Allen, 2009). Unsurprisingly, it is usually the victim's family who are the first support network the perpetrator attempts to separate the victim from (Stark, 2007, 2023). In these circumstances, the perpetrator is likely to threaten the victim's family with violence or threaten to hire others to harm her family with the intention of creating this separation (Douglas et al., 2019; Harris & Woodlock, 2019; Monckton Smith et al., 2014; Stark, 2023; Woodlock, 2017). Little empirical research has been conducted to consider this overspill of abuse to victims' families' and, as such, this will be discussed more comprehensively in Chapter 5.

A perpetrator of coercive control often puts limitations on the length of time the victim is allowed to see her family or he may forbid her from seeing them completely (Madhok et al., 2013; Stark, 2023). Moreover, the perpetrator may put pressure on the victim to choose between him and her family (Stark, 2007, 2023). Others can also be involved in the victim's isolation such as the perpetrator's family. This is particularly common in migrant communities where the watchful eyes of extended family members are ever-present (Chowdhury & Winder, 2022; Stark, 2023). In some cultures the family unit is patrifocal, meaning that the perpetrator is considered the head of the family, with his relatives playing an important role in the couple's lives (Georgas et al., 2006; Stark, 2023). As such, the perpetrator's family may prevent the victim from seeing her children if she does not comply with the perpetrator's demands.

Another potential rival for the perpetrator's affection is the victim's friends. The victim's friends are an extremely important part of her overall support network, especially in terms of her sense of self (Rose et al., 2000). The perpetrator may also belong to this social network so friends may actually pose more of a threat to the perpetrator than the victim's family (Dutton & Goodman, 2005; Goodman & Smyth, 2011; Stark, 2007, 2023). Perpetrators may choose to keep the victim's abuse hidden, use overt threats towards them or carry out the abuse in front of the victim's friends as an isolation tactic (Fontes, 2015; Stark, 2007, 2023). Likewise, perpetrators may spread rumours about the victim to drive a wedge between her and her friends (Fontes, 2015). Perpetrators may also turn up to social gatherings without warning or invite, employ spies to check up on the victim or forbid contact entirely (Stark, 2007, 2013). Again, this 'me or them' test of loyalty may also extend to friends. In some circumstances, women may be reluctant to forge new relationships based on their experiences of mistrust and fear demonstrated by the perpetrator, they may isolate themselves from friends as a means to keep the peace in their relationship, or they may remain isolated in order to keep their private troubles from becoming public (Stark, 2007; Fontes, 2015; Rose et al., 2000).

Isolation from work is another technique used within coercive control (Stark, 2007, 2023). Hartmann (1939) emphasises the need for a space which is free of conflict and describes work as one of these spaces designated as a safety zone (Stark, 2007, 2023). In many ways, work can act as a sanctuary for women in abusive relationships. It also symbolises life after abuse as it creates a space where women can resist the domination channelled through coercive control (Hayes, 2013; Rajah, 2007; Showalter, 2016; Stark, 2007, 2023). It allows women to push back against abuse and enables them to reclaim their autonomy (Hayes, 2013; Rajah, 2007). Rajah (2007: 210) goes further by exploring the term "edgework" in which she suggests that:

> ... the embodied experience of successful edgework may lead women to identify contradictions in their social position, which may, in turn, lead to changes in consciousness that counteract their oppression.

As such, Rajah (2007) is describing a form of resistance to abuse which women can engage in that provides them with a sense of authorship or accomplishment having challenged the limitations put in place by an abusive partner. Where Stark (2007, 2023) refers to this as a 'safety zone', others have considered this 'safety work' or 'space for action' (Kelly, 1988, 2003, 2012; Vera-Gray, 2018). However, 'safety work' is considered as part of the broader sexual violence literature and not within the context of intimate partner homicide.

With that being said, coercive control can negatively affect women's employability considering victims are likely to have gaps in employment, long periods of absence and/or issues relating to tardiness (Stark, 2007, 2023; Munteanu, 2021). In instances where the perpetrator is met with resistance, they may employ tactics discussed earlier, resulting in the victim losing her job. Similarly, the aforementioned 'check-ins' may also extend to the victim's workplace. Given that these tactics are used more by perpetrators of coercive control, many workplaces are starting to introduce awareness of absenteeism, stress, employee turnover, sick days and decreased productivity into their HR polices with reference to employees experiencing domestic abuse (Bennett et al., 2019, 2021; Equality and Human Rights Commission, 2013).

ISOLATION FROM FORMAL SUPPORT

As discussed previously, perpetrators can also isolate the victim from support providers which fall outside of the victim's social network. Formal support can include professionals working in the criminal justice system, police, legal representatives, social services, mental and physical healthcare staff, religious leaders, domestic abuse advocates, shelter staff, and community aid (Latta & Goodman, 2011; Liang et al., 2005; Rose et al., 2000; Stark, 2007, 2023; Trotter & Allen, 2009). This support differs from the emotional support sought from family and friends, instead being instrumental in nature (Rose et al., 2000;

Trotter & Allen, 2009). Instrumental support comprises of material assistance and physical support such as providing financial help, clothing, food, work opportunities and/or permanent housing solutions (Hasbullah et al., 2016; Kyriakakis, 2014; Liang et al., 2005).

In instances where victims are isolated from formal support, perpetrators may interfere with calls to the police, perhaps by calling them first or positioning themselves as victims (Hester, 2009; Miller, 2001; Monckton Smith et al., 2014; Stark, 2007, 2023). They may also use the criminal justice system as a means of enacting further abuse. For example, perpetrators may utilise their own abuse of the victim to create a set of circumstances whereby the victim could appear guilty of commissioning a crime (Roberts, 2022), the purpose of this being to reestablish power and control. Arguably, it also reaffirms their version of social order (Roberts, 2022; Wilcox, 2006). Similarly, perpetrators may report victims to statutory bodies such as children's/social services or the Department of Work and Pensions (DWP) as a further mechanism of control (Hester et al., 2007; Roberts, 2015, 2022). They may also threaten the victim with violence if they disclose the abuse to mental and/or physical healthcare professionals. It is clear that perpetrators go to extreme lengths to control victims and conceal abuse.

The 'Control' in Coercive Control

The final dimension which brings coercive control full circle is the element of control. Control is used to enable women's subordination within abusive relationships where the sole focus of the abuse is to dominate the victim (Stark, 2007, 2023). By way of domination, perpetrators seek to exploit their partner's material and personal resources for their own gain, preventing the victim's escape and establishing traditional gender roles (Stark, 2007, 2023). Control within abusive relationships is effective as inequality already exists as part of the patriarchal structures within society. Power is relative to gender. This extends to other intersections such as race, age and even class (McCue, 2008; Pain, 2014; Smith, 2005; Stark, 2012). Stark (2012) suggests that there may be a few instances where women could use coercive control over men. One of these instances is where privilege could be used in terms of a woman's class or income (Sharp-Jeffs, 2022). However, given the structural inequalities that already exist for women, it makes it even more difficult for them to leave abusive relationships (Stark, 2007, 2023).

Arguably, control is more consistent in cases of abuse than violence (Adams, 2007; Stark, 2007; Websdale, 2010). This has been previously highlighted earlier in this chapter. Control permeates every part of women's daily lives, impacting their sexual activities, bodily functions, eating patterns, their own perception of reality, and who they can see and what they can do at the most basic level (Stark, 2007, 2023). Similar to 'capture crimes', coercive control differs significantly from other forms of domestic abuse (Stark, 2023).

CONTROL AND ECONOMIC ABUSE

As briefly mentioned earlier, coercion and, indeed, control can be linked to economic abuse (Dutton & Goodman, 2005; Pollet, 2011; Stark, 2007, 2023). While the term 'financial abuse' tends to be used in a UK context, it does not fully consider the control of all economic resources, hence its omission from the title of this subsection (Sharp-Jeffs, 2022: 3). Instead, 'financial abuse' focuses more on monetary control and finances so could be considered a sub-category of economic abuse (Littwin, 2012; Sharp-Jeffs, 2015). Economic abuse continues to be under-researched globally so the scale of the issue is little understood (Westmarland, 2015). It has also often been coupled with emotional abuse, resulting in definitional issues and a lack of focus in terms of policy and practice (Sharp-Jeffs, 2021). The wider definition used within academic settings, and which has been used within the *Domestic Abuse Act 2021*, was developed by Adams et al. (2008: 564) who indicate that economic abuse "involves behaviours that control a person's ability to acquire, use, or maintain economic resources, thus threatening their economic security and potential for self-sufficiency".

According to the Crime Survey for England and Wales, 67.5% of women experienced non-physical abuse, including emotional and financial abuse, in the year ending March 2023 (ONS, 2024). Men are marginally less likely to experience this type of abuse with the percentage being around 65%. With that being said, emotional and financial abuse are combined in official statistics so it is difficult to pinpoint more concrete figures relating to financial abuse specifically. As part of the Crime Survey for England and Wales, data is collected on why victims do not leave shared accommodation with an abusive partner and 12.3% stated that this was due to being financially dependent on that person (ONS, 2024). The results are hardly surprising given that men tend to hold economic power by default when it comes to the legal system (Littwin, 2012; Sharp-Jeffs, 2022). For instance, it was not until the early 1960s that women were able to keep half of the savings provided as part of their allowance from their husband due to the introduction of the *Married Women's Property Act 1964*. Similarly, the *Equal Pay Act 1970* disallowed women from being paid less than men by employers. However, women still needed a signature from a male guarantor to secure a mortgage and could not apply for a loan or credit until 1974 when the *Equal Credit Opportunity Act* was decreed (Issa, 2023; Sharp-Jeffs, 2022). Arguably, men are still expected to manage money even now (Postmus et al., 2018). Due to the ingrained nature of gendered concepts, particularly in terms of economic resources, it is often a challenge to change behaviour adhering to these gender norms (Sharp-Jeffs, 2022).

Perpetrators can either deprive the victim of money, deny them access to their money or take possession of their finances (Adams et al., 2008; Pollet, 2011; Sharp-Jeffs, 2022; Stark, 2007, 2023). This limits victims' capacity to resist coercive control as their access to material resources is diminished (Dutton & Goodman, 2005). This is prevalent in almost half of all cases of coercive control, with many formal services not taking this issue seriously (Stark, 2023). In the case of women unable to find £100 at short notice, research shows that they are over three times more likely to experience domestic abuse (Walby & Allen, 2004; Sharp-Jeffs, 2022). There is also a link between economic abuse and suicide (Aitken & Munro, 2018; Sharp-Jeffs, 2022).

As illustrated earlier in the section on "Neglect and Sexual Abuse", poverty can increase women's risk of abuse, particularly in relationships characterised by unequal power relations (Lyon, 2000; Sanders & Schnabel, 2004). This means that women are often put in the position where they are choosing between staying in a controlling relationship or facing food insecurity or, possibly, even homelessness by leaving the relationship (Brandhorst & Clark, 2022; Frost et al., 2023; Lentz, 2018; Rahman et al., 2013; Sanders & Schnabel, 2004; Sharp-Jeffs, 2022; Zorza, 1991). Irrespective of the family income, the finances are often dispensed in favour of the man in the case of abusive relationships (Stark, 2007, 2023). This goes back to the previous discussions regarding the gendered nature of intimate partner abuse where the perpetrator owns the victim and thus, has exclusive 'property rights' (Franzway et al., 2019; Stark, 2006, 2007, 2023). This also extends to the victim's income. As a consequence of this, victims often feel extremely vulnerable and, in some cases, completely dependent on the perpetrator (Dutton & Goodman, 2005). This can, ultimately, put women who leave abusive relationships at a massive disadvantage in both divorce or custody proceedings as they cannot provide for their families (Stark, 2023). Likewise, these every-day controls are usually taken for granted and, more often than not, go completely unnoticed within our society (Stark, 2007, 2023).

The Case of Economic Abuse and Homicide

Jen is the sister of 31-year-old Nessa who was murdered by her ex-fiancé, Paton, in 2016. Nessa had been in a relationship with Paton for nearly ten years before deciding to end the relationship after a number of abusive incidents. Jen recalled Nessa meeting Paton in a supermarket around nine or ten years prior. Jen explained that both Nessa and Paton had lived separately on a number of occasions, with Nessa moving closer to Jen in 2013 until the beginning of 2014. This was prior to Nessa and Paton's final breakup. They also shared three children together. Jen explained that Paton held all the cards literally and figuratively in terms of Nessa's economic position:

> … he wouldn't put her name on the mortgage so she had no … this is where the financial control comes in. Nessa never had any money, she worked full-time but she never had a penny to her name but he always had money … yeah, she had nothing and he had everything so he wouldn't put her name on the mortgage, wouldn't do any of that stuff because he knew she would have some control. If she left then he would have to give her half and the marriage thing as well, if he's not married to her what control does she have? She has none. You know, it's very difficult unless you've been with someone a very long time and so that was kind of how their relationship was really …

This case shows how economic abuse can be perpetrated in an intimate relationship as a means of power and control. Economic abuse is perhaps one of the subtler forms of abuse (Johnson & Hotton, 2003, Sharp-Jeffs, 2021). While economic abuse alone has not directly been related to intimate partner homicide, it is important to consider the entire 'web of abuse' with homicide falling at the very end of the spectrum (Johnson & Hotton, 2003). However, it does share a connection with suicide (Aitken & Munro, 2018; Sharp-Jeffs, 2022). With that being said, more research needs to be conducted to further explore this link.

Conclusion

Risk factors for intimate partner homicide have been extensively researched. However, no research has considered this using victims' family narratives to enrich existing literature. Co-victims can provide detailed accounts of coercive control towards their loved ones, thereby contributing narratives underscoring the reality of abuse. With the inclusion of case studies, this chapter sought to explore risk factors for intimate partner homicide using the 'web of abuse' as a way of encapsulating all overlapping and interlinking dynamics involved in the anatomy of coercive control. It has covered the motivations for intimate partner homicide and the range of tactics used by perpetrators to maintain control. While it has not considered all risk factors for intimate partner homicide, it has outlined those which were highlighted by victims' families', thereby adding a new dimension to an existing field of research.

References

Abramson, K., 2014. Turning up the lights on gaslighting. *Philosophical Perspectives*, 28 (1), pp. 1–30.

Adams, A., Sullivan, C., Bybee, D. & Greeson, M., 2008. Development of the scale of economic abuse. *Violence Against Women*, 14 (5), pp. 563–587.

Adams, D., 2007. *Why Do They Kill? Men Who Murder Their Intimate Partners.* Nashville, TN: Vanderbilt University Press.

Adinkrah, M., 2017. When a wife says "no": Wife sexual refusal as a factor in husband–wife homicides in Ghana. *Journal of Interpersonal Violence*, 36 (3–4), pp. 1–27.

Aitken, R., & Munro, V., 2018. *Domestic Abuse and Suicide: Exploring the Links with Refuge's Client Base and Work Force* [online]. London: Refuge. Available at: https://wrap.warwick.ac.uk/id/eprint/103609/1/WRAP-Domestic-abuse-and-suicide-Munro-2018.pdf [Accessed 19 March 2025].

Aldridge, M. L., & Browne, K. D., 2003. Perpetrators of spousal homicide: A review. *Trauma, Violence, & Abuse*, 4 (3), pp. 265–276.

Aloyce, D., Mshana, G., Peter, E., Malibwa, D., Buller, A. M., Mchome, Z., Kapiga, S. & Stöckl, H., 2023. Pathways of romantic jealousy to intimate partner violence in Mwanza, northern Tanzania. *Family Relations*, 73 (2), pp. 843–857.

Aloyce, D., Stöckl, H., Malibwa, D., Peter, E., Mchome, Z., Dwarumpudi, A., Buller, A. M., Kapiga, S., & Mshana, G., 2022. Men's reflections on romantic jealousy and intimate partner violence in Mwanza, Tanzania. *Violence Against Women*, 29 (6–7), pp. 1299–1318.

Anderson, K. L. 2005., Theorizing gender in intimate partner violence research. *Sex Roles*, 52 (1112), pp. 853–865.

Andrews, D. A., & Bonta, J., 2006. *The Psychology Of Criminal Conduct*. Toronto, Ontario: Anderson Publishing.

Arnold, G., 2009. A battered women's movement perspective of coercive control. *Violence Against Women*, 15, pp. 1432–1443.

Bahrami, M., Shokrollahi, P., Kohan, S., Momeni, G., & Rivaz, M., 2015. Reaction to and coping with domestic violence by Iranian women victims: A qualitative approach. *Global Journal of Health Science*, 8 (7), pp. 100–109.

Baldwin, S. B., Fehrenbacher, A. E., & Eisenman, D. P., 2015. Psychological coercion in human trafficking. *Qualitative Health Research*, 25, pp. 1171–1181.

Barlow, C. F., 2016. *Coercion and Women Co-Offenders: A Gendered Pathway into Crime*. Bristol: Policy Press.

Belfrage, H., & Rying, M. 2004. Characteristics of spousal homicide perpetrators: Study of all cases of spousal homicide in Sweden 1990–1999. *Criminal Behavor & Mental Health*, 14, pp. 121–133.

Bennett, A., Wibberley, G., & Paterson, A., 2021. "It's not just a private matter": Developing effective policy and procedure for addressing the impact of domestic abuse in the workplace. CIPD Applied Research Conference, Manchester, UK, 21 January. London: CIPD, pp. 1–9.

Bennett, T., Wibberley, G. & Jones, C., 2019. The legal, moral and business implications of domestic abuse and its impact in the workplace. *Industrial Law Journal*, 48 (1), pp. 137–142.

Bhatti, M. M., Shuja, K. H., Aqeel, M., Bokhari, Z., Gulzar, S. N., Fatima, T. & Sama, M., 2023. Psychometric development and validation of victim gaslighting questionnaire (VGQ): Across female sample from Pakistan. *International Journal of Human Rights in Healthcare*, 16 (1), pp. 4–18.

Bion, W. R., 1992. *Cogitations*. London: Karnac.

Boonzaier, F. & de la Rey, C., 2004. Woman abuse: The construction of gender in women and men's narratives of violence. *South African Journal of Psychology*, 34 (3), pp. 443–463.

Bostock, J., Plumpton, M., & Pratt, R., 2009. Domestic violence against women: Understanding social processes and women's experiences. *Journal of Community and Applied Social Psychology*, 19, pp. 95–110.

Bouffard, L. A., 2010. Exploring the utility of entitlement in understanding sexual aggression. *Journal of Criminal Justice*, 38 (5), pp. 870–879.

Bowstead, J., 2011. Space and place as constraints and resources in women's strategies to escape domestic violence. *Metronome*, 1, pp. 9–17.

Bracewell, K., Hargreaves, P. & Stanley, N., 2020. The consequences of the COVID-19 lockdown on stalking victimisation. *Journal of Family Violence*, 37, pp. 951–957.

Brady, P. Q., & Nobles, M. R., 2017. The dark figure of stalking: Examining law enforcement response. *Journal of Interpersonal Violence*, 32 (20), pp. 3149–3173.

Brandhorst, S., & Clark, D. L., 2022. Food security for survivors of intimate partner violence: Understanding the role of food in survivor well-being. *Health and Social Care in the Community*, 30, doi: 10.1111/hsc.14064.

Buss D. M., 2013. Sexual jealousy. *Psychological Topics*, 22 (2), pp. 155–182.

Campbell, J., & Glass, N., 2009. Safety planning, danger, and lethality assessment. In: Mitchell, C., & Anglin, D., eds. *Intimate Partner Violence: A Health-Based Perspective*. Oxford:Oxford University Press, pp. 319–334.

Campbell, J., Glass, N., Sharps, P., Laughon, K., & Bloom, T., 2007. Intimate partner homicide: Review and implications of research and policy. *Trauma, Violence & Abuse*, 8 (3), pp. 246–269.

Campbell, J., Webster, D., Koziol-McLain, J., Block, C., Campbell, D., Curry, M. & Laughon, K., 2003. Risk factors for femicide in abusive relationships: Results from a multisite case control study. *American Journal of Public Health*, 93 (7), pp. 1089–1097.

Canter, D. V., & Ioannou, M., 2004. A multivariate model of stalking behaviours. *Behaviormetrika*, 31 (2), pp. 113–130.

Cavanagh, K., Dobash, R. E., Dobash, R. P. & Lewis, R., 2001. "Remedial work": Men's strategic responses to their violence against intimate female partners. *Sociology*, 35(3), pp. 695–714.

Chowdhury, R., & Winder, B., 2022. A web model of domestic violence and abuse in Muslim communities – A multi perspective IPA approach. *Social Sciences*, 11, p. 354.

Copelon, R., 1994. Intimate terror: Understanding domestic violence as torture. In: Cook, R. J., ed. *Human Rights of Women: National and International Perspectives*. Philadelphia, Pennsylvania: University of Pennsylvania Press, pp. 116–152.

Crossman, K. A., & Hardesty, J. L., 2018. Placing coercive control at the center: What are the processes of coercive control and what makes control coercive? *Psychology of Violence*, 8 (2), pp. 196–206.

Daly, M., & Wilson, M., 1998. The evolutionary social psychology of family violence. In: Crawford, C., and Krebs, D., eds. *Handbook of Evolutionary Psychology: Ideas, Issues and Applications*. Mahwah, NJ: Lawrence Erlbaum, pp. 431–456.

Dawson, R., & Gartner, R., 1998. Differences in the characteristics of intimate femicides: The role of relationship state and relationship status. *Homicide Studies*, 2, pp. 378–399.

Debbane, E., 2011. Envy and its relation to destructiveness. *Canadian Journal Psychoanalysis*, 19, pp. 108–124.

DeGue, S., DiLillo, D. & Scalora, M., 2010. Are all perpetrators alike? Comparing risk factors for sexual coercion and aggression. *Sexual Abuse*, 22, pp. 402–426.

Devries, K. M., Mak, J. Y., Bacchus, L. J., Child, J. C., Falder, G., Petzold, M., Astbury, J., & Watts, C. H., 2013. Intimate partner violence and incident depressive symptoms and suicide attempts: A systematic review of longitudinal studies. *PLoS Medicine*, 10, doi: 10.1371/journal.pmed.1001439.

Dobash, R. E., & Dobash, R., 1980. *Violence Against Wives*. New York: Free Press.

Dobash, R. E., & Dobash, R. P., 2011. What were they thinking? Men who murder an intimate partner. *Violence Against Women*, 17, pp. 111–134.

Dobash, R. E., Dobash, R. P., & Cavanagh, K., 2009. "Out of the blue": Men who murder an intimate partner. *Feminist Criminology*, 4, pp. 194–225.

Dobash, R. P., Dobash, R. E., Cavanagh, K. & Lewis, R., 2004. Not an ordinary killer-just and ordinary guy: When men murder an intimate woman partner. *Violence Against Women*, 10, pp. 577–605.

Dorpat, T. L., 1994. On the double whammy and gaslighting. *Psychoanalysis & Psychotherapy*, 11 (1), pp. 91–96.

Dorpat, T. L., 1996. *Gaslighting, the Double Whammy, Interrogation, and Other Methods of Covert Control in Psychotherapy and Analysis*. Northvale, NJ: Jason Aronson Inc.

Douglas, H., Harris, B. A. & Dragiewicz, M., 2019. Technology-facilitated domestic and family violence: Women's experiences. *British Journal of Criminology*, 59 (3), pp. 1–20.

Duron, J. F., Johnson, L., Hoge, G. L. & Postmus, L. L., 2021. Observing coercive control beyond intimate partner violence: Examining the perceptions of professionals about common tactics used in victimization. *Psychology of Violence*, 11 (2), pp. 144–154.

Dutton, D. G., 2007. *The Abusive Personality: Violence and Control in Intimate Relationships*. 2nd ed. New York: The Guilford Press.

Dutton, D. G., & Kerry, G., 1999. Modus operandi and personality disorder in incarcerated spousal killers. *International Journal of Law & Psychiatry*, 22, pp. 287–299.

Dutton, M. A., & Goodman, L. A., 2005. Coercion in intimate partner violence: Toward a new conceptualization. *Sex Roles*, 52, pp. 743–756.

Enander, V., Krantz, G., Lysell, H. & Örmon, K., 2021. Before the killing: Intimate partner homicides in a process perspective, Part I. *Journal of Gender-Based Violence*, 5 (1), pp. 59–74.

Equality and Human Rights Commission, 2013. *Managing and Supporting Employees Experiencing Domestic Abuse* [online]. London: Chartered Institute of Personnel and Development. Available at: chrome-extension://efaidnbmnnnibpcajpcglclefindmkaj/https://www.equalityhumanrights.com/sites/default/files/domesticabuseguide.pdf [Accessed 28 August 2024].

Eriksson, L., & Mazerolle, P., 2013. A general strain theory of intimate partner homicide. *Aggression and Violent Behavior*, 18 (5), pp. 462–470.

Faver, C. A., & Strand, E. B., 2003. Domestic violence and animal cruelty: Untangling the web of abuse. Special section: Domestic violence and social work education. *Journal of Social Work Education*, 39 (2), pp. 237–248.

Faver, C. A., & Strand, E. B., 2008. Unleashing compassion: Social work and animal abuse. In: Ascione, F. R., ed. *The International Handbook of Animal Abuse and Cruelty: Theory, Research and, Application*. Indiana: Purdue University Press, pp. 175–196.

Feldman, H., & de Paola, H., 1994. An investigation into the psychoanalytic concept of envy. *International Journal of Psychoanalysis*, 75, pp. 217–234.

Ferraro, K. F., 1996. Women's fear of victimisation: Shadow of sexual assault? *Social Forces*, 75 (2), pp. 667–690.

Follingstad, D. R., & De Hart, D. D., 2000. Defining psychological abuse of husbands towards wives. *Journal of Interpersonal Violence*, 15 (9), pp. 891–920.

Fontes, L. A., 2015. *Invisible Chains: Overcoming Coercive Control in Your Intimate Relationship*. New York: Guilford Publications, Inc.

Foucault, M., 1991. *Discipline and Punish: The Birth of Prison*. London: Penguin.

Franzway, S., Moulding, N., Wendt, S., Zuffrey, C. & Chung, D., 2019. *Sexual Politics of Gendered Violence and Women's Citizenship*. Bristol: Policy Press.

Fraser, C., Olsen, E., Lee, K., Southworth, C. & Tucker, S., 2010. The new age of stalking: Technological implications for stalking. *Juvenile & Family Court Journal*, 61 (4), pp. 39–55.

French, J. R. P., Jr., & Raven, B., 1959. The bases of social power. In: Cartwright, D., ed. *Studies in Social Power*. Oxford: University of Michigan, pp. 150–167.

Frost, E. L., Fawole, O. I., Okedare, O. O., Salawu, M. M., Kiene, S. M., Augusto, C., & Reed, E., 2023. Money, economic abuse, and food insecurity: A qualitative study among young Nigerian women with a history of intimate partner violence. *Adolescents*, 3, pp. 330–342.

García-Moreno, C., 2013. *Global and Regional Estimates of Violence Against Women: Prevalence and Health Effects of Intimate Partner Violence and non-Partner Sexual Violence*. Geneva, Switzerland: World Health Organization.

Gavey, N., 2003. Writing the effects of sexual abuse. In: Reavey, P., & Warner, S., eds. *New Feminist Stories of Child Sexual Abuse*. Oxon: Routledge, pp. 187–205.

Georgas, J., Berry, J. W., Van der Vijver, F. J. R., Kağitçıbaşi, C. & Poortinga, Y. H., 2006. *Families Across Cultures: A 30-Nation Psychological Study*. Cambridge: Cambridge University Press.

George, A., & Harris, B., 2014. *Landscapes of Violence: Women Surviving Family Violence in Regional and Rural Victoria* [online]. Geelong: Deakin University. Available at: https://www.deakin.edu.au/__data/assets/pdf_file/0003/287040/Landscapes-of-Violence-online-pdf-version.pdf [Accessed 12 July 2024].

Goodman. L. A., & Smyth, K. F., 2011. A call for a social network-oriented approach to services for survivors of intimate partner violence. *Psychology of Violence*, 1 (2), pp. 79–92.

Gordon, M. T., & Riger, S., 1991. *The Female Fear: The Social Cost of Rape*. Urbana, Chicago: University of Illinois Press.

Gosse, C., 2021. "Not the real world": Exploring experiences of online abuse, digital dualism, and ontological labor. In: Bailey, J., Flynn, A., & Henry, N., eds. *The Emerald International Handbook of Technology-Facilitated Violence and Abuse*. Leeds: Emerald Publishing Limited, pp. 47–64.

Graham, L. M., Macy, R. J., Rizo, C. F. & Martin, S. L., 2022. Explanatory theories of intimate partner homicide perpetration: A systematic review. *Trauma, Violence & Abuse*, 23 (2), pp. 408–427.

Grann, M., & Wedin, M., 2002. Risk factors for recidivism among spousal assault and spousal homicide offenders. *Psychology, Crime & Law*, 8, pp. 5–23.

Guerrero, L. K., Trost, M. L. & Yoshimura, S. M., 2005. Emotion and communication in the context of romantic jealousy. *Personal Relationships*, 12, pp. 233–252.

Harris, B. A., & Woodlock, D., 2019. Digital coercive control: Insights from two landmark domestic violence studies. *British Journal of Criminology*, 59 (3), pp. 530–550.

Hartmann, H., 1939. *Ego Psychology and the Problem of Adaptation*. New York: International Universities Press.

Hasbullah, M., Kahar, R. & Ahmad, S., 2016. *A preliminary study of instrumental, emotional, and social support for domestic violence survivors in Selangor, Malaysia*. Proceedings of the 3rd World Conference On Integration Of Knowledge, Malaysia, 28–29 November 2016. Langkawi, Malaysia: WorldConferences.net.

Hayes, B. E., 2013. Women's resistance strategies in abusive relationships. *SAGE Open*, 3 (3), pp. 1–11.

Hayes, S., & Jeffries, S., 2016. Romantic terrorism? An auto-ethnographic analysis of gendered psychological and emotional tactics in domestic violence. *Journal of Research in Gender Studies*, 6 (2), pp. 38–61.

Hellman, A. N., & Hurley, S., 2023. Looking for the hidden hurts: When radiological findings suggest presence of intimate partner violence. *Journal of Radiology Nursing*, 42 (2), pp. 166–171.

Hester, M., 2009. Who Does What to Whom? Gender and Domestic Violence Perpetrators, *European Journal of Criminology*, 10 (5), pp. 1–19.

Hester, M., 2010. Gender and Sexuality. In: C. Itzin, A. Taket and S. Barter-Godfrey, eds., *Domestic and Sexual Violence and Abuse: Tackling the Health and Mental Health Effects*. London: Routledge, pp. 99–131.

Hester, M., Pearson, C., Harwin, N. & Abrahams, H., 2007. *Making an Impact: Children and Domestic Violence*. London: Jessica Kingsley.

Holub, A. M., & Barbaro, N., 2018. Homicide adaptation theory. In: Shackelford, T. K., & Weekes-Shackelford, V. A., eds. *Encyclopedia of Evolutionary Psychological Science*. Cham: Springer, pp. 1–4.

Ingala-Smith, K., 2018. Femicide. In: Lombard, N., ed. *The Routledge Handbook of Gender and Violence*. Oxon: Routledge, pp. 185–198.

Issa, E. E., 2023. Women and credit through the decades: The 1970s [online]. *NerdWallet*. Available at: https://www.nerdwallet.com/article/credit-cards/women-credit-decades-70s [Accessed 10 October 2024].

Jayasuriya, V., Wijewardena, K. & Axemo, P., 2011. Intimate partner violence against women in the Capital Province of Sri Lanka: Prevalence, risk factors, and help seeking. *Violence Against Female*, 17 (8), pp. 1086–1102.

James, D. V., & Farnham, F. R., 2003. Stalking and serious violence. *Journal of the American Academy of Psychiatry and the Law Online*, 31(4), pp. 432–439.

Johnson, H., 2012. When feminism meets evolutionary psychology: The enduring legacy of Margo Wilson. *Homicide Studies*, 16 (4), pp. 332–345.

Johnson, H., Eriksson, L., Mazerolle, P., & Wortley, R., 2019. Intimate femicide: The role of coercive control. *Feminist Criminology*, 14 (1), pp. 3–23.

Johnson, H., & Hotton, T., 2003. Losing control: Homicide risk in estranged and intact intimate relationships. *Homicide Studies*, 7 (1), pp. 58–84.

Johnson, M. P., 2006. Conflict and control: Gender symmetry and asymmetry in domestic violence. *Violence Against Women*, 12 (11), pp. 1003–1018.

Johnson, M. P., 2008. *A Typology of Domestic Violence: Intimate Terrorism, Violent Resistance, and Situational Couple Violence*. Boston, Massachusetts: Northeastern University Press.

Jurgenson, N., 2011. Digital dualism versus augmented reality [online]. Maryland: The Society Pages: Cyborgology. Available at: https://thesocietypages.org/cyborgology/2011/02/24/digital-dualism-versus-augmented-reality/ [Accessed 8 March 2024].

Kaighobadi F., Shackelford T. K. & Goetz A. T., 2009. From mate retention to murder: Evolutionary psychological perspectives on men's partner-directed violence. *Review of General Psychology*, 13 (4), pp. 327–334.

Karakurt, G., & Silver, K. E., 2013. Emotional abuse in intimate relationships: The role of gender and age. *Violence & Victims*, 28 (5), pp. 804–821.

Kelly, L., 1988. *Surviving Sexual Violence*. Cambridge: Polity.

Kelly, L., 2003. The wrong debate: Reflections on why force is not the key issue with respect to trafficking in women for sexual exploitation. *Feminist Review*, 73, pp. 139–144.

Kelly, L., 2012. Standing the test of time? Reflections on the concept of the continuum of sexual violence. In: Brown, J. and Walklate, S., eds. *Handbook on Sexual Violence*. London: Routledge, pp. xvii–xxvi.

Kennedy, M. C., 2022. Digital coercive control: A male perspective. In: Gavin, H., ed., *Women and the Abuse of Power*. Leeds: Emerald Publishing Limited, pp. 105–122.

Kirkwood, C., 1993. *Leaving Abusive Partners: From the Scars of Survival to the Wisdom for Change*. London: Sage Publications.

Kivisto, A. J., 2015. Male perpetrators of intimate partner homicide: A review and proposed typology. *Journal of the American Academy of Psychiatry and the Law*, 43, pp. 300–312.

Klein, M., 1997. *Envy and Gratitude and Other Works 1946–1963*. London: Vintage.

Knight, L., & Hester, M., 2016. Domestic violence and mental health in older adults. *International Review of Psychiatry*, 28 (5), pp. 464–474.

Kyriakakis, S., 2014. Mexican immigrant women reaching out: The role of informal support networks in the process of seeking help for IPV. *Violence Against Women*, 20 (9), pp. 1097–1116.

Lammers, M., 2002. Women's experience of emotional abuse in intimate relationships: A qualitative study [online]. Ph.D. thesis, University of Waikato. Available at: https://researchcommons.waikato.ac.nz/bitstream/handle/10289/14047/thesis.pdf?sequence=1&isAllowed=y [Accessed 19 June 2024].

Lammers, M., Richie, J. & Robertson, N., 2005. Women's experience of emotional abuse in intimate relationships. *Journal of Emotional Abuse*, 5 (1), pp. 29–64.

Latta, R. E., & Goodman, L. A., 2011. Intervening in partner violence against women: A grounded theory exploration of informal network members' experiences. *The Counseling Psychologist*, 39 (7), pp. 973–1023.

Lentz, E. C., 2018. Complicating narratives of women's food and nutrition insecurity: Domestic violence in rural Bangladesh. *World Development*, 104, pp. 271–280.

Leve, A., 2017. Trump Is gaslighting America – Here's how to survive. *Business Insider UK* [online], 18 March. Available at: https://www.businessinsider.com/trump-is-gaslighting-america-heres-how-to-survive-2017-3 [Accessed 31 July 2024].

Liang, B., Goodman, L., Tummala-Narra, P. & Weintraub, S., 2005. A theoretical framework for understanding help-seeking processes among survivors of intimate partner violence. *American Journal of Community Psychology*, 36(1/2), pp. 71–84.

Liem, M., & Roberts, D. W., 2009. Intimate partner homicide by presence or absence of a self-destructive act. *Homicide Studies*, 13 (4), pp. 339–354.

Little, J., 2023. Violence, the body and the spaces of intimate war. In: Carter, S. & Woodyer, T., eds. *Domesticating Geopolitics*. Oxon: Routledge, pp. 74–93.

Littwin, A., 2012. Coerced debt: The role of consumer credit in domestic violence. *California Law Review*, 100 (4), pp. 951–1026.

Logan, T. K., Cole, J. & Shannon, L., 2007. A mixed-methods examination of sexual coercion and degradation among women in violent relationships who do and do not report forced sex. *Violence and Victims*, 22 (1), pp. 71–94.

Logan T., & Walker R., 2009. Partner stalking: Psychological dominance or business as usual? *Trauma, Violence, and Abuse*, 10, pp. 247–270.

Lyon, E., 2000. *Welfare, Poverty, and Abused Women: New Research and Its Implications. Building Comprehensive Solutions to Domestic Violence* [online]. Harrisburg, PA: National Resource Center on Domestic Violence. Available at: https://vawnet.org/sites/default/files/materials/files/2016-09/BCS10_POV.pdf [Accessed 25 September 2024].

MacMillan, C., 2022. An omnipresent gaze: Men's enactment of coercive control in the private sphere. *Journal for Social Thought*, 6 (1), pp. 1–13.

Madhok, S., Philips, A. & Wilson, K., 2013. *Gender, Agency and Coercion*. Basingstoke: Palgrave Macmillan.

Marshall, A. D., & Holtzworth-Munroe, A., 2002. Varying forms of husband sexual aggression: Predictors and subgroup differences. *Journal of Family Psychology*, 16, pp. 286–296.

Marshall, L. L., 1992a. Development of the Severity of Violence Against Men scales. *Journal of Family Violence*, 7, pp. 189–203.

Marshall, L. L., 1992b. Development of the Severity of Violence Against Women scales. *Journal of Family Violence*, 7, pp. 103–121.

Martinez, C. T., 2015. Engendered expressions of aggression: The role of gender, proprietary behaviours, and jealousy in intimate partner violence. *Violence and Gender*, 2 (2), pp. 112–118.

Matias, A., Gonçalves, M., Soeiro, C. & Matos, M., 2020. Intimate partner homicide: A meta-analysis of risk factors. Aggression and Violent Behavior, 50.

McCue, M. L., 2008. *Domestic Violence*. Oxford: ABC-CLIO.

McFarlane, J.M., Campbell, J.C., Sachs, C.J., Ulrich, Y., & Xu, X., 1999. Stalking and Intimate partner Femicide. *Homicide Studies*, 394, pp. 300–316.

McFarlane, J., Campbell, J., & Watson, K., 2002. Intimate partner stalking and femicide: Urgent implications for women's safety. *Behavioral Sciences and the Law*, 20, pp. 51–68.

McGlynn, C., Johnson, K., Rackley, E., Henry, N., Gavey, N., Flynn, A. & Powell, A., 2021. "It's torture for the soul": The harms of image-based sexual abuse. *Social and Legal Studies*, 30 (4), pp. 541–562.

McLachlan, F., & Harris, B., 2022. Intimate risks: Examining online and offline abuse, homicide flags, and femicide. *Victims & Offenders*, 17 (5), pp. 623–646.

McNulty, J. K., 2020. Highlighting the dark side of forgiveness and the need for a contextual approach. In: Worthington, E. L. Jr. and Wade, N. G., eds. *Handbook of Forgiveness*. New York: Routledge, pp. 33–42.

Meloy, J. R., 1996. Stalking (obsessional following): A review of some preliminary studies. *Aggression and Violent Behaviour*, 1, pp. 147–162.

Melton, H. C., 2007. Stalking in the context of intimate partner abuse. *Feminist Criminology*, 2 (4), pp. 347–363.

Miller, S. L., 2001. The paradox of women arrested for domestic violence. *Violence Against Women*, 7, pp. 1339–1376.

Mitchell, J. E., & Raghavan, C., 2019. The impact of coercive control on use of specific sexual coercion tactics. *Violence Against Women*, 27 (2), pp. 187–206.

Monckton Smith, J., Szymanska, K. & Haile, S., 2017. *Exploring the Relationship between Stalking and Homicide* [online]. Gloucester, England: University of Gloucester. Available at: chrome-extension://efaidnbmnnnibpcajpcglclefindmkaj/https://eprints.glos.ac.uk/4553/1/NSAW%20Report%2004.17%20-%20finalsmall.pdf [Accessed 12 August 2024].

Monckton Smith, J., Williams, A. & Mullane F., 2014. *Domestic Abuse, Homicide and Gender*. London: Palgrave Macmillan.

Moracco, K. E., Runyan, C. W. & Butts, J. D., 1998. Femicide in North Carolina, 1991–1993: A state-wide study of patterns and precursors. *Homicide Studies*, 2, pp. 422–446.

Moreschi, C., Da Broi, U., Zamai, V., & Palese, F., 2016. Medico legal and epidemiological aspects of femicide in a judicial district of north eastern Italy. *Journal of Forensic and Legal Medicine*, 39, pp. 65–73.

Morris, A., 2009. Gendered dynamics of abuse and violence in families: Considering the abusive household gender regime. *Child Abuse Review*, 18 (6), pp. 414–427.

Mršević, Z., & Hughes, D. M., 1997. Violence against women in Belgrade, Serbia: SOS Hotline 1990–1993. *Violence Against Women*, 3 (2), pp. 101–128.

Mullen, P. E., Pathé, M. & Purcell, R., 2009. *Stalkers and their Victims*. Cambridge: Cambridge University Press.

Munk, T., & Kennedy, M., 2024. *Victimisation in the Digital Age: An Online/Offline Continuum Approach*. Oxon: Routledge.

Munteanu, V., 2021. Examining the impact of domestic abuse survivors on employee performance and recommendations for the employer [online]. M.A. thesis, National College of Ireland. Available at: chrome-extension://efaidnbmnnnibpcajpcglclefindmkaj/https://norma.ncirl.ie/5336/1/violetamunteanu.pdf [Accessed 28 August 2024].

Myhill, A., 2015. Measuring coercive control: What can we learn from national population surveys? *Violence Against Women*, 21 (3), pp. 355–375.

Myhill, A., & Hohl, K., 2016. The "golden thread": Coercive control and risk assessment for domestic violence. *Journal of Interpersonal Violence*, 34 (21–22), pp. 4477–4497.

Nicolaidis, C., Curry, M. A., Ulrich, Y., Sharps, P., McFarlane, J., Campbell, D., Gary, F., Laughton, K., Glass, N. & Campbell, J., 2003. Could we have known? A qualitative analysis of data from women who survived an attempted homicide by an intimate partner. *Journal of General Internal Medicine*, 18, pp. 788–794.

Norris, S., Huss, M. & Palarea, R. E., 2011. A pattern of violence: Analyzing the relationship between intimate partner violence and stalking. *Violence and Victims*, 26 (1), pp. 103–115.

Office for National Statistics (ONS), 2023. *Stalking: Findings from the Crime Survey for England and Wales* [online]. England and Wales: Office for National Statistics. Available at: https://www.ons.gov.uk/peoplepopulationandcommunity/crimeandjustice/datasets/stalkingfindingsfromthecrimesurveyforenglandandwales [Accessed 16 August 2024].

Office for National Statistics (ONS), 2024. *Partner Abuse in Detail, England and Wales: Year Ending March 2023* [online]. England and Wales: Office for National Statistics. Available at: https://www.ons.gov.uk/peoplepopulationandcommunity/crimeandjustice/articles/partnerabuseindetailenglandandwales/yearendingmarch2023 [Accessed 10 October 2024].

Pain, R. 2014. Everyday terrorism: Connecting domestic violence and global terrorism. *Progress in Human Geography*, 38 (4), pp. 531–550.

Pence, E., & Paymar, M., 1993. *Education Groups for Men Who Batter: The Duluth Model*. New York: Springer Publishing Company.

Pereira, A. R., Vieira, D. N. & Magalhães, T., 2013. Fatal intimate partner violence against women in Portugal: A forensic medical national study. *Journal of Forensic and Legal Medicine*, 20, pp. 1099–1107.

Petric, D., 2018. Gaslighting and the knot theory of mind. *Medicine*, 4, pp. 1–4.

Pitman, T. M., 2010. The legacy of domestic violence: How the dynamics of abuse continue beyond separation [online]. Ph.D. thesis, University Of Tasmania. Available at: https://doi.org/10.25959/23210972.v1 [Accessed 29 May 2024].

Polk, K., 1994. *When Men Kill: Scenarios of Masculine Violence*. Cambridge: Cambridge University Press.

Pollet, S. L., 2011. Economic abuse: The unseen side of domestic violence. *New York State Bar Journal*, 83 (2), pp. 40–44.

Porter, A., Montgomery, C. O., Montgomery, B. E., Eastin, C., Boyette, J. & Snead, G. 2019. Intimate partner violence-related fractures in the United States: An 8 year review. *Journal of Family Violence*, 34 (7), pp. 601–609.

Postmus, J., Hoge, G., Breckenridge, J., Sharp-Jeffs, N. & Chung, D., 2018. Economic abuse as an invisible form of domestic violence: A multicountry review. *Trauma, Violence & Abuse*, 21 (2), pp. 261–283.

Raghavan, C., Beck, C. J., Menke, J. M., & Loveland, J. E., 2019. Coercive controlling behaviors in intimate partner violence in male same-sex relationships: A mixed-methods study. *Journal of Gay & Lesbian Social Services*, 31 (3), pp. 370–395.

Raghavan, C., Cohen, S. & Tamborra, T., 2014. Development and preliminary validation of the Multidimensional Sexual Coercion Questionnaire (MSCQ). *Journal of Sexual Aggression*, 21, pp. 271–289.

Rahman, M., Nakamura, K., Seino, K., & Kizuk, M., 2013. Intimate partner violence and chronic undernutrition among married Bangladeshi women of reproductive age: Are the poor uniquely disadvantaged? *European Journal of Clinical Nutrition*, 67, pp. 301–307.

Rajah, V., 2007. Resistance as edgework in violent intimate relationships of drug-involved women. *British Journal of Criminology*, 47, pp. 196–213.

Raven, B. H., 1993. The bases of power: Origins and recent developments. *Journal of Social Psychology*, 49 (4), pp. 227–251.

Rawls, J., 1971. *A Theory of Justice*. Cambridge, Massachusetts: Harvard University Press.

Rees, A., Agnew-Davies, R. & Barkham, M., 2006. *Outcomes for women escaping domestic violence at refuge. In: Society for Psychotherapy Research Book of Abstracts*. The University of Edinburgh, Scotland, 21–24 June 2006.

Richards, B., 2000. The anatomy of envy. *Psychoanalytic Studies*, 2 (1), pp. 65–76.

Richards, L., 2016. Stalking: Murder in slow motion. *Huffington Post* [online], 21 April. Available at: https://www.huffingtonpost.co.uk/laura-richards1/stalking-murder-in-slow-motion_b_9746844.html [Accessed 16 August 2024].

Rietdijk, N., 2018. (You drive me) crazy: How gaslighting undermines autonomy [online]. Master's thesis, Utrecht University. Available at: chrome-extension://efaidnbmnnnibpcajpcglclefindmkaj/https://studenttheses.uu.nl/bitstream/handle/20.500.12932/31075/RMA%20Thesis%20Natascha%20Rietdijk.pdf?sequence=2&isAllowed=y [Accessed 31 July 2024].

Riger, S., & Gordon, M. T., 1981. The fear of rape: A study in social control. *Journal of Social Issues*, 37 (4), pp. 71–92.

Roberts, J., 2015. "It was do or die" – how a woman's experience of domestic abuse can influence her involvement in crime: A qualitative investigation of the experiences of community-based female offenders. Ph.D. thesis, University of Leicester.

Roberts, J., 2022. *Gendered Justice? How Women's Attempts to Cope With, Survive, or Escape Domestic Abuse Can Drive Them into Crime*. Leeds: Emerald Publishing Limited.

Rose, L. E., Campbell, J. & Kub, J., 2000. The role of social support and family relationships in women's responses to battering. *Health Care for Women International*, 21, pp. 27–39.

Rose, D., Trevillion, K., Woodall, A., Morgan, C., Feder, G., & Howard, L., 2011. Barriers and facilitators of disclosures of domestic violence by mental health service users: Qualitative study. *British Journal of Psychiatry*, 198, pp. 189–194.

Ross, J. M., 2012. Self-reported fear in partner violent relationships: Findings on gender differences from two samples. *Psychology of Violence*, 2 (1), pp. 58–74.

Salari, S., & LeFevre Sillito, C., 2016. Intimate partner homicide suicide: Perpetrator primary intent across young, middle, and elder adult age categories. *Aggression and Violent Behavior*, 26, pp. 26–34.

Sanders, C. K., & Schnabel, M., 2004. Organizing for economic empowerment of battered women: Women's savings accounts. *Journal of Community Practice*, 14 (3), pp. 47–68.

Sanderson, C., 2008. *Counselling Survivors of Domestic Abuse*. London: Jessica Kingsley Publishers.

Scarr, L., & Kennedy, M. C., 2023. "They didn't want to upset the client": Stalking in hands-on occupations. In: Mellins, M., Wheatley, R. & Flowers, C., eds. *Young People, Stalking Awareness and Domestic Abuse*. Cham, Switzerland: Palgrave Macmillan, pp. 201–223.

Schechter, S., 1982. *Women and Male Violence: The Visions and Struggles of the Battered Women's Movement*. Boston: South End Press.

Scott, A. J., 2020. Stalking: How perceptions differ from reality and why these differences matter. In: Bull, R. and Blandón-Gitlin, I., eds. *The Routledge International Handbook of Legal and Investigative Psychology*. Oxon: Routledge, pp. 238–254.

Scott, A. J., Lloyd, R. & Gavin, J., 2010. The influence of prior relationship on perceptions of stalking in the United Kingdom and Australia. *Criminal Justice and Behavior*, 37 (11), pp. 1185–1194.

Serran, G., & Firestone, P., 2004. Intimate partner homicide: A review of the male proprietariness and the self-defense theories. *Aggression and Violent Behavior*, 9 (1), pp. 1–15.

Sharma, K., 2023. Behind closed doors: Confronting the reality of domestic abuse. *VIDHIGYA: The Journal of Legal Awareness*, 18 (1–2), pp. 44–60.

Sharp-Jeffs, N., 2015. *A Review of Research and Policy on Financial Abuse within Intimate Partner Relationships*. London: CWASU.

Sharp-Jeffs, N., 2021. Understanding the economics of abuse: An assessment of the economic abuse definition within the Domestic Abuse Bill. *Journal of Gender-based Violence*, 5 (1), pp. 163–173.

Sharp-Jeffs, N., 2022. *Understanding and Responding to Economic Abuse*. Leeds: Emerald Publishing Limited.

Sharp-Jeffs, N., Kelly, L. & Klein, R., 2018. Long journeys toward freedom: The relationship between coercive control and space for action – Measurement and emerging evidence. *Violence Against Women*, 24 (2), pp. 163–185.

Showalter, K., 2016. Women's employment and domestic violence: A review of the literature. *Aggression and Violent Behavior*, 31, pp. 37–47.

Smith, A., 2005. Looking to the future: Domestic violence, women of color, the state and social change. In: Sokoloff, N. J., and Pratt, C., eds. *Domestic Violence at the Margins: Readings on Race, Class, Gender and Culture*. Piscataway, New Jersey: Rutgers University Press, pp. 416–434.

Solot, D., 1997. Untangling the animal abuse web. *Society and Animals*, 5 (3), pp. 257–265.

Southworth, C., Finn, J., Dawson, S., Fraser, C. & Tucker, S., 2007. Intimate partner violence, technology, and stalking. *Violence Against Women*, 13 (8), pp. 842–856.

Spencer, C. M., 2018. A meta-analysis of risk factors for intimate partner homicide: Examining male perpetration and female victimization [online]. Ph.D. thesis, Kansas State University. Available at: https://krex.k-state.edu/server/api/core/bitstreams/dbd914ee-c187-4cde-8f6f-73d9775e0cfc/content [Accessed 14 May 2024].

Spencer, C. M., & Stith, S. M., 2020. Risk factors for male perpetration and female victimization of intimate partner homicide: A meta-analysis. *Trauma, Violence & Abuse*, 21 (3), pp. 527–540.

Spencer, C. M., Stith, S. M. & Cafferky, B., 2022. What puts individuals at risk for physical intimate partner violence perpetration? A meta-analysis examining risk markers for men and women. *Trauma, Violence, & Abuse*, 23 (1), pp. 36–51.

Stark, E., 2006. Commentary on Johnson's "Conflict and control: Gender symmetry and asymmetry in domestic violence". *Violence Against Women*, 12 (11), pp. 1019–1025.

Stark, E., 2007. *Coercive Control: How Men Entrap Women in Personal Life*. New York: Oxford University Press.

Stark, E., 2009. Rethinking coercive control. *Violence Against Women*, 15 (12), pp. 1509–1525.

Stark, E., 2010. Do violent acts equal abuse? *Sex Roles*, 62, pp. 201–211.

Stark, E., 2012. Looking beyond domestic violence: Policing coercive control [Special issue]. *Journal of Police Crisis Negotiations*, 12, pp. 199–217.

Stark, E., 2013. Coercive control. In: Lombard, N. and McMillan, L., eds. *Violence against Women: Current Theory and Practice in Domestic Abuse, Sexual Violence and Exploitation*. London: Jessica Kingsley, pp. 17–33.

Stark, E., 2017. Foreword. In: McOrmond-Plummer, L., Levy-Peck, J. Y. & Easteal, P., eds. *Perpetrators of Intimate Partner Sexual Violence*. Oxon: Routledge, pp. xx–xxv.

Stark, E., 2018. Coercive control as a framework for responding to male partner abuse in the UK. In: Lombard, N., ed. *The Routledge Handbook or Gender and Violence*. Oxon: Routledge, pp. 15–27.

Stark, E., 2023. *Coercive Control: How Men Entrap Women in Personal Life*. 2nd ed. New York: Oxford University Press.

Stark, E., & Hester, M. 2018. Coercive control: Update and review. *Violence Against Women*, 25 (1), pp. 81–104.

Stern, R., 2007. *The Gaslight Effect: How to Spot and Survive the Hidden Manipulation Others Use to Control Your Life*. New York: Harmony Books.

Stern, R., 2018. *The Gaslight Effect: How to Spot and Survive the Hidden Manipulation Others Use to Control Your Life*. 2nd ed. New York: Harmony Books.

Stewart, D. E., MacMillan, H. & Kimber, M., 2021. Recognizing and responding to intimate partner violence: An update. *The Canadian Journal of Psychiatry*, 66 (1), pp. 71–106.

Suzy Lamplugh Trust, 2021. Press release (Suzy Lamplugh: 35 Years) [online]. Available at: https://www.suzylamplugh.org/news/press-release-suzy-lamplugh-35-years [Accessed 3 July 2024].

Sweet, P. L., 2019. The sociology of gaslighting. *American Sociological Review*, 84 (5), pp. 851–875.

Tahna, M., Beck, C. J. A., Figueredo, A. J. & Raghavan, C., 2010. Sex differences in intimate partner violence and the use of coercive control as a motivational factor for intimate partner violence. *Journal of Interpersonal Violence*, 10 (5), pp. 1–19.

Thiel de Bocanegra, H., Rostovtseva, D. P., Khera, S. & Godhwani, N., 2010. Birth control sabotage and forced sex: Experiences reported by women in domestic violence shelters. *Violence Against Women*, 16 (5), pp. 601–612.

Tolman, R., 1989. The development of a measure for the psychological maltreatment of women by their male partners. *Violence and Victims*, 4, pp. 159–177.

Toprak, S., & Ersoy, G., 2017. Femicide in Turkey between 2000 and 2010. *PLoS ONE*, 12 (8), pp. 1–16.

Trotter, J. L., & Allen, N. E., 2009. The good, the bad, and the ugly: Domestic violence survivors' experiences with their informal social networks. *American Journal of Community Psychology*, 43, pp. 221–231.

Tyner, J. A., 2012. *Space, Place, and Violence: Violence and the Embodied Geographies of Race, Sex and Gender*. New York: Routledge.

Vatnar, S., Friestad, C. & Bjerkly, S., 2017. Intimate partner homicide in Norway 1990–2012. *Psychology of Violence*, 7 (3), pp. 395–405.

Vera-Gray, F., 2018. *The Right Amount of Panic: How Women Trade Freedom for Safety*. Bristol: Policy Press.

Viñas-Racionero, R., Raghavan, C., Soria-Verde, M. Á., Scalora, M. J., Santos-Hermoso, J., González-Álvarez, J. L. & Garrido-Antón, M. J., 2023. Enhancing the assessment of coercive control in Spanish femicide cases: A nationally representative qualitative analysis. *Journal of Family Violence*, 40, pp. 1–12.

Walby, S., & Allen, J., 2004. *Domestic Violence, Sexual Assault and Stalking: Findings from the British Crime Survey*[online]. London:Home Office. Available at:https://op

enaccess.city.ac.uk/id/eprint/21697/1/Domesticviolencefindings_2004_5BritishCrimeSurvey276.pdf[Accessed 19 March 2025].

Walby, S., & Towers, J., 2018. Untangling the concept of coercive control: Theorizing domestic violent crime. *Criminology & Criminal Justice*, 18 (1), pp. 7–28.

Walker, L. E., 1984. *The Battered Women Syndrome*. New York: Springer.

Warshaw, C., Lyon, E., Bland, P. J., Phillips, H. & Hooper, M., 2014. *Mental Health and Substance Use Coercion Surveys: Report from the National Center on Domestic Violence, Trauma, & Mental Health and the National Domestic Violence Hotline* [online]. Chicago, Illinois: US Department of Health and Human Services. Available at: chrome-extension://efaidnbmnnnibpcajpcglclefindmkaj/https://www.thehotline.org/wp-content/uploads/media/2024/07/2012-Mental-Health-Coercion-Survey.pdf [Accessed 6 August 2024].

Weare, S. F., & Barlow, C. F., 2019. Women as co-offenders: Pathways into crime and offending motivations. *The Howard Journal of Criminal Justice*, 58 (1), pp. 86–103.

Websdale, N., 2010. *Familicidal Hearts: The Emotional Styles of 211 Killers*. Oxford: Oxford University Press.

Westmarland, N., 2015. *Violence Against Women: Criminological Perspectives on Men's Violences*. New York: Routledge.

Wilcox, P., 2006. *Surviving Domestic Violence: Gender, Poverty and Agency*. Basingstoke: Palgrave Macmillan.

Wilson, D., & Daly, M., 1992. The man who mistook his wife for a chattel. In: Barkow, J. H., Cosmides, L. & Tooby, J., eds. *The Adapted Mind: Evolutionary Psychology and the Generation Of Culture*. New York: Oxford University Press, pp. 289–322.

Wilson, D., & Daly, M., 1993. An evolutionary psychological perspective on male sexual proprietariness and violence against wives. *Violence and Victims*, 8 (3), pp. 271–294.

Woodlock, D., 2017. The abuse of technology in domestic violence and stalking. *Violence Against Women*, 25 (5), pp. 584–602.

Zorza, J., 1991. Woman battering: A major cause of homelessness. *Clearinghouse Review*, 25 (4), pp. 421–429.

4 Online Harm

Emerging Risk Factors in the Web of Abuse

Introduction

The focus of this chapter is to provide a comprehensive review of existing literature and research, considering online harm in relation to intimate partner abuse and homicide. The purpose of this is to highlight victims' families' perspectives in terms of how the online environment enables and amplifies harm. As families often have an unobstructed view of abuse, they are well positioned to describe the abuse which occurs across the online environment. The importance of this discussion is to place online harm alongside offline harm as a risk factor for intimate partner homicide, which has only recently been acknowledged.

It is important to note that Chapter 3 and this chapter are intrinsically linked as they are part of the same continuum – the continuum of online-offline harm (Munk & Kennedy, 2024). As a reminder, this school of thought suggests that the online and offline environments cannot exist in isolation and are, as such, more complicated than the binary approaches taken previously (Gosse, 2021). There has and continues to be a tendency for criminology to be focused on "theoretical binary oppositions", which are largely unhelpful as they have bolstered the separation of both criminology and the digital technology fields (Brown, 2006: 223). Instead, there needs to be a recognition that harm extends across both spaces. This is further discussed by Jurgenson (2011: para. 2) regarding "digital dualism", which considers offline or physical space as *real* and online or virtual space as *less real* (Munk & Kennedy, 2024). This has particularly problematic consequences for victim-survivors who experience harm or victimisation intersecting both spaces (Munk & Kennedy, 2024). Often the harm perpetrated online is considered *less harmful* than the harm perpetrated offline. This understanding is present in cases where the harm is less visible and it is largely how this type of harm is framed by the media and other public debates (McGlynn et al., 2021; McLachlan & Harris, 2022).

While this chapter is placed after the discussion on risk factors relating to intimate partner abuse and homicide from an offline perspective, it is not to suggest that online harm is less important or less harmful than offline harm. Instead, and as mentioned earlier, it should be considered part of this

DOI: 10.4324/9781003464488-4

continuum of online-offline harm. In the same way Chapter 3 linguistically uses 'offline' to discuss the harms occurring within the in-person or physical sphere, this chapter uses 'online' to describe the harms occurring within the virtual environment (Gosse, 2021; McLachlan & Harris, 2022; Munk & Kennedy, 2024). However, this is not without its own issues as 'online' is an indistinct term similar to 'technology', which Murphie and Potts (2003: 3) suggest is "generalized to the point of abstraction". Using this term captures some but not all experiences of harm due to lack of clarity in regards to what counts as digital technologies and whether these technologies need a mobile phone or internet connection (McLachlan & Harris, 2022).

Conceptualising Digital Coercive Control

There are many debates relating to terminology and definitions surrounding the online environment and our understandings of it. These debates extend to intimate partner abuse as mentioned in Chapter 1. Terminology relating to online harm includes technology-enabled dating and relationship violence (Reyns et al., 2013); technology-enhanced abuse (Fraser et al., 2010); technology-facilitated abuse (Bailey et al., 2021; Hand et al., 2009; Rees et al., 2011; Woodlock, 2017); online violence against women (Abdul Aziz, 2017); digital dating abuse (Reed et al., 2017); technology-facilitated domestic and family violence (Douglas et al., 2019); technology-facilitated intimate partner violence (McLachlan & Harris, 2022); technology-facilitated intimate partner abuse (Leitão, 2021); technology-facilitated coercive control (Dragiewicz et al., 2018); and digital coercive control (Harris & Woodlock, 2019, 2023).

Similar to Chapter 3, this chapter utilises Stark's (2007, 2023) framework of coercive control to unpack the ways in which digital technologies are used to perpetrate abuse. This is what Harris and Woodlock (2019: 533) have called "digital coercive control". The rationale for using this term rather than the others listed above is that digital coercive control captures the "… method (digital), intent (coercive behaviour) and impact (control of an ex/partner)" of abuse where devices and digital media are utilised to abuse partners or ex-partners (Harris & Woodlock, 2019: 533). It also avoids blame being placed on the medium in which the harm is communicated, thereby taking into account existing gender inequality which facilitates harm against women in society (Harris & Woodlock, 2019; Vera-Gray, 2017). Coercive control is also criminalised in England and Wales as per Section 76 of the *Serious Crime Act 2015* which provides a legislative framework whereby perpetrators can be prosecuted for demonstrating such behaviour. As mentioned in Chapter 2, evidence of coercive control can include online harm but this is not referred to as a risk factor for intimate partner homicide (CPS, 2023).

In the same way Stark (2007, 2023) and Hester (2010) frame coercive control as a product of structural gender inequality, digital coercive control follows the same understanding. It also expands discourse surrounding the mechanisms of abuse which are not typically considered serious forms of abuse (Harris &

Woodlock, 2019, 2023; Stark, 2007, 2023). Digital coercive control is treated in the same manner as coercive control with many responses considering this form of abuse as less serious than others. This is in line with Stark's work on the violent incident model in which it is demonstrated that policy, legal and criminal justice responses to intimate partner abuse, up until recently, considered the severity of abuse based on violent incidents and the extent of physical injury or threatened physical injury (Stark, 2012). Instead, digital coercive control should be considered a pattern of abuse as per the current statutory guidance provided by the Crown Prosecution Service (CPS) which is an extension of abuse already being perpetrated (CPS, 2023; Harris & Woodlock, 2019; Lyndon et al., 2011; McLachlan & Harris, 2022).

By way of comparison to coercive control again, Stark (2007) draws attention to the spatiality of this form of abuse stating that it is "spatially diffuse" (Stark, 2007: 208). Consequently, the modes of perpetration can move freely between private and public domains, meaning that coercive control does not just occupy the 'home' space. Due to the nature of digital coercive control, it can be considered spaceless as it exceeds fixed borders in the physical world (Harris & Woodlock, 2019, 2023; McLachlan & Harris, 2022). However, the term 'home' and its conceptualisations are highly contested (Dutton & Goodman, 2005; Stark, 2007; Tyner, 2012). The home is not simply a place or 'dwelling' which is lived in. This space allows us to learn gender roles, behaviours and expectations, some of which may influence our perceptions of other intersections such as sex, age, race and class. Gregson and Lowe (1995: 226) have explained this further by suggesting that the home has:

> a multiplicity of meanings suggests[ing] that rather than seeing things in terms of a single ideology of home, we need to think of home in terms of dominance and resistance.

As such, this shows the importance of space and place in terms of digital coercive control and intimate partner abuse. Space, place, safety and harm are juxtaposed in these instances. The home may not be a place or space of safety, and instead may be considered a place or space where abuse is normalised (Harris & Woodlock, 2019). This speaks to the notion of privacy whereby abuse is often "permit[ed], encourage[d], and reinforce[d]" (Schneider, 1994: 36). While the "veil of privacy" was challenged by the second wave of feminism bringing private troubles to light in the public sphere, formal responses still continue to be limited (Fineman, 1994: xiii; Harris, 2016). In order to contextualise and situate the notions of place, space and spacelessness, Harris and Woodlock (2019) use de Certeau's (1984) spatial framework to describe how space manifests in both practical and ideological ways. Scott and Hogg (2015: 172) go further to suggest that space can also be conceptualised as "mental space or symbolic landscapes" moving beyond simple physical geography. While this discussion considers rurality, it can also be applied to the digital environment.

The mechanisms of digital coercive control prevent women's "space for action" (Harris & Woodlock, 2019: 537). These spaces represent one way in which women can cope, resist and challenge abuse. Given the 'spaceless' nature of digital coercive control, it means women can be vulnerable to harm anywhere at any time (Harris & Woodlock, 2019; Woodlock, 2013). As such, the abuse is no longer tied to the private domain or the 'home' as discussed previously. The digital environment enables perpetrator omnipresence and omnipotence, meaning that women are never really able to leave an abusive relationship (McLachlan & Harris, 2022; Stark, 2012). They can never feel safe (Hand et al., 2009). The permanence of the internet and digital technologies allows for abuse to be extended and thereby exacerbates the impact on victims (Kings-Ries, 2011; Lucero et al., 2014). Arguably, coercive control operates in this way but the digital element provides more opportunities for abuse and surveillance, further diminishing the possibility of escape (McLachlan & Harris, 2022). In fact, it renders the concept of escape non-existent.

However, it is unclear how feminist understandings of coercive control, and indeed digital coercive control, can map across to the LGBTIQA+ community in terms of gender and power (Harris & Woodlock, 2023; Hester & Donovan, 2009). This is a particularly difficult area in regards to lesbian relationships where the dynamics of abuse may differ (Renzetti, 1992). It has been suggested that the "impact and meanings of sexuality, race, and ethnicity as locations of power and control" also need to be taken into account (Harris & Woodlock, 2023: 16). Similarly, Ristock (2002) has commented that a deep-seated heterosexual bias is rooted within the concept of coercive control. Others have suggested that the concept of coercive control cannot be applied to or speak for Indigenous populations given that they believe experiences of victimisation and perpetration go beyond this binary construct (Harris & Woodlock, 2023). Furthermore, it does not factor in the policies, laws and institutions that are governed by racialised heteronormative ideologies which have persisted for centuries (Harris & Woodlock, 2023).

While much of the literature and research on digital coercive control considers its link to intimate partner abuse, few studies go further to discuss its implications for homicide. The premise of this book is not only to highlight examples of how digital coercive control is observed by co-victims but also to show that digital coercive control should be considered a legitimate risk factor for intimate partner homicide. As mentioned in Chapter 2, few studies have made this connection, with much of the research utilising secondary data with a distinct quantitative focus (McLachlan & Harris, 2022). McLachlan and Harris (2022) analysed coroner and police files in order to perform a statistical analysis of digital coercive control in cases of intimate partner homicide. While this provides a picture of the incidence of the problem, it does not take into account the nuance involved in these cases. Moreover, the links to the digital environment could not be determined in many of these cases due to incomplete data. Consequently, the empirical research used in this book provides the first qualitative inquiry into the mechanisms of digital coercive control in intimate partner homicide cases from the perspective of victims' families' in England and Wales.

Importance of Digital Technologies

Empirical research and existing literature has and continues to place the use of new technologies and digital media into two camps in terms of intimate partner abuse:

> ... using technology is like having a super power: you can use it for good or you can use it for evil.
>
> (Fasnacht & Griffith, 2009: 6)

New technologies and digital media are therefore either considered beneficial or problematic in terms of victimisation and resistance, specifically in relation to intimate partner abuse (Douglas et al., 2019; Freed et al., 2017). Other scholars concur with this (Al-Alosi, 2020; Baughman, 2009; Bumb, 2017). As discussed previously, this chapter shows how this way of thinking also extends to intimate partner homicide. Digital technologies comprise of devices and software used for the purpose of communication. This includes smartphones, mobile applications (e.g., WhatsApp, Kik Messenger), global positioning systems (GPS), social networking sites (e.g., Facebook) and the Internet of Things (Douglas et al., 2019; Kennedy, 2022).

While much of the discourse focuses on the negative effects of digital technologies in the context of intimate partner abuse, there are some positive applications which must be noted. At its most basic level, digital technology enables women to access information and resources (Al-Alosi, 2020). This can be crucial for victims who face other barriers to support such as time, location, disability or communication (Al-Alosi, 2020). For instance, video conferencing can be employed to aid in treatment options for women in rural areas (Hassija & Gray, 2011). Digital technologies can also prove useful in terms of collecting evidence of abusive behaviours or actions and holding perpetrators to account (Al-Alosi, 2020; Douglas & Burton, 2018). However, there are a number of obstacles that need to be overcome in order for this type of evidence to be considered in criminal proceedings (Baughman, 2009).

Digital media can also be utilised as a tool of empowerment for victim-survivors of intimate partner abuse (Al-Alosi, 2020; Baughman, 2009). It enables victim-survivors to extend their social network allowing access to informal support networks such as online self-help groups (Baughman, 2009) or family and friends (Fugate et al., 2005; Hand et al., 2009; Moe, 2007). This may be beneficial for women who are not yet ready to seek formal support or who are still dealing with the consequences of abuse (Baughman, 2009). As discussed in Chapter 3, there is evidence to suggest that women tend to confide in informal support networks prior to contacting more formal support such as the police (Hand et al., 2009; Moe, 2007). Research shows that digital media's empowering nature can be multifaceted in that it can enable women to rebuild their lives, to break down barriers economically and to challenge other harmful behaviour such as misogyny (Al-Alosi, 2020; Capel et al., 2017; Dragiewicz et al., 2018). Women in situations where abuse is normalised and commonplace often have issues related to shame and embarrassment which may prevent them from discussing experiences in a formal setting (Bagshaw et al., 2000; Feder et al., 2006; Fugate et al., 2005; Rempel et al., 2019). As such, the anonymity and the immediate perpetual accessibility the internet provides allows these women to start making sense of their experiences (Al-Alosi, 2020; Douglas et al., 2019; Hand et al., 2009).

Given the broader reach of the internet, some victims have voiced feeling more open to discuss their experiences online as it limits the negativity from others (Tarzia et al., 2017). Similarly, it gives women access to information regarding the support services available to them, their rights and information relating to safety planning (Kranz & Nakamura, 2002). Arguably, digital technologies can also enhance women's safety as well as providing them with a tool which may assist with their recovery from abuse (Baughman, 2009; Fraser et al., 2010; Southworth et al., 2005). This can include both physical or online tools such as CCTV cameras, watches, panic buttons and web-based applications that allow women to develop safety plans (Al-Alosi, 2020). They may also provide opportunities to engage with alternative forms of justice. Hashtag activism is one medium in which women can speak out about their experiences, transforming the online sphere into a space of virtual resistance (Al-Alosi, 2020; Dobrin, 2020). With that being said, it can also open up women to other forms of victimisation, including harassment, hate speech, and dismissive and/or minimising comments from others (Al-Alosi, 2020; Suler, 2004).

However, the internet and digital technologies are not accessible to all, especially those in developing countries or those with other socio-demographic factors limiting their access (Al-Alosi, 2020). Although some victims may be privileged enough to have access to digital technologies, they may lack digital literacy or have a poor internet connection which impedes their ability to make use of the online environment (Thomas et al., 2018). This can be linked to age, language skills or the sheer amount of information available online (Rempel et al., 2019; Thomas et al., 2018). Similarly, affordability is also a significant factor for individual victims and service providers, especially in the current economic climate (Al-Alosi, 2018, 2020). Other issues include the posting of misinformation or inappropriate information online, and a reduction in face-to-face contact with service providers which has the potential to leverage cuts in staffing (Snook, Chayne & SafeLives, 2017; Sorenson et al., 2014).

In addition, the online environment also provides more opportunities to perpetrators of intimate partner abuse. It makes victims more accessible to perpetrators as there is no need for physical access (Al-Alosi, 2020; Baughman, 2009; Douglas et al., 2019; Muise et al., 2009; Runions et al., 2013; Suler, 2004). It also extends and intensifies the abuse being perpetrated, providing perpetrators more scope to intimidate and control victims (Dimond et al., 2011; Douglas et al., 2019; Fraser et al., 2010; Hand et al., 2009; Southworth et al., 2007). Other forms of abuse can be incorporated as a result of the digital environment, such as economic abuse being carried out through online banking (Al-Alosi, 2017). This can have significant consequences for victims' mental health (Fraser et al.,

2010; Woodlock, 2017). Moreover, the online environment provides more opportunities for control in new and innovative ways which has impacted women's sense of 'feeling safe', thereby destroying this idea of a 'safe distance' between the victim and perpetrator (Hand et al., 2009: 3; McLachlan & Harris, 2022). It is important to note that perpetrators' incessant contact can lead to chronic fear (Stark, 2007, 2023). Of course, each victim's experience is very personal and unique to them, meaning that chronic fear can be instilled regardless of how much contact ensues (Stark, 2007, 2023; Woodlock, 2017).

While support is available for women in these circumstances, with agencies in Australia and the UK acknowledging issues with digital technology through charitable campaigns and developing safe practices, much of the guidance recommends women take a "technology detox" or disconnect from digital media as a response to online harm (Levy, 2015: 687). Other researchers in the field have termed this a "digital detox" (Al-Alosi, 2020: 9). Douglas et al. (2019) highlight a number of issues related to this guidance: (i) it discriminates against the victim as it places responsibility on them for the harm caused, meaning that they face consequences for the perpetrator's actions (United Nations Development Programme and UN Women, 2015); (ii) the practicalities of disconnecting from digital media are unrealistic given the intertwined nature of our lives with digital media; and (iii) often support requires a digital connection resulting in victims becoming more isolated and less able to engage with other parts of their lives such as work or education.

Furthermore, resistance to abuse can endanger victims further, especially in terms of email or browser history deletion (Al-Alosi, 2020). For example, victims may delete emails but overlook checking the 'sent' and 'deleted' email folders to eradicate all traces of communication. Similarly, deleting browser history can also spark suspicion (Baughman, 2009; Mason & Magnet, 2012). Research shows that perpetrators may delete evidence collected by victims before it is reported, thereby impacting their credibility (Al-Alosi, 2020; Fraser et al., 2010). Al-Alosi (2020: 8) comments on "tweet and delete" behaviours which perpetrators employ to abuse or humiliate victims by posting a defaming message or information temporarily, and then deleting it before it can be reported or addressed. Other difficulties lie in practitioner competence with technology, practitioner support of technology with victims, a lack of technology maintenance or technology giving a false sense of security to victims (Al-Alosi, 2020).

Technologies of Abuse

As digital technologies evolve with the emerging online environment, it is important to show the types of technologies that have been used to control victims in abusive relationships. For example, research conducted by Hand et al. (2009) shows that mobile and landline phones have been employed to orchestrate 'check-ins', allowing perpetrators to work out whom the victim is contacting whether that be family, friends or co-workers. Given the rise and availability of technology, check-ins have become easier to plan and carry out, enabling perpetrators to increase surveillance (Hand et al., 2009; Kennedy, 2022; Stark, 2012). Regular phone calls to victims can provide a reference point in terms of loyalty, with any unanswered calls potentially being seen as a sign of infidelity or cheating (Kennedy, 2022; Stark, 2007, 2023). Perpetrators have been known to check their partner's call history to ensure they are not in contact with anyone not previously approved (Hand et al., 2009; Kennedy, 2022). Similarly, short message service (SMS) texts, more commonly known as text messages, may also be the subject of inspection (Kennedy, 2022; Kotka, 2005). These so-called inspections can be overt or covert, or may be demanded as a test of loyalty or under the assumption of trust. In situations where victims are unwilling to provide their phone for inspection, perpetrators may be under the impression they have something to hide (Chung, 2003; Kennedy, 2022). As discussed in Chapter 3, this sense of ownership over the victim can actively encourage negative self-talk, resulting in self-blame, among those being controlled and monitored (Hand et al., 2009; Kennedy, 2022). Abuse can also be perpetrated through this medium by sending upsetting, threatening or bullying text messages (Rocque, 2021). The use of global positioning systems (GPS) has also been reported as a means of controlling victims whereby a person's location can be accessed through their mobile phone (Chen, 2017; Hand et al., 2009; Mason & Magnet, 2012). These tools have been used in other situations such as stalking (Burke et al., 2011; Cole, 2014; Kennedy, 2022; Melander, 2010; Southworth et al., 2007).

Since the launch of smartphones in the early 21st century, smartphone camera capabilities have improved and advanced significantly. This has enabled perpetrators to take pictures, videos and audio recordings which can aid in remote monitoring behaviour. This can and has been used in the non-consensual creation, production and distribution of images, videos and texts created to control, intimidate and threaten victims – particularly women (Hand et al., 2009; McGlynn & Rackley, 2017; Paradiso et al., 2023; Powell et al., 2019). This has been referred to as image-based sexual abuse and encompasses a range of harms and abusive behaviours, including upskirting, deepfake pornography (Fido et al., 2022; McGlynn & Rackley, 2017), revenge pornography, non-consensual pornography, cyber-rape or involuntary porn (Citron & Franks, 2014; Maddocks, 2018), and sextortion (O'Malley & Holt, 2020; Paradiso et al., 2023; Powell et al., 2019). Back in the early 2000s, this was referred to as 'digital voyeurism', including many of the behaviours outlined above which have now been given their own terminology and category (Kee, 2005: 20). Similar to the earlier discussion around phone calls and text messages, these behaviours can be perpetrated overtly or covertly, with or without consent. For women in abusive relationships, this type of behaviour(s) can occur during the course of the relationship or may occur post-separation (Al-Alosi, 2020; Fraser et al., 2010; Hand et al., 2009; Stark, 2007, 2023). In situations where women are recorded without the use of mobile technologies, other mediums have been reportedly utilised such as webcams, pinhole cameras and hidden sound equipment (Bagshaw et al., 2000; Kotka, 2005; Southworth et al., 2005).

Other research has focused on the capabilities of the internet and computer software in the commission of covert surveillance. For example, a study conducted by Southworth and colleagues (2007) found five methods perpetrators used to control and monitor victims behaviour online, including computer monitoring software, keystroke logging, instant messaging and chat rooms, checking browser history (Hertlein & van Dyck, 2020; Schokkenbroek et al., 2023), and email tampering. Despite spyware's original purpose being to monitor children's internet usage, it has also been employed by perpetrators to monitor current and/or ex-partners (Southworth et al., 2005, 2007). Its range of uses is extensive depending on the software set up for surveillance. For instance, some software has been reported to record browser history clearance and/or deletion, and keypad activity including saving email passwords (Southworth et al., 2005, 2007) It has also enabled perpetrators access to chatroom conversations with support agencies (Kee, 2005) and allowed for gaslighting behaviour using emails (Baum et al., 2009; Burke et al., 2011; Douglas et al., 2019; Kee, 2005; Kranz & Nakamura, 2002; Woodlock, 2017). A number of studies have identified the ways gaslighting is carried out in these instances. Perpetrators check, intercept or redirect emails to their own accounts in order to monitor their partner and they have also been known to read emails and mark them as unread so as not to arouse suspicion (Kee, 2005; Kranz & Nakamura, 2002).

In addition to so-called older methods of communication, monitoring behaviour has been made more accessible with instant messaging platforms and social networking sites. As previously discussed in this chapter, this has allowed abuse and monitoring behaviour to move from the private to public domain more readily (Burke et al., 2011; Harris & Woodlock, 2019; Melander, 2010). Melander (2010) suggested that more harm could potentially be caused by embarrassing or humiliating a partner on social media than the abuse experienced in private. Perpetrators' surveillance tactics are facilitated by the options on social networking sites such as Facebook where the 'check-in' function enables victims' whereabouts to be known (Cole, 2014; Mason & Magnet, 2012). This function could potentially impact victim safety even though they have voluntarily used the function on Facebook. Other mediums in which locations can become known include the default geotag function which is set to automatically embed GPS information into photographs taken on smartphones. This allows anyone who has access to these photographs information on the location of the photographs, meaning that victims could be traced in this way (Cole, 2014). Without knowledge of geotag information in photographs, victims could be putting themselves at risk without realising it by simply uploading a photograph to Facebook or other social networking sites. Perpetrators also have the opportunity to create false social media accounts to abuse and monitor victims, especially given the lax policies these platforms often operate (Baughman, 2009; Dimond et al., 2011). Other studies have indicated that perpetrators have been known to install other types of location-based tracking applications and devices covertly on victims' mobile phones (Burke et al., 2011; Douglas et al., 2019; Woodlock, 2017).

The estimates of online harm victimisation and perpetration are notoriously difficult to measure due to a number of issues, including conflicting definitions, significant underreporting, and the lack of recognition of this type of harm by victims and support agencies (Navarro, 2015; McLachlan & Harris, 2022). However, Brown and Hegarty (2018) have provided some scope by suggesting the rates of victimisation as being between <1% to 91% and perpetration being between 3% to 94%. However, much of the research concerning prevalence rates considers adolescent populations (Cavezza & McEwan, 2014; McLachlan & Harris, 2022). Harris and Woodlock (2023) have indicated the incidence of victimisation being closer to 10–15% but also ranging up to 94%. While this offers some insight into the scale of the issue, this is only the tip of the iceberg when it comes to online harm. In detailing the technologies of abuse, some of the ways in which digital technologies are utilised to abuse and monitor victims in intimate relationships become evident. However, as the internet and digital technologies evolve, newer forms of online harm continue to be discovered as victims come to light. As such, researchers, practitioners, service providers and the criminal justice system must follow in hot pursuit.

Digital Coercive Control and Technologies of Abuse

Digital technologies are used in one of two ways to perpetrate coercive control. They are either used to communicate abuse or to monitor behaviour. This can be understood through Harris and Woodlock's (2019) discussion of digital coercive control, and the 'spaceless' nature of this type of online harm. In considering Stark's (2007, 2023) original understanding of coercive control, the second and third dynamic involved in the technology of coercive control, namely intimidation and isolation, are the main driving forces for digital coercive control (Kennedy, 2022; Stark, 2007, 2012, 2023).

As mentioned in Chapter 3, the purpose of intimidation is to scare and silence victims ensuring faithfulness and reliance on the perpetrator (Karakurt & Silver, 2013; Kennedy, 2022; Salari & LeFevre Sillito, 2016; Stark, 2007, 2023). This can be achieved through the use of threats, gaslighting, surveillance and monitoring behaviour, stalking, mircroregaulation, and degradation and shaming (Stark, 2007, 2023). On the other hand, isolation can be the motivation for or may be the result of digital coercive control (Myhill & Hohl, 2016; Stark, 2007, 2023). This is closely tied to emotional isolation discussed in more depth in Chapter 3. For perpetrators who use isolation as a control tactic, the aim is to whittle down the victim's support circle whether that be informal or formal support (Duron et al., 2021). This, in turn, impedes victims' abilities to seek help from anyone outside of the perpetrator's physical or virtual grasp (Dutton & Goodman, 2005; Stark, 2007, 2023). Both facets of coercive control have significant consequences for victims.

Table 4.1 Conceptualising Online Harm and Coercive Control

Types of Online Harm	*Link to Coercive Control*	*Characteristics of Online Harm*
Communicating abuse	Intimidating behaviour Use of active and passive threats Gaslighting Degradation and shaming Microregulation	Communicating incessantly via landline/mobile phones, text messages or other digital means Sending upsetting, threatening or bullying text messages Sending or threatening to distribute sexually explicit text messages, images or videos to others
Monitoring behaviour	Intimidating behaviour Surveillance and monitoring behaviour Stalking Microregulation Isolation	Arranging 'check-ins' Checking call history Examining text messages Taking pictures, videos and audio recordings with the intent to share them with others Recording via webcams, pinhole cameras and/or hidden sound equipment Checking internet browser history Keystroke logging Inspecting instant and chat room messages Reading, tampering with and intercepting emails Installing location-based tracking applications Impersonating friends or family by creating new social media accounts

Sources: Al-Alosi, 2020; Chung, 2003; Bagshaw et al., 2000; Baughman, 2009; Baum et al., 2009; Burke et al., 2011; Cole, 2014; Dimond et al., 2011; Douglas et al., 2019; Hand et al., 2009; Kee, 2005; Kennedy, 2022; Kotka, 2005; Kranz & Nakamura, 2002; Melander, 2010; McGlynn & Rackley, 2017; Paradiso et al., 2023; Powell et al., 2019; Rocque, 2021; Southworth et al., 2005, 2007; Stark, 2007, 2012, 2023; Woodlock, 2017.

Note: Not an exhaustive list.

Mediums for Communicating Abuse

The internet and digital technologies can be used to carry out a range of behaviours which enable perpetrators to frighten, humiliate, denigrate or belittle victims (Douglas et al., 2019; McLachlan & Harris, 2022). The use of active threats is one way in which this behaviour can be perpetrated, showing synergy between the offline and online environment (Pain et al., 2014; Stark, 2007, 2023; Stewart et al., 2021; Tyner, 2012; Walby & Towers, 2018). (For more information on active threats, see Chapter 3). While image-based sexual abuse is considered a separate harm, it is the use of active threats which allows it to be considered within the scope of digital coercive control. In particular, sextortion incorporates the coercive behaviours encountered in abusive relationships, whereby perpetrators have acquired nude, sexual or sexually explicit images or videos of the victim with the intent to share these images without the victim's consent (Henry & Powell 2015; McGlynn et al., 2017; Powell & Henry, 2017; Wittes et al., 2016; Wolak & Finkelhor, 2016). Sextortion is used as a means of blackmail, where if the perpetrator's demands are not met, they share said images or videos as punishment (Woolford, 2019). The impact of this harm on the victim can be devastating, creating a culture of fear, humiliation and vulnerability (Powell & Henry, 2017; Wolak & Finkelhor 2016). Many victims report feelings of powerlessness (Woolford, 2019). This is one of many examples of how the online environment can be used to communicate abuse.

Of course, this is not a new phenomenon but is facilitated due to the ubiquity of mobile technologies and the accessibility of the internet (McGlynn & Rackley, 2017). As mentioned earlier, perpetrators of sextortion use blackmail to gain something from the victim, whether it be more sexual content, money or in-person sexual activities (Woolford, 2019). This can be described as a 'private crime' which initially occurs between the victim and perpetrator. However, there can be threats of public exposure, but these tend not to be carried out since the victim typically complies with the perpetrator's demands (Patchin & Hinduja, 2018). As opposed to Wolak et al. (2018), Patchin and Hinduja's (2018) research suggests sextortion perpetrators can be someone known to the victim. In addition to being used within sex-trafficking contexts and already highlighted above, sextortion can also be used as a control mechanism within relationships characterised by intimate partner abuse (Henry & Powell, 2014) and digital coercive control. Similarly, it can be used to seek revenge in regards to an ex-partner or to serve the purpose of pornography (McGlynn et al., 2017; Powell & Henry, 2017).

The Case of Sextortion

Shena is the mother Jamielee, a 17-year-old mum-to-be, who was murdered by her ex-partner Bruce in 2013. Jamielee and Bruce starting dating after Jamielee's 16th birthday. Shena believed the relationship was characterised by controlling behaviour. While Jamielee and Bruce separated on several occasions, Jamielee returned to Bruce and her relationship with her mother became strained due to Shena's concerns about her daughter's whereabouts. Shena had contacted the police multiple times but they were unable to give specifics about Jamielee's location due to her being over the age of 16 years. With that being said, Shena described her daughter as:

> … a cool kid cheeky, spoilt, loved, mental as a box of frogs, very loving …

In addition to other forms of coercive control, Jamielee was subjected to threats relating to the release and sharing of intimate images and videos she shared with Bruce. It is unclear to Shena whether Jamielee had volunteered these images and videos or whether they had been taken without Jamielee's consent:

> He was going to post her videos he had taken of her and pictures all over social media. He was going to send them to me, her dad, she even told the police about that, I think three minutes before he murdered her ... and they still haven't got him ... sexually explicit pictures of her that he had taken of her ... some of them she might have done, she might have sent a chest shot, you know, I'm not having a go at her, it's the thing that they do, its peer pressure and they're all doing it ...

Sextortion in this case appears to have been used to prevent the victim leaving the relationship (Henry & Powell, 2014). Furthermore, the perpetrator's intent may have been to further isolate the victim from family and friends due to feelings of embarrassment or shame (Howard, 2019; Williams, 2012). Despite the perpetrator not distributing the images and videos of the victim, the creation and threat of distribution of these images and videos was enough to concern the victim, hence her contact with the police. This use of active threats correlates with the behaviours attributed to image-based sexual abuse (Powell & Henry, 2017). Similarly, these behaviours can be ascribed to this sense of male entitlement and privilege previously discussed in Chapter 3 (Bouffard, 2010; Martinez, 2015; Powell & Henry, 2017; Stark, 2007, 2023; Wilson & Daly, 1992, 1993). It is not within the remit of this chapter to go into depth about sextortion but simply to illustrate that this is another means to communicate abuse which is facilitated by the online environment.

Mediums for Monitoring Behaviour

In addition to communicating abuse and threats, the online environment can also be utilised as a tool for surveillance and/or monitoring behaviour in a number of different ways. Mobile technologies have increasingly made it easier for perpetrators to spy on victims, thereby depriving them of privacy (Stark, 2007, 2023). As mentioned in Chapter 3, this monitoring can occur on an implicit or explicit level with the aim being to create a sense of omnipresence and omnipotence (Douglas et al., 2019; Stark, 2007, 2023). Stark (2007: 255) indicates that, at times, perpetrators may openly use digital technologies as a provision that "let[s] the victim know she is being watched or overheard". In other circumstances, perpetrators may use a clandestine approach to monitoring where victims are unaware of being tracked (Burke et al., 2011; Douglas et al., 2019; Woodlock, 2017). This situation can be worsened by victims' lack of knowledge and understanding of technology (Douglas et al., 2019; Thomas et al., 2018). Tracking of victims can be carried out exclusively by perpetrators or they can employ other proxies to help with surveillance activities (Douglas et al., 2019).

Arguably, monitoring behaviour draws parallels with stalking which often occurs simultaneously with coercive control (Norris et al., 2011; Monckton Smith et al., 2017). The main focus of stalking is to incite fear as a result of unwanted, relentless behaviour (Canter & Ioannou, 2004; Logan & Walker,

2009; Melton, 2007; Mullen et al., 2009; Woodlock, 2017). However, stalking is considered a separate form of abuse similar to sextortion discussed earlier. There is clear evidence to suggest that stalking can occur in-person or online, or it can take place in both spaces at the same time. This is indicative of the continuum of online-offline harm discussed at the beginning of this chapter (Munk & Kennedy, 2024). Due to the intertwined nature of digital technologies and our lives, it is increasingly difficult to separate these two forms of harm (Gosse, 2021). Stalking should be considered stalking regardless of how it is perpetrated, but both environments should be given the same attention.

The Case of Total Digital Surveillance

As a reminder, Jen sister's Nessa was killed by her ex-fiancé, Paton, in 2016. Her death was a result of a decade of controlling behaviour where Nessa attempted to regain control on multiple occasions by leaving Paton and moving nearer her sister. More details about Nessa can be found in Chapter 3. After ending a very controlling and manipulative relationship, Nessa had begun seeing someone new from work, Simmy, at the time of her murder. Jen suggested Nessa was drawn to Simmy as he was thoughtful:

> … from what Kay [Jen's other sister] has said he showed something that she'd never had and that's just being thoughtful when she was working and she hadn't had time to make that packed lunch, she'd been getting the kids off to school, actually coming back from Marks and Spencer's with a sandwich and a cup of coffee was huge. It might not be for some people but it was huge for Nessa.

Jen also described the three sisters as being close: "Just we're close, me Kay and Nessa have always been close …". She also believed Nessa to be fiercely protective of her children:

> … and the one thing she would never have done was leave those children and when he turned around and said she'd gone away for a few days, I just I was like no, she would have told me, Kay or my mum if she was going anywhere she would have told somebody but she would have never ever ever have left the children with him. She just wouldn't have done, whether she was going away and she brought the children up here or to Kay or to my mum, she would have never left them in the house with him. Just never in a million years would she have done that …

The extent to which Paton monitored and, arguably, stalked Nessa was immense. This behaviour was perpetrated through incessant phone calls, email tampering and microregulation of social media. Jen gave numerous examples of times when Paton's monitoring of Nessa was extensive to the point where he asked others to confirm her location:

> ... with her phone he would be texting her continually and ringing her continually to check up where she is, where are you? Who are you with you know? And Kay [Nessa's sister] was saying that one time they were at the zoo and he'd phoned and she was like "I'm at the zoo with Kay", "put Kay on the phone then" ... No so Kay had to say hi Paton I'm here, you know, for him to actually believe that she was actually with Kay yeah so the phone was a really big thing and when I think about it now I always sort of said to Nessa "oh will you get off that bloody phone you are driving me nuts cos you know you're on it constantly" but actually a lot of time it was because he was messaging her continually what you doing? Who you talking to? What, you know, where are you? Why have you not called me? That kind of thing so there was a lot of it ...

This account shows clear links to microsurveillance, which is a facet of coercive control that seeks to remove the victim's autonomy by controlling every part of the victim's life (Stark, 2007, 2023). In this instance, the perpetrator controlled where the victim went and who she saw, and wanted proof she was complying with his demands. Surveillance of this kind introduces fear into routine everyday activities (Dobash & Dobash, 1979; Pain & Smith 2008; Pain, 2014; Stark, 2007, 2023). It is unlike any other kind of oppression (Stark, 2007, 2023). It also makes intimidation portable. Women are essentially hostages without rights or liberties (Stark, 2007, 2012; Woodlock, 2017). In addition to constant phone calls, Paton also carried out 'check-ins' covertly by accessing Nessa's emails and other messages:

> I remember one time as well he did actually hack into her emails ... yeah he did and I can remember that, it was quite a while ago but she messaged me and said I think Paton's been in my email account and I was like "what makes you say that?" She said "because he's read something and I know I haven't read it cos obviously once you click on it it's open" so I said just change all your passwords, just change everything, change every single password and then you'll soon see if it's him. I think she'd said she'd found some stuff on the computer and it was all like I don't know if it was like some kind of code or I'm not into the techy at all but she'd found something on his computer that was supposed to help you get into various apps and help you break passwords and she found that on his laptop. Well yeah he did, he found, he obviously got a picture of Simmy [Nessa's new partner] from somewhere because he knew what he looked like ... He'd got messages off her phone, he'd definitely taken messages off her phone because did somebody say – I think he messaged Simmy and told him to back off ... so he had to have got something off of the phone to have done that yeah but he definitely got some stuff off of her phone but that was when he'd, I think what he's done is he's got into it and then Nessa's [changed] her passwords and then the next time he's gone ... to get back in again to check-up he's ended up locking it which is when she's had to go to

> the Apple shop. And that's when the guy at the Apple shop has obviously said "you are aware whoever this is isn't the first time they've done it" and there's this this and this on your phone …
>
> (Jen, Sister)

Similarly, this highlights the extent of the perpetrator's spatial and temporal tactics in terms of coercive control. It also shows that his control did extend outside of the usual physical parameters to the digital environment (Douglas et al., 2019; Hand et al., 2009; Harris & Woodlock, 2019; Stark, 2007, 2023; Woodlock, 2017). Moreover, it provides empirical evidence for proprietariness or proprietary behaviours discussed in Chapter 3, which is enhanced by the online sphere (Bouffard, 2010; Martinez, 2015; Stark, 2007, 2023; Wilson & Daly, 1992, 1993). This is comparable to the notion of property rights discussed in more detail in the previous chapter. In this example, Paton believed he had "exclusive possession" of the victim, thereby giving him the right to ward off any new potential suitors (Stark, 2007: 207). As such, the digital environment was able to facilitate the perpetrator's rights to exclusivity.

Paton's microsurveillance of Nessa was boosted further by social media, with Jen explaining that Paton had "… deleted all the men off her [Nessa's] Facebook at one stage …". This narrative considers the concept of spaceless microregulation where coercive control perpetrated across social networking platforms transcends geographic boundaries, thus no longer being bound to the 'private' domain (Hand et al., 2009; Harris & Woodlock, 2019). Omnipresence was a clear consequence of this microregulation (Stark, 2007, 2023). This can be further illustrated by Foucault's notion of panopticism (Pain, 2014). In situations like this, the perpetrator will have complete control over the victim. As the victim never knows when they are being watched, they will constantly regulate their behaviour as a way of appeasing the perpetrator (May et al., 2010; Monckton Smith et al., 2014; Roberts, 2019; Stanko, 1996, 2001; Stark, 2010). As outlined above, the perpetrator's gaze extended to the victim's social networking whereby male friends were not seen as a necessity. Together with chronic fear, this account shows that the perpetrator wanted to further instil this notion of ownership and a sense of exclusive control to the victim and may have also wanted to prevent the likelihood of disclosure to more formal support services (Crossman & Hardesty, 2018; Jasinski et al., 2014). This case study provides a detailed qualitative account which explores how digital technologies broaden and intensify monitoring behaviours through digital coercive control.

Implications for Intimate Partner Homicide

Although the field of digital media and intimate partner abuse has continued to grow and develop over the past two decades, with research being conducted across the globe, few studies have made the link between intimate partner abuse and intimate partner homicide (Dimond et al., 2011; Douglas et al., 2019; Fraser et al., 2010; Hand et al., 2009; Southworth et al., 2005, 2007; Wiederhold, 2013;

Woodlock, 2017; Yardley & Wilson, 2014). Of these few studies, many have been conducted in Australia using secondary forms of data rather than first-hand accounts (Douglas et al., 2019; Harris & Woodlock, 2023; McLachlan & Harris, 2022; Woodlock, 2017). While still in its infancy, there is a growing body of research highlighting the existence of both digital coercive control and offline abuse in serious intimate partner abuse or intimate partner homicide cases (Dragiewicz et al., 2019; Harris & Woodlock, 2019). Arguably, research data from McLachlan and Harris's (2022) Queensland Domestic and Family Violence Death Review Unit (DFVDRU) study can potentially predict the presence of online abuse in cases where homicide may be a real possibility. Hence, the importance for digital coercive control to be considered a risk factor for intimate partner homicide.

Given that there is a distinct lack of consideration in terms of digital coercive control, this can lead to missed opportunities for intervention. This is particularly important in regards to prevention of fatal abuse or homicide (McLachlan & Harris, 2022). Existing risk factors discussed in Chapter 3 considered as precursors to intimate partner homicide can be identified and evidenced through perpetrators' use of online harm. As highlighted earlier in this chapter, perpetrators can use digital media and mobile technologies to enact facets of coercive control which both extend and amplify existing abuse. Digital coercive control can, therefore, provide intelligence for intimate partner homicide (McLachlan & Harris, 2022). From analysing case files, including coroners' reports and police investigations as part of the DFVDRU, McLachlan and Harris (2022) were able to determine that intimate partner homicide is more likely to occur in cases where digital coercive control is present. Research on filicide has also indicated that incessant contact can be considered a "homicide flag" (Dwyer & Miller, 2014; McLachlan & Harris, 2022: 630). Similarly, stalking or monitoring behaviour has also been given this classification (Dragiewicz et al., 2019; Harris, 2020; Woodlock, 2017). McLachlan and Harris (2022) found a sevenfold increase in stalking behaviour in cases where digital coercive control was present. The case studies included in this chapter, complied from interviews with victims' families', also provide empirical evidence of digital coercive control used in abusive relationships which resulted in homicide. This emphasises the importance of unpacking and conducting further research on this online-offline continuum and its connection to intimate partner homicide.

Moreover, existing risk factors such as potential or actual separation can exacerbate monitoring or stalking behaviours where digital media and mobile technologies enable contact beyond the physical plane (McLachlan & Harris, 2022; Spencer & Stith, 2020; Woodlock, 2017). Potential or actual separation is a well-established risk factor for homicide within the literature (Campbell et al., 2007; Spencer & Stith, 2020; Woodlock, 2017). In a recent study, Dragiewicz et al. (2019) reported that all participants who experienced online harm did so as a result of separation or that online harm worsened at the point of separation. Of note, more than half of participants were aware that online harm occurred during the relationship, with the rest suggesting that online harm was experienced post-separation. In addition, digital media and mobile technologies are often used in cases of shared custody of children or where visitation needs to be arranged between the victim and perpetrator (McLachlan & Harris, 2022). In these cases, children can be used as a conduit to further abuse or monitor the victim under the pretence of co-parenting (Stark & Hester, 2019).

The case studies included in this chapter also provide evidence in terms of the mechanisms of digital coercive control used in abusive relationships which resulted in homicide. In a similar vein, they highlight the nature of digital coercive control in these relationships where this online harm was used to further abuse and monitor the victims in ways which would not be possible without the digital environment. This emphasises the importance of unpacking and conducting further research on this online-offline continuum and its connection to intimate partner homicide. As such, more research into this field of study is likely to positively impact and influence responses to fatal abuse and intimate partner homicide, especially where digital coercive control is a major factor.

Conclusion

While different categories of harm within the online environment have not all necessarily been criminalised or recognised, we know digital media and mobile technologies are increasingly used to perpetrate abuse, particularly in intimate relationships. There are significant differences between cases with and without digital coercive control. Digital coercive control is spaceless, indicating that there is no legitimate means of escape. The spaceless nature of this type of harm also impacts temporal barriers so constant contact can ensue. Perpetrators can, therefore, seem omnipotent and omnipresent. As the online and offline environment are intrinsically linked, digital coercive control must be considered a risk factor for intimate partner homicide. There is a clear relationship between known risk factors for intimate partner homicide and the execution of digital coercive control.

References

Abdul Aziz, Z., 2017. *Due Diligence and Accountability for Online Violence Against Women* [online]. Boston, Massachusetts: Association for Progressive Communications. Available at: chrome-extension://efaidnbmnnnibpcajpcglclefindmkaj/https://esem.org.mk/pdf/Najznachajni%20vesti/2018/1/DDP-OVAW.pdf [Accessed 12 November 2024].

Al-Alosi, H., 2017. Cyber-violence: Digital abuse in the context of domestic violence. *University of New South Wales Law Journal*, 40 (4), pp. 1573–1603.

Al-Alosi, H., 2018. Technology is both a weapon and a shield for those experiencing domestic violence. *The Conversation* [online], 17 June. Available at: https://theconversation.com/technology-is-both-a-weapon-and-a-shield-for-those-experiencing-domestic-violence-97776.

Al-Alosi, H., 2020. Fighting fire with fire: Exploring the potential of technology to help victims combat intimate partner violence. *Aggression and Violent Behavior*, 52, pp. 1–10.

Bagshaw, D., Chung, D., Couch, M., Lilburn, S. & Wadham, B., 2000. *Reshaping Responses to Domestic Violence* [online]. Commonwealth of Australia: University of

South Australia. Available at: chrome-extension://efaidnbmnnnibpcajpcglclefindmkaj/https://wesnet.org.au/wp-content/uploads/2012/07/PADV-Reshaping-responses.pdf [Accessed 28 October 2024].

Bailey, J., Flynn, A. & Henry, N., 2021. *The Emerald International Handbook of Technology-Facilitated Violence and Abuse* (Emerald Studies In Digital Crime, Technology and Social Harms). Leeds: Emerald Group Publishing.

Baughman, L. L., 2009. Friend request or foe? Confirming the misuse of internet and social networking sites by domestic violence perpetrators. *Widener Law Journal*, 19, pp. 933–966.

Baum, K., Catalano, S., Rand, M. & Rose, K., 2009. *Stalking Victimization in the United States*. Washington, DC: Department of Justice. Available at: https://www.justice.gov/archive/ovw/docs/bjs-stalking-rpt.pdf [Accessed 19 March 2025].

Bouffard, L. A., 2010. Exploring the utility of entitlement in understanding sexual aggression. *Journal of Criminal Justice*, 38 (5), pp. 870–879.

Brown, S., 2006. The criminology of hybrids: Rethinking crime and law in technosocial networks. *Theoretical Criminology*, 10 (2), pp. 223–244.

Brown, C., & Hegarty, K., 2018. Digital dating abuse measures: A critical review. *Aggression and Violent Behavior*, 40, pp. 44–59.

Burke, S. C., Wallen, M., Vail-Smith, K. & Knox, D., 2011. Using technology to control intimate partners: An exploratory study of college undergraduates. *Computers in Human Behavior*, 27, pp. 1162–1167.

Bumb, M. L., 2017. Domestic violence law, abusers' intent, and social media: How transaction-bound statutes are the true threats to prosecuting perpetrators of gender-based violence. *Brooklyn Law Review*, 82 (2), pp. 917–960.

Campbell, J., Glass, N., Sharps, P., Laughon, K. & Bloom, T., 2007. Intimate partner homicide: Review and implications of research and policy. *Trauma, Violence & Abuse*, 8 (3), pp. 246–269.

Canter, D. V., & Ioannou, M., 2004. A multivariate model of stalking behaviours. *Behaviormetrika*, 31(2), pp. 113–130.

Capel, T., Vyas, D. & Brereton, M., 2017. *Women in crisis situations: Empowering and supporting women through ICTs*. IFIP Conference on Human-Computer Interaction. INTERACT, pp. 64–84.

Cavezza, C., & McEwan, T. E., 2014. Cyberstalking versus off-line stalking in a forensic sample. *Psychology, Crime & Law*, 20 (10), pp. 955–970.

de Certeau, M., 1984. *The Practice of Everyday Life*. Berkeley: University of California Press.

Chen, B. X., 2017. When you should (and shouldn't) share your location using a smartphone. *New York Times* [online], 12 July. Available at: https://www.nytimes.com/2017/07/12/technology/personaltech/using-location-sharing-apps.html.

Chung, D., 2003. Is she really going out with him: Young people's understandings and experiences of sex, love and violence in intimate heterosexual relationships. Ph.D. thesis, University of Adelaide.

Citron, D. K., & Franks, M. A., 2014. Criminalizing revenge porn. *Wake Forest Law Review*, 49 (2), pp. 345–392.

Cole, M., 2014. Post-breakup emotion and obsessive relational intrusion in the mediated world [online]. Ph.D. thesis, Arizona State University. https://www.proquest.com/openview/48d81b143c0d2390edd18283df76787c/1?pq-origsite=gscholar&cbl=18750 [Accessed 26 November 2024].

Crossman, K. A., & Hardesty, J. L., 2018. Placing coercive control at the center: What are the processes of coercive control and what makes control coercive? *Psychology of Violence*, 8 (2), pp. 196–206.

Crown Prosecution Service (CPS), 2023. *Controlling or Coercive Behaviour in an Intimate or Family Relationship* [online]. London: Crown Copyright. Available at: https://www.cps.gov.uk/legal-guidance/controlling-or-coercive-behaviour-intimate-or-family-relationship [Accessed 14 November 2024].

Dimond, J. P., Fiesler, C., & Bruckman, A. S. 2011. Domestic violence and information communication technologies. *Interacting with Computers*, 23, pp. 413–421.

Dobash, R. E., & Dobash, R., 1979. *Violence Against Wives: A Case Against the Patriarchy*. New York: Free Press.

Dobrin, D., 2020. The hashtag in digital activism: A cultural revolution. *Journal of Cultural Analysis and Social Change*, 5 (1), pp. 1–14.

Douglas, H., & Burton, M., 2018. Legal responses to non-consensual smartphone recordings in the context of domestic and family violence. *University of New South Wales Law Journal*, 4 (1), pp. 157–184.

Douglas, H., Harris, B. A. & Dragiewicz, M., 2019. Technology-facilitated domestic and family violence: Women's experiences. *British Journal of Criminology*, 59 (3), pp. 551–570.

Dragiewicz, M., Burgess, J., Matamoros-Fernández, A., Salter, M., Suzor, N. P., Woodlock, D. & Harris, B., 2018. Technologies of coercive control: Digital domestic violence and the competing roles of social media platforms. *Feminist Media Studies*, 18, pp. 609–625.

Dragiewicz, M., Harris, B., Woodlock, D., Salter, M., Easton, H., Lynch, A., Campbell, H., Leach, J. & Milne, L., 2019. *Domestic Violence and Communication Technology: Survivor Experiences of Intrusion, Surveillance, and Identity Crime* [online]. Brisbane, Australia: The Australian Communications Consumer Action Network and Queensland University of Technology. Available at: chrome-extension://efaidnbmnnnibpcajpcglclefindmkaj/https://eprints.qut.edu.au/131143/1/Domestic%2Bviolence%2Band%2Bcommunication%2Btechnology%2BSurvivor%2Bexperience%2Bof%2Bintrusion%2Bsurveillance%2Band%2Bidentity%2Bcrime.pdf [Accessed 30 December 2024].

Duron, J. F., Johnson, L., Hoge, G. L. & Postmus, L. L., 2021. Observing coercive control beyond intimate partner violence: Examining the perceptions of professionals about common tactics used in victimization. *Psychology of Violence*, 11 (2), pp. 144–154.

Dutton, M. A., & Goodman, L. A., 2005. Coercion in intimate partner violence: Toward a new conceptualization. *Sex Roles*, 52, pp. 743–756.

Dwyer, J., & Miller, R., 2014. *Working With Families Where an Adult Is Violent: Best Interest Case Practice Model Specialist Practice Resource* [online]. Victoria, Australia: Department of Health and Human Services. Available at: chrome-extension://efaidnbmnnnibpcajpcglclefindmkaj/https://www.cpmanual.vic.gov.au/sites/default/files/Working%20with%20families%20where%20an%20adult%20is%20violent%20specialist%20resource%203017.pdf [Accessed 30 December 2024].

Fasnacht, L. D., & Griffith, T., 2009. *Using Technology to Stalk And Harass* [online]. Pennsylvania: Middpenn Matters. Available at: https://perma.cc/NBU9-5FVF [Accessed 28 October 2024].

Feder, G. S., Hutson, M., Ramsay, J. & Taket, A. R., 2006. Women exposed to intimate partner violence: expectations and experiences when they encounter health care professionals: A meta-analysis of qualitative studies. *Archives of Internal Medicine*, 166 (1), pp. 22–37.

Fido, D., Rao, J. & Harper, C. A., 2022. Celebrity status, sex, and variation in psychopathy predicts judgements of and proclivity to generate and distribute deepfake pornography. *Computers in Human Behavior*, 129. doi:10.1016/j.chb.2021.107141.

Fineman, M. A., 1994. Preface. In: Fineman, M. A., & Mykitiuk, R., eds. *The Public Nature of Private Violence: The Discovery of Domestic Abuse*. Oxon: Routledge, pp. xi–xvii.

Fraser, C., Olsen, E., Lee, K., Southworth, C. & Tucker, S., 2010. The new age of stalking: Technological implications for stalking. *Juvenile and Family Court Journal*, 61 (4), pp. 39–55.

Freed, D., Jackeline, P., Minchala, D., Levy, K., Ristenpart, T. & Dell, N., 2017. Digital technologies and intimate partner violence: A qualitative analysis with multiple stakeholders. *Proceedings ACM Human-Computer Interaction*, 1 (46), pp. 1–22.

Fugate, M., Landis, L., Riordan, K., Naureckas, S. & Engel, B., 2005. Barriers to domestic violence help seeking: Implications for intervention. *Violence Against Women*, 11 (3), pp. 290–310.

Gosse, C., 2021. "Not the real world": Exploring experiences of online abuse, digital dualism, and ontological labor. In: Bailey, J., Flynn, A. & Henry, N., eds. *The Emerald International Handbook of Technology-Facilitated Violence and Abuse*. Leeds: Emerald Publishing Limited, pp. 47–64.

Gregson, N., & Lowe, M., 1995. Home-making: On the spatiality of daily social reproduction in contemporary middle-class Britain. *Transactions, Institute of British Geographers*, 20, pp. 224–235.

Hand, T., Chung, D. & Peters, M., 2009. *The Use of Information and Communication Technologies to Coerce and Control in Domestic Violence and Following Separation* [online]. Sydney: Australian Domestic and Family Violence Clearinghouse. Available at: https://advocacy4oromia.files.wordpress.com/2015/03/stakeholderpaper_6.pdf [Accessed 28 October 2024].

Harris, B., 2016. Violent landscapes: A spatial study of family violence. In: Harkness, A., Harris, B., & Baker, D., eds. *Locating Crime in Context and Place: Perspectives on Regional, Rural and Remote Australia*. Alexandria, New South Wales: The Federation Press, pp. 70–84.

Harris, B., 2020. *Technology, Domestic and Family Violence: Perpetration, Experiences and Responses* [online]. Queensland, Australia: Queensland University of Technology Centre for Justice. Available at: chrome-extension://efaidnbmnnnibpcajpcglclefindmkaj/https://www2.dvac.org.au/wp-content/uploads/2021/03/Briefing-paper-series-April-2020-Issue-4.pdf [Accessed 30 December 2024].

Harris, B. A., & Woodlock, D., 2019. Digital coercive control: Insights from two landmark domestic violence studies. *British Journal of Criminology*, 59 (3), pp. 530–550.

Harris, B. A., & Woodlock, D., 2023. *Technology and Domestic and Family Violence: Victimisation, Perpetration and Responses*. Oxon: Routledge.

Hassija, C. M, & Gray M. J., 2011. The effectiveness and feasibility of videoconferencing technology to provide evidence-based treatment to rural domestic violence and sexual assault populations. *Telemed e-Health*, 17 (4), pp. 309–315.

Henry, N., & Powell, A., 2014. The dark side of the virtual world. In: Henry, N., & Powell, A., eds. *Preventing Sexual Violence: Interdisciplinary Approaches to Overcoming a Rape Culture*. Basingstoke: Palgrave Macmillan, pp. 84–104.

Henry, N., & Powell, A., 2015. Beyond the "sext": Technology-facilitated sexual violence and harassment against adult women. *Australian and New Zealand Journal of Criminology*, 48 (1), pp. 104–188.

Hertlein, K. M., & van Dyck, L. E., 2020. Predicting engagement in electronic surveillance in romantic relationships. *Cyberpsychology, Behavior, and Social Networking*, 23 (9), pp. 604–610.

Hester, M., 2010. Gender and sexuality. In: Itzin, C., Taket, A. & Barter-Godfrey, S., eds., *Domestic and Sexual Violence and Abuse: Tackling the Health and Mental Health Effects*. Oxon: Routledge, pp. 99–131.

Hester, M., & Donovan, C., 2009. Researching domestic violence in same-sex relationships – A feminist epistemological approach to survey development. *Journal of Lesbian Studies*, 13 (2), pp. 161–173.

Howard, T., 2019. Sextortion: Psychological effects experienced and seeking help and reporting among emerging adults [online]. Ph.D. thesis, Walden University. Available at: chrome-extension://efaidnbmnnnibpcajpcglclefindmkaj/https://scholarworks.waldenu.edu/cgi/viewcontent.cgi?article=7863&context=dissertations.

Jasinski, J., Blumenstein, L. & Morgan, R., 2014. Testing Johnson's typology: Is there gender symmetry in intimate terrorism? *Violence and Victims*, 29, pp. 73–88.

Jurgenson, N., 2011. Digital dualism versus augmented reality [online]. Maryland: The Society Pages, Cyborgology. Available at: https://thesocietypages.org/cyborgology/2011/02/24/digital-dualism-versus-augmented-reality/ [Accessed 8 March 2024].

Karakurt, G., & Silver, K. E., 2013. Emotional abuse in intimate relationships: The role of gender and age. *Violence & Victims*, 28 (5), pp. 804–821.

Kee, J., 2005. *Cultivating Violence through Technology: Exploring the Connections between Information and Communication Technologies (ICT) and Violence Against Women (VAW)* [online]. Geneva: Association of Progressive Communications' Women's Networking Support Programme. Available at: https://www.apc.org/sites/default/files/VAW_ICT_EN_0.pdf [Accessed 19 March 2025].

Kennedy, M. C., 2022. Digital coercive control: A male perspective. In: Gavin, H., ed. *Women and the Abuse of Power*. Leeds: Emerald Publishing Limited, pp. 105–122.

Kings-Ries, A., 2011. Teens, technology, and cyberstalking: The domestic violence wave of the future? *Texas Journal of Women and the Law*, 20, pp. 131–164.

Kotka, I., 2005. Stalking and cyberstalking in South Australia. BA Social Work thesis, University of South Australia.

Kranz, A. L., & Nakamura, K., 2002. Helpful or harmful? How innovative communication technology affects survivors of intimate violence [online]. University of Minnesota: Minnesota Center Against Violence and Abuse. Available at: https://citeseerx.ist.psu.edu/document?repid=rep1&type=pdf&doi=f2df923b800f71b1690d97bc381fa9b721d516ba [Accessed 19 March 2025].

Leitão, R., 2021. Technology-facilitated intimate partner abuse: A qualitative analysis of data from online domestic abuse forums. *Human-Computer Interaction*, 36 (3), pp. 203–242.

Levy, K., 2015. Intimate surveillance. *Idaho Law Review*, 51, pp. 679–693.

Logan T., & Walker R., 2009. Partner stalking: Psychological dominance or business as usual? *Trauma, Violence, and Abuse*, 10, pp. 247–270.

Lucero, J. L., Weisz, A. N., Smith-Darden, J., & Lucero, S. M., 2014. Exploring gender differences: Socially interactive technology use/abuse among dating teens. *Journal of Women and Social Work*, 29, pp. 478–491.

Lyndon, A., Bonds-Raacke, J., & Cratty, A. D., 2011. College students' Facebook stalking of ex-partners. *Cyberpsychology, Behavior and Social Networking*, 14, pp. 711–716.

Maddocks, S., 2018. From non-consensual pornography to image-based sexual abuse: Charting the course of a problem with many names. *Australian Feminist Studies*, 33(97), pp. 345–361.

Martinez, C. T., 2015. Engendered expressions of aggression: The role of gender, proprietary behaviours, and jealousy in intimate partner violence. *Violence and Gender*, 2 (2), pp. 112–118.

Mason, C., & Magnet, S., 2012. Surveillance studies and violence against women. *Surveillance & Society*, 10 (2), pp. 105–118.

May, D., Rader, N. E. & Goodrum, S., 2010. A gendered assessment of the "threat of victimization": Examining gender differences in fear of crime, perceived risk, avoidance, and defensive behaviors. *Criminal Justice Review*, 3, pp. 1–24.

Melton, H. C., 2007. Stalking in the context of intimate partner abuse. *Feminist Criminology*, 2 (4), pp. 347–363.

Mullen, P. E., Pathé, M. & Purcell, R., 2009. *Stalkers and Their Victims*. Cambridge: Cambridge University Press.

McGlynn, C., Johnson, K., Rackley, E., Henry, N., Gavey, N., Flynn, A. & Powell, A., 2021. "It's torture for the soul": The harms of image-based sexual abuse. *Social and Legal Studies*, 30 (4), pp. 541–562.

McGlynn, C., & Rackley, E., 2017. Image-based sexual abuse. *Oxford Journal of Legal Studies*, 37 (3), pp. 534–561.

McGlynn, C., Rackley, E. & Houghton, R., 2017. Beyond "revenge porn": The continuum of image-based sexual abuse. *Feminist Legal Studies*, 25, pp. 25–46.

McLachlan, F., & Harris, B., 2022. Intimate risks: Examining online and offline abuse, homicide flags, and femicide. *Victims & Offenders*, 17 (5), pp. 623–646.

Melander, L. A., 2010. College students' perceptions of intimate partner cyber harassment. *Cyberpsychology, Behavior, and Social Networking*, 13, pp. 263–268.

Moe, A., 2007. Silenced voices and structured survival: Battered women's help seeking. *Violence Against Women*, 13 (7), pp. 676–699.

Monckton Smith, J., Szymanska, K. & Haile, S., 2017. *Exploring the Relationship between Stalking and Homicide* [online]. Gloucester: University of Gloucester. Available at: chrome-extension://efaidnbmnnnibpcajpcglclefindmkaj/https://eprints.glos.ac.uk/4553/1/NSAW%20Report%2004.17%20-%20finalsmall.pdf [Accessed 12 August 2024].

Monckton Smith, J., Williams, A., & Mullane F., 2014. *Domestic Abuse, Homicide and Gender*. London: Palgrave Macmillan.

Muise, A., Christofides, E. & Desmarais, S. 2009. more information than you ever wanted: Does Facebook bring out the green-eyed monster of jealousy? *Cyberpsychology and Behavior*, 12 (4), pp. 441–444.

Munk, T., & Kennedy, M., 2024. *Victimisation in the Digital Age: An Online/Offline Continuum Approach*. Oxon: Routledge.

Murphie, A., & Potts, J., 2003. *Culture and Technology*. London: Red Globe Press.

Myhill, A., & Hohl, K., 2016. The "golden thread": Coercive control and risk assessment for domestic violence. *Journal of Interpersonal Violence*, 34 (21–22), pp. 4477–4497.

Navarro, J., 2015. Cyberabuse and cyberstalking. In: Navarro, J. N., Clevenger, S., & Marcum, C. D., eds. *The Intersection Between Intimate Partner Abuse, Technology and Cybercrime: Examining the Virtual Enemy*. Durham, North Carolina: Carolina Academic Press, pp. 125–140.

Norris, S., Huss, M., & Palarea, R. E., 2011. A pattern of violence: Analyzing the relationship between intimate partner violence and stalking. *Violence and Victims*, 26 (1), pp. 103–115.

O'Malley, R. L., & Holt, K. M., 2020. Cyber sextortion: An exploratory analysis of different perpetrators engaging in a similar crime. *Journal of Interpersonal Violence*, 37 (1–2), pp. 1–26.

Pain, R., 2014. Everyday terrorism: Connecting domestic violence and global terrorism. *Progress in Human Geography*, 38 (4), pp. 531–550.

Pain, R., & Smith, S. J., 2008. *Fear: Critical Geopolitics and Everyday Life*. Aldershot: Ashgate.

Paradiso, M. N., Rollè, L. & Trombetta, T., 2023. Image-based sexual abuse associated factors: A systematic review. *Journal of Family Violence*, 39, pp. 931–954.

Patchin, J. W., & Hinduja, S., 2018. Sextortion among adolescents. Results from a national survey of U.S. youth. *Sexual Abuse*, 32 (1), pp. 1–25.

Powell, A., & Henry, N., 2017. *Sexual Violence in a Digital Age*. London: Palgrave Macmillan.

Powell, A., Henry, N., Flynn, A. & Scott, A. J., 2019. Image-based sexual abuse: The extent, nature, and predictors of perpetration in a community sample of Australian residents. *Computers in Human Behavior*, 92, pp. 393–402.

Reed, L. A., Toleman, R. M. & Ward, L. M., 2017. Gender matters: Experiences and consequences of digital dating abuse victimization in adolescent dating relationships. *Journal of Adolescence*, 59, pp. 79–89.

Rees, S., Silove, D., Chey, T., Ivancic, L., Steel, Z., Creamer, M., Teesson, M., Bryant, R., McFarlane, A. C., Mills, K. L., Slade, T., Carragher, N., O'Donnell, M. & Forbes, D., 2011. Lifetime prevalence of gender-based violence in women and the relationship with mental disorders and psychosocial function. *Journal of the American Medical Association*, 306, pp. 513–521.

Rempel, E., Donelle, L., Hall, J. & Rodger, S., 2019. Intimate partner violence: A review of online interventions. *Informatics for Health and Social Care*, 44 (2), pp. 204–219.

Renzetti, C. M., 1992. *Violent Betrayal: Partner Abuse in Lesbian Relationships*. London: Sage.

Reyns, B. W., Burek, M. W., Henson, B. & Fisher, B. S., 2013. The unintended consequences of digital technology: Exploring the relationship between sexting and cybervictimization. *Journal of Crime Justice*, 36, pp.1–17.

Ristock, J., 2002. *No More Secrets: Violence in Lesbian Relationships*. New York: Routledge.

Roberts, N. J., 2019. Gender, sexual danger and the everyday management of risks: The social control of young females. *Journal of Gender-Based Violence*, 3 (1), pp. 29–44.

Rocque, R., 2021. Digital abuse: Awareness is preparedness. *International Journal of Nursing Education and Research*, 9 (4), pp. 1–4.

Runions, K., Shapka, J. D., Dooley, J. & Modecki, K., 2013. Cyber-aggression and victimization and social information processing: Integrating the medium and the message. *Psychology of Violence*, 3 (1), pp. 9–26.

Salari, S., & LeFevre Sillito, C., 2016. Intimate partner homicide suicide: Perpetrator primary intent across young, middle, and elder adult age categories. *Aggression and Violent Behavior*, 26, pp. 26–34.

Schneider, E. M., 1994. The violence of privacy. In: Fineman, M. A., & Mykitiuk, C., eds. *The Public Nature of Private Violence: The Discovery of Domestic Abuse*. Oxon: Routledge, pp. 26–58.

Schokkenbroek, J. M., Ponnet, K. & Hardyns, W., 2023. Technology-facilitated harm and abuse in intimate relationships. In: Shackelford, T. K., ed. *Encyclopedia of Domestic Violence*. Cham: Springer International Publishing, pp. 1–16.

Scott, J., & Hogg, R., 2015. Strange and stranger ruralities: Social constructions of rural crime in Australia. *Journal of Rural Studies*, 39, pp. 171–179.

Snook, Chayne & SafeLives, 2017. *Tech vs. Abuse: Research Findings* [online]. London: Comic Relief. Available at: chrome-extension://efaidnbmnnnibpcajpcglclefindmkaj/https://safelives.org.uk/wp-content/uploads/Tech-vs-abuse-report.pdf.

Sorenson, S. B., Shi, R., Zhang, J. & Xue, J., 2014. Self-presentation on the web: Agencies serving abused and assaulted women. *American Journal of Public Health*, 104 (4), pp. 702–707.

Southworth, C., Dawson, S., Fraser, C. & Tucker, S., 2005. *A High-tech Twist on Abuse: Technology, Intimate Partner Stalking, and Advocacy* [online]. University of Minnesota: Center Against Violence and Abuse. Available at: https://www.acesdv.org/wp content/uploads/2014/06/NNEDV_HighTechTwist_PaperAndApxA_English08.pdf [Accessed 28 October 2024].

Southworth, C., Finn, J., Dawson, S., Fraser, C. & Tucker, S., 2007. Intimate partner violence, technology, and stalking. *Violence Against Women*, 13 (8), pp. 842–856.

Spencer, C. M. & Stith, S. M., 2020. Risk factors for male perpetration and female victimization of intimate partner homicide: A meta-analysis. *Trauma, Violence & Abuse*, 21 (3), pp. 527–540.

Stanko, E., 1996. Reading danger: Sexual harassment, anticipation and self-protection. In: Hester, M., Kelly, L. & Radford, J., eds. *Women, Violence and Male Power: Feminist Research, Activism and Practice*. Milton Keynes: Open University Press, pp. 50–62.

Stanko, E., 2001. Women, danger, and criminology. In: Renzetti, C. M., & Goodstein, L., eds. *Women, Crime, and Criminal Justice*. Los Angeles: Roxbury Publishing Company, pp. 13–26.

Stark, E., 2007. *Coercive Control: How Men Entrap Women in Personal Life*. New York: Oxford University Press.

Stark, E., 2010. Do violent acts equal abuse? *Sex Roles*, 62, pp. 201–211.

Stark, E., 2012. Looking beyond domestic violence: Policing coercive control [Special issue]. *Journal of Police Crisis Negotiations*, 12, pp. 199–217.

Stark, E., 2023. *Coercive Control: How Men Entrap Women in Personal Life*. 2nd ed. New York: Oxford University Press.

Stark, E., & Hester, M., 2019. Coercive control: Update and review. *Violence against Women*, 25 (1), pp. 81–104.

Stewart, D. E., MacMillan, H. & Kimber, M., 2021. Recognizing and responding to intimate partner violence: An update. *The Canadian Journal of Psychiatry*, 66 (1), pp.71–106.

Suler, J., 2004. The online disinhibition effect. *Cyberpsychology & Behavior*, 7 (3), pp. 321–326.

Tarzia, L., Deepthi, I., Thrower, E. & Hegarty, K., 2017. "Technology doesn't judge you": Young Australian women's views on using the internet and smartphones to address intimate partner violence. *Journal of Technology in Human Services*, 35 (3), pp. 199–218.

Thomas, J., Wilson, C. K. & Park, S., 2018. Australia's digital divide is not going away [online]. *The Conversation*, 29 March Available at: https://theconversation.com/australias-digital-divide-is-not-going-away-91834.

Tyner, J. A., 2012. *Space, Place, and Violence: Violence and the Embodied Geographies of Race, Sex and Gender*. New York: Routledge.

United Nations Development Programme and UN Women, 2015. *Combatting Online Violence against Women & Girls: A Worldwide Wake- up Call* [online]. New York: Broadband Commission. Available at: chrome-extension://efaidnbmnnnibpcajpcglcle

findmkaj/https://www.broadbandcommission.org/Documents/publications/bb-wg-gender-report2015-highlights.pdf.

Vera-Gray, F., 2017. "Talk about a cunt with too much idle time": Trolling feminist research. *Feminist Review*, 115, pp. 61–78.

Walby, S., & Towers, J., 2018. Untangling the concept of coercive control: Theorizing domestic violent crime. *Criminology & Criminal Justice*, 18 (1), pp. 7–28.

Wiederhold, B. K., 2013. Are "Facebook murders" a growing trend? *Cyberpsychology, Behavior and Social Networking*, 16, pp. 1–2.

Williams, J. L., 2012. Teens, sexts, & cyberspace: The constitutional implications of current sexting & cyberbullying laws. *William & Mary Bill of Rights Journal*, 20 (3), pp. 1018–1050.

Wilson, D., & Daly, M., 1992. The man who mistook his wife for a chattel. In: Barkow, J. H., Cosmides, L. & Tooby, J., eds. *The Adapted Mind: Evolutionary Psychology and the Generation of Culture*. New York: Oxford University Press, pp. 289–322.

Wilson, D., & Daly, M., 1993. An evolutionary psychological perspective on male sexual proprietariness and violence against wives. *Violence and Victims*, 8 (3), pp. 271–294.

Wittes, B., Poplin, C., Jurecic, Q. & Spera, C., 2016. *Sextortion: Cybersecurity, Teenagers, and Remote Sexual Assault* [online]. Washington, DC: The Brookings Institute. Available at: https://www.brookings.edu/wp-content/uploads/2016/05/sextortion1-1.pdf [Accessed 19 March 2025].

Wolak, J., & Finkelhor, D., 2016. *Sextortion: Findings from a Survey of 1,631 Victims* [online]. Durham, University of New Hampshire: Crimes Against Children Research Center. Available at: https://www.wearethorn.org/wp-content/uploads/2016/08/Sextortion_Report.pdf [Accessed 27 June 2019].

Wolak, J., Finkelhor, D., Walsh, W. & Treitman, L., 2018. Sextortion of minors: Characteristics and dynamics. *Journal of Adolescent Health*, 62, pp. 72–79.

Woodlock, D., 2013. *Technology-facilitated Stalking: Findings and Recommendations from the SmartSafe Project* [online]. Collingwood, Victoria: Domestic Violence Resource Centre. Available at: https://techsafety.org.au/wp-content/uploads/2023/08/Woodlock-Technology-facilitated-Stalking-Findings-and-Recommendations-from-the-SmartSafe-Project-2013-smartsafe.org_.au_.pdf [Accessed 19 March 2025].

Woodlock, D., 2017. The abuse of technology in domestic violence and stalking. *Violence Against Women*, 25 (5), pp. 584–602.

Woolford, S. M., 2019. Victim blaming and cyber sexual victimization: An exploratory study on the influence of gender and political ideology on victim blaming attitudes towards sextortion [online]. Ph.D. thesis, Pennsylvania State University. Available at: https://etda.libraries.psu.edu/files/final_submissions/20560 [Accessed 10 March 2020].

Yardley, L., & Wilson, D., 2014. Making sense of "Facebook murder"? Social networking sites and contemporary homicide. *The Howard Journal of Criminal Justice*, 54 (2), pp. 109–134.

5 Overspill of Abuse

Introduction

The central facet of this chapter is to highlight the mechanisms by which perpetrators extend abuse to victims' families, friends and their wider social circle. As previously stated in Chapter 1, individuals considered outside of the direct victim pool are often referred to as co-victims (Bastomski & Duane, 2019; Hertz et al., 2005; Jackson et al., 2022; MacVane et al., 2003). They are not necessarily the initial target for abuse but their abuse is incorporated into the victim's experience as a means of intimidation, isolation and control as part of the larger 'web of abuse'. As discussed in Chapter 3, the web of abuse is wide-ranging, indicating that abuse can go beyond the victim to others in their social circle (Faver & Strand, 2008; Solot, 1997). This can include active threats aimed at the family, wider family unit and pets (Douglas et al., 2019; Harris & Woodlock, 2019; Monckton Smith et al., 2014; Stark, 2007, 2023; Woodlock, 2017). It can also encompass behaviours which isolate the victim emotionally and physically from their informal support network (Baldwin et al., 2015; Duron et al., 2021). This has been referred to as social abuse in older literature (Bagshaw et al., 2000). It often involves ongoing rudeness from the perpetrator towards family and friends of the victim which eventually limits contact in addition to other forms of isolation mentioned above (Bagshaw et al., 2000). Moreover, this abuse can be perpetrated offline and online, again speaking to this continuum of online-offline harm discussed in earlier chapters (Chapters 2, 3 and 4) (Munk & Kennedy, 2024).

As this area of study is vastly under-researched, literature is limited with much of the focus being on victims' experiences. Often the overspill of abuse to victims' families' and friends tends to receive little attention and is not usually the overall focus of the research. Instead, the majority of empirical studies consider the victim-perpetrator dichotomy despite others potentially being targeted for abuse. Interestingly, while some research exists in relation to co-victims of intimate partner abuse (Gregory, 2017), none considers the link to co-victims of intimate partner homicide. Some research has taken a literature-based approach to the gendered dynamics of abuse in families, briefly mentioning "multi-abuses perpetrated on family members" (Morris, 2009: 414) but

DOI: 10.4324/9781003464488-5

not providing any further context in terms of this issue. Other research considers "bystanders" in the context of the victim's situation where individuals are aware of abusive incidents but do not know the victim intimately and are not directly involved in such incidents, instead being viewed as witnesses (Gregory, 2017: 1). Studies considering bystander interactions with the victim tend to focus on the role they play in these situations, with an emphasis on understanding and responsibility (Beeble et al., 2008; Klein, 2012; Sylaska & Edwards, 2014). Many are also related to college students which is a very narrow victim pool (Borsky et al., 2016; Storer et al., 2016). As such, this chapter seeks to fill this gap in the literature and explore the overspill of abuse to others connected to the victim, with the focus being on victims' families in cases of intimate partner homicide.

The Impact of Co-victims' Informal Support

As a reminder, co-victims can include anyone with a familial or kinship relationship or friendship with the victim(s) (Bastomski & Duane, 2019). While older literature focused mostly on co-victims defined as family and friends, this definition has been broadened given the ever-changing family structures that exist within and outside the Western world (Jackson et al., 2022). Individuals who fall into this category are considered a source of informal support for those experiencing abuse (Goodman & Smyth, 2011; Latta & Goodman, 2011; Liang et al., 2005; Rose et al., 2000; Trotter & Allen, 2009; Stark, 2007, 2023). As mentioned in Chapter 3, they can provide a range of support on both an emotional and/or instrumental level (Hasbullah et al., 2016; Liang et al., 2005; Rose et al., 2000). With the current global estimates of intimate partner abuse being around 30% in terms of lifetime prevalence, the majority of the population are likely to witness and/or support a relative, friend, co-worker or neighbour who is experiencing intimate partner abuse (Gregory, 2017; WHO, 2021). In many of these cases, victims' families' and other sources of support are often aware of the abuse being perpetrated against their loved one, with many being the first point of contact for disclosure (Gregory, 2017; Klein, 2012; Williamson & Hester, 2009). This places a huge responsibility on them in terms of help-seeking behaviours beyond the first initial disclosure. Their reaction, behaviours and judgments are likely to hinder or facilitate future disclosures and help-seeking practices when it comes to victims seeking more formal support (Gregory, 2017; Klein, 2012). For those victims whose abuse is fatal, co-victim support is much more complicated as those individuals are left behind following the homicide. Given that in 2023, 51,100 women were killed by an intimate partner or family member globally, there is a high likelihood that many co-victims may be in this position (UNODC and UN Women, 2023).

As such, the impact of providing informal support is of interest. Physical and psychological repercussions were most commonly reported (Gregory et al., 2017). Co-victims endured physical health impacts as a result of losing someone to intimate partner homicide, witnessing abuse first-hand or supporting an intimate partner abuse victim long-term (Gregory et al., 2017). As discussed in Chapter 1, the aftermath of supporting a victim of intimate partner homicide is very difficult to comprehend as the physical health consequences can be related to a number of other ongoing or emergent issues which are irrelevant to the homicide (Gregory et al., 2017). This can include general ageing in addition to caring for children with trauma (Hardesty et al., 2008; Spencer-Carver, 2008). Physical fatigue is also a common factor for those who support loved ones experiencing abuse, particularly where long-term support is needed (Latta, 2008). Similar reports have been made by informal supporters in the context of caring for those with long-term physical health conditions (Bucki et al., 2012; Nahm et al., 2010). In addition, post-traumatic stress disorder (PTSD) is typical in those who witness abuse (Gregory et al., 2017).

Furthermore, there are significant mental health consequences to supporting individuals in the situations described above. Within a healthcare context, these consequences have been described as acute or chronic (Gregory et al., 2017). Co-victims who experience the death of a loved one report trauma, shock and fear in addition to complex feelings related to their own history of victimisation where this is a factor (Hardesty et al., 2008; Latta, 2008). As mentioned in Chapter 1, the process of grief is much more complicated for co-victims in this position (Connolly & Gordon, 2015; Costa et al., 2017; Stretesky et al., 2010; Persons, 1990; Prigerson et al., 1999). Similarly, their caring responsibilities may change as a result of the death (Spencer-Carver, 2008). Other researchers have suggested that the psychological and emotional trauma experienced by those affected by death is comparable to those who witness abuse (Erlingsson et al., 2009). Some family members have reported fearing for their own safety and that then impacting the support they are willing to provide for the victim (Goodkind et al., 2003; Hobart, 2002; Riger et al., 2002).

From a chronic perspective, other emotions were apparent such as "grief, guilt, shame, sadness, hopelessness, powerlessness, worry, isolation, reduced confidence, anger, and frustration" (Gregory et al., 2017: 566). The persistence of grief was commonly reported, particularly for those affected by intimate partner homicide (McNamara, 2008). This was complicated further by stigma associated with homicide (Costa et al., 2017; Gregory et al., 2017; Spencer-Carver, 2008). Guilt and regret were also frequently reported by co-victims, with many of them feeling guilty for not recognising abuse or wishing they had intervened sooner (Hardesty et al., 2008; Latta, 2008; McNamara, 2008). This psychological toll was also felt alongside emotions related to sadness and hopelessness (Erlingsson et al., 2009; Gregory et al., 2017; McNamara, 2008). Co-victims disclosed feelings of isolation, particularly from larger society as well as their own informal networks due to being the only surviving relative who was aware of intimate partner abuse in the victim's life (Latta, 2008). In addition, both anger and frustration were also discussed in relation to the perpetrator directly, victims disregarding advice, and criminal justice responses to intimate partner homicide specifically (Erlingsson et al., 2009; Latta, 2008; Gregory et al., 2017; Spencer-Carver, 2008).

Understanding the Overspill of Harm

As mentioned previously, there is a very limited body of research which has considered the overspill of abuse to co-victims (Gregory, 2017; Gregory et al., 2017; Hobart, 2002; Latta, 2008; Morris, 2009; Riger et al., 2002; Stark, 2007, 2023). This is narrower still in terms of intimate partner homicide. This chapter takes the same approach as Chapters 3 and 4 with regards to discussing the spillage of abuse from both an offline and online harm perspective. The same rationale also applies concerning the linguistic benefits and challenges of using the terms 'offline' and 'online'. However, it allows for the harms to be described in their respective environments, with the caveat that these two environments cannot be separated due to their inherent connection as noted earlier. Instead, they should be considered as part of the continuum of online-offline harm (Munk & Kennedy, 2024).

Offline Harm

In addition to the impacts discussed earlier, existing literature has shown that many co-victims experience direct physical impacts from the perpetrator. This can include verbal abuse, threatening behaviour, physical harm and an increased risk of fatal abuse (Goodkind et al., 2003; Gregory, 2017; Gregory et al., 2017; Hobart, 2002; Latta, 2008; Riger et al., 2002). As discussed in Chapter 3, threats are part of the perpetrator's repertoire of abuse. Threats are used to intimidate victims and threats of harm or threats to kill are specific examples of active threats (Pain et al., 2014; Stark, 2007, 2023; Stewart et al., 2021; Tyner, 2012; Walby & Towers, 2018). These types of threats are considered more direct and are potentially more fear inducing, thereby encouraging compliance from victims (Monckton Smith et al., 2014; Pain, 2014; Stark, 2007, 2023). It is important to remember that threats are part of the anatomy of coercive control. As such, this notion of harm spilling over into the lives of co-victims is another significant factor in coercive control (Stark, 2007, 2023). This may lead victims to isolate themselves further from family and friends to prevent them from becoming further recipients of abuse (Monckton Smith et al., 2014; Stark, 2007, 2023).

In particular, threats to kill were a real possibility for some co-victims. To give an estimate of the number of co-victims killed during the same incident in which the intimate partner homicide occurred, Hobart (2002) reported ten adult family members and friends being murdered in addition to three new partners and one co-worker. In Salari's (2007) study, 16 co-victims were injured or killed often after a period of ongoing abuse. Dobash and Dobash (2015: 59) have termed this "collateral killing", with Wilson and Daly (1985) describing this phenomenon as "killing the competition" especially where the victim is acquainted with a new partner. Wolf et al. (2000) suggested that where protection orders were in place for women, they were often less likely to be subjected to physical abuse, with their family and friends having an increased risk of this form of harm. This also extended to co-workers (Gregory et al., 2017; Swanberg & Logan, 2005; Swanberg et al., 2007). Threats of harm have also been noted in the literature. These types of threats occurred repeatedly towards co-workers in addition to other intimidating behaviour, and were often used by the perpetrator to obtain information on the victim (Gregory et al., 2017; Latta, 2008; Riger et al., 2002; Swanberg & Logan, 2005; Swanberg et al., 2006, 2007).

The Overspill of Threats to Shena

As a reminder, Shena's daughter Jamielee was killed in 2013 while she was pregnant with her first child. This was a result of escalating controlling behaviour perpetrated by Bruce who subjected Jamielee to a barrage of controlling tactics, including sextortion, which is discussed in more detail in Chapter 4. However, this abuse also extended to her mother in the form of threats to kill:

> I was in the house and I thought cos I used to wash up with earphones on yeah in the house, don't matter I'm in my house nothing's going to happen, and I thought on a few occasions I felt something behind me and when I'd gone to look the backdoor has slammed on two occasions. He'd told Jamielee it was him [Bruce] that he was going to do [kill] me so we was on high alert anyway for months, I literally thought it was me he was going to kill cos that's what he told her. If you don't fucking behave I'll have your mum so there was all this going on …
>
> (Shena, Mother).

In this case, threats to kill could arguably be linked to stalking behaviour, which is one of the facets of coercive control and intimate partner homicide (Bracewell et al., 2020; Brady & Nobles, 2017; Scarr & Kennedy, 2023; Campbell et al., 2007; Canter & Ioannou, 2004; McFarlane et al., 1999; Melton, 2007; Monckton Smith et al., 2014; Stark, 2007, 2023). These active threats were communicated to the victim as a way of ensuring compliance (Stark, 2007, 2023). For the most part, stalkers do not act on threats but this was not the case as per the above account (Meloy, 2000). The perpetrator knew the victim's mother's routine and was able to intimidate the victim by getting her to imagine what he was capable of doing to her mother (Kelly, 1988; Stark, 2007, 2023). Threats towards Shena were not limited to threats to kill but also extended to sexual abuse:

> He was waiting outside for Duncan [Shena's partner] to go to the flat to come in and he told Jamielee that he was going to rape me and put me in hospital, she'd watch, she'd be watching him switch off my life support so Duncan didn't go and he didn't come in so we ended up, I think Jamielee told One Foot Forward and they informed the police, I rang the police as well and we had the helicopters over the house all weekend that weekend …
>
> (Shena, Mother).

Threats of sexual abuse are often directed towards the victim as a form of coercion but in this case they were aimed at the victim's mother. Similar to threats of lethal violence, this also fits into the wider context of coercive control (Stark, 2007, 2023). The communication of this threat was explicit with the perpetrator's aim being for the victim to submit to him. In order to protect her mother, the victim had no choice but to submit to the perpetrator but this also led to the victim becoming more isolated from her support system (Dutton & Goodman, 2005; Stark, 2007, 2023). It is important to note that compliance is very much dependant on women's perceptions of what happens next, especially in terms of sexual abuse (Kelly, 1988). The victim's sexual relationship with the perpetrator may have fuelled her fear, with the verbal threat accentuating it (Kelly, 1988). This threat also violated the place where the victim perhaps felt most safe: at home. This continuum of fear and threat described above extends from being limited to particular individuals, to affecting each and every part of women's lives (Kelly, 1988; Stark, 2007, 2023). As mentioned previously, this case shows two types of offline harm perpetrated towards the victim's mother. While threats to kill and threats of harm are considered commonplace to some extent in intimate partner abuse and homicide cases, little research has discussed this in terms of their extension to family members (Gregory, 2017). Similarly, threats of sexual abuse are completely absent from the literature, and this is a newer finding in relation to the overspill of abuse.

Online Harm

As discussed, there is a small body of literature considering offline harm in relation to co-victims of abuse with the majority focusing on intimate partner abuse cases (Gregory, 2017; Gregory et al., 2017; Hobart, 2002; Latta, 2008; Morris, 2009; Riger et al., 2002; Stark, 2007, 2023). However, minimal research has shown the link to online harm (Douglas et al., 2019), or indeed, online harm in cases of intimate partner homicide in general. Chapter 4 outlines the concept of digital coercive control, highlighting the need for the digital environment to be considered another realm where harm can be communicated, and where victims can be monitored (Burke et al., 2011; Douglas et al., 2019; McLachlan & Harris, 2022; Woodlock, 2017). Similar to the earlier discussion on offline harm, threats of harm can be communicated through the medium of digital media. This can be orchestrated through phone calls, text messages or social media (Douglas et al., 2019).

Gaslighting is a form of manipulation used to intimidate and control victims, and has been likened to psychological abuse (Abramson, 2014; Dutton, 2007; Hayes & Jeffries, 2016; Petric, 2018; Rietdijk, 2018; Sweet, 2019). As mentioned in Chapter 3, its purpose is to make the victim question their own perception of reality as a way of removing their identity, freedom and decision-making capabilities (Dorpat, 1994, 1996). Up until recently, gaslighting's social context has been absent from the literature, with Sweet (2019) unpacking its gendered connotations for the first time. As Sweet (2019) suggests that gaslighting holds the same gendered and sexually unequal hallmarks as coercive control, it can be leveraged by perpetrators in the same manner. Gaslighting is not only harmful by its very nature, but can also impact help-seeking behaviour by those affected (Warshaw et al., 2014). However, gaslighting is not a well-researched area of study, with much of its focus within psychological literature. As such, it needs further exploration, especially within the context of intimate partner abuse and homicide.

The Extension of Gaslighting to the Victim's Immediate Family

As a reminder, Tam's daughter Blair was murdered in 2013 by an acquaintance, Jackson. Tam believed Blair's murder to be consequence of unrequited love. As mentioned previously, Blair was good friends with the perpetrator who wanted more from their relationship. Unfortunately, she did not feel the same way. In addition to exhibiting jealousy and proprietary behaviours, gaslighting was also perpetrated in this case using mobile technologies and the online environment:

> … we had a text back saying I'm out with me mates, I'm probably going to stop at Emma's [Blair's friend]. And she said I'll probably stay at … but it wasn't Blair, it was him. And he had obviously studied Blair's texts because he ended it with 3 kisses like she always did …
>
> (Tam, Father)

> I had done a couple of texts to who I thought was Blair but it was obviously him, and then he then sent back one that was really cryptic wasn't it in that it was something like "I won't be able to message anymore cos my phone's died … too", so it was very cryptic so my phone's died but Blair had already died anyway.
>
> (Tam, Father)

Firstly, this case reflects prior planning on the part of the perpetrator which is typical of perpetrators who have a strong sexual motivation for committing homicide (Chan and Heide, 2009; Kerr et al., 2013; Kocsis et al., 2002; Meloy, 2000; Schlesinger, 2004). By using the victim's phone to contact her parents, the perpetrator was able to protect his identity without raising alarm (Beech et al., 2005; Meloy, 2000). As described above, the victim's father suggests the perpetrator had studied his daughter's text messages in order to mimic her. This also enabled the perpetrator to have more time with the victim (Beauregard & Proulx, 2002; Chan & Heide, 2009). It also highlights how the online environment positively enabled the perpetrator in terms of evading apprehension, allowing him more time with the victim and extending his fantasy to the victim's parents. The perpetrator's gaslighting stretched beyond the victim's parents to her sibling as well:

> I rang and left a message and he didn't – cos we had his telephone number – I rang he didn't answer that, but Sandy contacted him, Blair's

> sister, on Facebook and he sent a message back. Oh, I don't know where she is, saying oh I don't know where she is [Blair] I had gone to bed. I was ill last night so I went to bed and I think Blair went down Wigtown with her mates, so he knew, you know, he knew what was going to happen ... he even put the rider in it to say I'll get in touch with everybody I can to try and find out where she is and he was still using it [Facebook] the following day ...
>
> (Tam, Father)

In addition to using text messages, the perpetrator also utilised Facebook as a tool for gaslighting. It allowed him to communicate his alibi to the victim's family and also gave him the opportunity to feign an interest in the victim's whereabouts, thereby rendering his guilt undetectable. Interestingly, he offered to help to search for the victim. As the online environment provided the perpetrator with a degree of anonymity, it enabled him to project an image deemed acceptable to others (Goffman, 1959; Levin & Fox, 2008; Monckton Smith et al., 2014; Woodworth et al., 2012). With the use of social media, he was able to look and act beyond suspicion, appearing completely innocent (Goffman, 1959; Levin & Fox, 2008). This goes hand in hand with other areas of focus such as benign disinhibition and dissociative imagination which are factors related to Suler's (2004) work on the online disinhibition effect. As such, the perpetrator in this case used the online environment to (i) behave in a different way to the way he behaved in real-life, and (ii) also saw his communication with the victim's sister as a game where the same rules and conventions did not apply to everyday life (Suler, 2004). The way in which gaslighting was used in this case is very specific but shows the lengths some perpetrators go to in order to manipulate those beyond the victim. It also underscores that online harm does, indeed, occur to those connected with the initial primary target. While gaslighting is not necessarily experienced by all victims, particularly as abuse can be very unique and individual, this emphasises the need for more research to be conducted in this area. As far as the author is aware, no research exists relating to gaslighting of co-victims of intimate partner abuse or homicide.

Communication from Prison

After criminal justice proceedings are finalised and the perpetrator has been held accountable for his actions, there is a chance for a victim's family to grieve and start making sense of their loved one's death (Connolly & Gordon, 2015). The accountability being discussed within this context is conventional justice in terms of a conviction and punitive sentence (McGlynn & Westmarland, 2018). However, conventional justice does not necessarily mend the harm or provide the resolution victims' families' want. For instance, many family members report feeling unsatisfied with the punitive sentence given to the perpetrator (Clements & Vigil, 2003; Connolly & Gordon, 2015; Rinear, 1988). As such, other forms of justice exist including kaleidoscope justice, restorative justice and bereaved family activism (Cook, 2020; Marshall, 1999; McGlynn &

Westmarland, 2018). Although this chapter's focus is not on justice, it is still worth noting the different types of justice considered by other scholars working in this field and the area of sexual violence. Nonetheless, this concludes the discussion on justice as it is not within the remit of the chapter to examine this in further detail.

With that being said, contact with victims' families does not always stop as a result of the perpetrator's incarceration. Their healing processes can be complicated further by the perpetrator being able to communicate with the family through the postal service. As perpetrators have limited to no access to the internet or other forms of digital media, hand-written letters are a means to exert further control and harm towards co-victims after incarceration. Arguably, this can be considered another element of online harm. As mentioned earlier, Stark (2007, 2023) has commented on perpetrators' abusive tactics moving beyond the primary victim as a mechanism of further control in a bid to undermine victims' social networks. This can often be exacerbated where the victim and perpetrator shared children or custody of children (Gregory, 2017). Similar to the discussion of online harm above, no research has been undertaken to explore this issue further.

A Case Involving Letters from Prison

As previously discussed in Chapter 4, Jen's sister Nessa was killed by her ex-fiancé in 2016 after ongoing abuse during their ten-year relationship. As a result of his incarceration, Paton was unable to communicate with his three surviving children. This was an agreement he made with the family court. However, Jen described receiving hand-written letters and a recording of *Stick Man* (a popular children's book) for Nessa's children whom she was now the guardian for:

> … he wrote two weeks after he was sent to prison, he wrote like when he was remanded he wrote a letter to me and I honestly don't know how I wasn't sick when I opened it because he'd agreed with the family courts because of the children, he'd agreed with the family courts that he would attempt to make no contact with the children which he, even after did this CD thing and he managed to persuade the entire prison that he was allowed to send this thing. This is how much of a salesman he is, he managed to persuade them that he was allowed to do it and they sent this CD out. This was after the letter but sort of two weeks after this letter turned up, it was odd cos it was this non-descript brown envelope, and I opened it and this drivel about how much he loved us as family and Nessa and all this kind of thing and that he hadn't done anything and he wasn't allowed to talk about the case and how much he loved her and us and I was like what is he doing? What is he playing at writing letters? He then sends this CD so … it was him reading a story, the Stick Man I think it is …

This case highlights the manipulative and devious nature of the perpetrator (Monckton Smith et al., 2014). Jen describes him as a "salesman". She suggested the perpetrator presented an alternative persona – one which was eager to please and thoughtful – when he wanted to be viewed in a favourable light to others (Goffman, 1959; Levin & Fox, 2008; Monckton Smith et al., 2014; Woodworth et al., 2012). This shows the perpetrator's skilful ability in terms of impression management (Goffman, 1959; Levin & Fox, 2008). Despite not being permitted to communicate with the victim's family, this perpetrator still managed to persuade the prison staff to forward his letter and CD. There is also evidence of denial in this letter (Monckton Smith et al., 2014; Woodworth et al., 2012). Similarly, the perpetrator speaks of his love for the victim and her family, attempting to reconnect with the family in terms of their grief. The perpetrator continued repeatedly to contact the victim's family:

> Well he's sent three or four letters now yeah, now he can't get them out with the mail service, he sends them with the social worker ... before it was basically how much he loved everybody and then the worst one I have to say was the second one when he used the line "I too have lost Nessa", and quite honestly if I'd been in a room in with him I'd have poked him in the eye for that. How dare you, how dare you put that into a letter when you're the man who has done this, you know, that's that's not acceptable ...
>
> (Jen, Sister).

This shows the persistent nature of the perpetrator in his continued insistence on making contact with the family. The perpetrator also plays the victim suggesting he "too" has lost his significant other. Again, this links to the notion of identity management whereby the perpetrator is attempting to relate to the victim's family (Goffman, 1959; Levin & Fox, 2008). To the perpetrator, this appears to be the most appropriate response. Jen's discussion in this case underscores another technique in which perpetrators can perpetuate abuse further than their initial target. Once perpetrators have lost that initial target, there appears to be a drive for them to continue harassing and abusing others associated with the victim. This draws synergies with literature concerning the continuation of abuse post-separation (Campbell et al., 2007; Dragiewicz et al., 2019; McLachlan & Harris, 2022; Spencer & Stith, 2020; Woodlock, 2017). In spite of this, there is a dearth of research considering abuse following imprisonment.

Conclusion

Empirical research, albeit scant, has been conducted to examine the impact of the spillage of abuse over to co-victims of intimate partner abuse. To date, this has considered threatened or actual physical abuse mostly towards friends of the primary victim. However, with the ease of mobile technologies and digital media, this abuse can extend to online harm. Such harm can be exerted beyond friends of the victim to family and others within their informal support network. This needs to be considered part of the 'web of abuse' which encompasses coercive control. In showing the range of tactics used by perpetrators to exceed the spatial and temporal dimensions of control towards the victim, this chapter has highlighted how the boundaries of abuse can be broadened. Furthermore, it has underscored how this overspill of abuse to victims' families can create an endless cycle of abuse, particularly within the context of intimate partner homicide.

References

Abramson, K., 2014. Turning up the lights on gaslighting. *Philosophical Perspectives*, 28 (1), pp. 1–30.

Bagshaw, D., Chung, D., Couch, M., Lilburn, S. & Wadham, B., 2000. *Reshaping Responses to Domestic Violence: Final Report* [online]. University of South Australia, Adelaide: Partnerships Against Domestic Violence Taskforce. Available at: https://wesnet.org.au/wp-content/uploads/2012/07/PADV-Reshaping-responses.pdf [Accessed 19 March 2025].

Baldwin, S. B., Fehrenbacher, A. E. & Eisenman, D. P., 2015. Psychological coercion in human trafficking. *Qualitative Health Research*, 25, pp. 1171–1181.

Bastomski, S., & Duane, M., 2019. *Losing a Loved One to Homicide: What We Know About Homicide Co-victims from Research and Practice Evidence* [online]. Washington, DC: Center for Victim Research. Available at: https://justiceresearch.dspacedirect.org/server/api/core/bitstreams/879bb0ce-3fc7-4215-b2ba-68dc3bae9090/content [Accessed 19 March 2025].

Beauregard, E., & Proulx, J., 2002. Profiles in the offending process of nonserial sexual murderers. *International Journal of Offender Therapy and Comparative Criminology*, 46, pp. 386–399.

Beeble, M., Post, L., Bybee, D. & Sullivan, C., 2008. Factors related to willingness to help survivors of intimate partner violence. *Journal of Interpersonal Violence*, 23 (12), pp. 1713–1729.

Beech, A., Fisher, D. & Ward, T., 2005. Sexual murderers' implicit theories. *Journal of Interpersonal Violence*, 20 (11), pp. 1366–1389.

Borsky, A., McDonnell, K., Rimal, R. & Turner, M., 2016. Assessing bystander behavior intentions toward friends to prevent dating violence: Development of the Bystander Behavior Intentions-Friends Scale through concept mapping and exploratory factor analysis. *Violence and Victims*, 31 (2), pp. 215–234.

Bracewell, K., Hargreaves, P. & N. Stanley., 2020. The consequences of the COVID-19 lockdown on stalking victimisation. *Journal of Family Violence*, 37, pp. 951–957.

Brady, P. Q., & Nobles, M. R., 2017. The dark figure of stalking: Examining law enforcement response. *Journal of Interpersonal Violence*, 32 (20), pp. 3149–3173.

Bucki, B., Spitz, E. & Baumann, M., 2012. Caring for a stroke victim: The emotional reactions of male and female caregivers. *Sante Publique*, 24, pp. 143–156.

Burke, S. C., Wallen, M., Vail-Smith, K. & Knox, D., 2011. Using technology to control intimate partners: An exploratory study of college undergraduates. *Computers in Human Behavior*, 27, pp. 1162–1167.

Campbell, J., Glass, N., Sharps, P., Laughon, K. & Bloom, T., 2007. Intimate partner homicide: Review and implications of research and policy. *Trauma, Violence & Abuse*, 8 (3), pp. 246–269.

Canter, D. V., & Ioannou, M., 2004. A multivariate model of stalking behaviours. *Behaviormetrika*, 31 (2), pp. 113–130.

Chan, H. C., & Heide, K. M., 2009. Sexual homicide: A synthesis of the literature. *Trauma, Violence & Abuse*, 10 (1), pp. 31–54.

Clements, P. T., & Vigil, G. J., 2003. Child and adolescent homicide survivors: Complicated grief and altered worldviews. *Journal of Psychosocial Nursing & Mental Health Services*, 41, pp. 30–39.

Connolly, J., & Gordon, R., 2015. Co-victims of homicide: A systematic review of the literature. *Trauma, Violence, & Abuse*, 16 (4), pp. 494–505.

Cook, E. A., 2020. Bereaved family activism. In: Tapley, J., & Davies, P., eds. *Victimology Research, Policy and Activism*. Cham, Switzerland: Palgrave Macmillan, pp. 115–134.

Costa, D. H. de., Njaine, K. & Schenker, M., 2017. Repercussions of homicide on victims' families: A literature review. *Ciência & Saúde Coletiva*, 22 (9), pp. 3087–3087.

Dobash, R. P., & Dobash, R. E., 2015. *When Men Murder Women*. New York: Oxford University Press.

Dorpat, T. L., 1994. On the double whammy and gaslighting. *Psychoanalysis & Psychotherapy*, 11 (1), pp. 91–96.

Dorpat, T. L., 1996. *Gaslighting, the Double Whammy, Interrogation, and Other Methods of Covert Control in Psychotherapy and Analysis*. Northvale, New Jersey: Jason Aronson Inc.

Douglas, H., Harris, B. A. & Dragiewicz, M., 2019. Technology-facilitated domestic and family violence: Women's experiences. *British Journal of Criminology*, 59 (3), pp. 1–20.

Dragiewicz, M., Harris, B., Woodlock, D., Salter, M., Easton, H., Lynch, A., Campbell, H., Leach, J. & Milne, L., 2019. *Domestic Violence and Communication Technology: Survivor Experiences of Intrusion, Surveillance, and Identity Crime* [online]. Brisbane, Australia: The Australian Communications Consumer Action Network and Queensland University of Technology. Available at: chrome-extension://efaidnbmnnnibpcajpcglclefindmkaj/https://eprints.qut.edu.au/131143/1/Domestic%2Bviolence%2Band%2Bcommunication%2Btechnology%2BSurvivor%2Bexperience%2Bof%2Bintrusion%2Bsurveillance%2Band%2Bidentity%2Bcrime.pdf [Accessed 30 December 2024].

Duron, J. F., Johnson, L., Hoge, G. L., & Postmus, L. L., 2021. Observing coercive control beyond intimate partner violence: Examining the perceptions of professionals about common tactics used in victimization. *Psychology of Violence*, 11 (2), pp. 144–154.

Dutton, D. G. 2007. *The Abusive Personality: Violence and Control In Intimate Relationships*. 2nd ed. New York: The Guilford Press.

Dutton, M. A., & Goodman, L. A., 2005. Coercion in intimate partner violence: Toward a new conceptualization. *Sex Roles*, 52, pp. 743–756.

Erlingsson, C., Carlson, S., Astrom, S. & Saveman, B., 2009. Dilemmas in witnessing elder abuse in caregiving situations: A family member perspective. *Southern Online Journal of Nursing Research*, 9 (1). Available at: https://www.researchgate.net/publication/238103518_Dilemmas_in_Witnessing_Elder_Abuse_in_Caregiving_Situations_A_Family_Member_Perspective [Accessed 13 March 2025].

Faver, C. A., & Strand, E. B., 2008. Unleashing compassion: Social work and animal abuse. In: Ascione, F. R., ed. *The International Handbook of Animal Abuse and*

Cruelty: Theory, Research and, Application. Indiana: Purdue University Press, pp. 175–196.

Goodkind, J., Gillum, T., Bybee, D. & Sullivan, C., 2003. The impact of family and friends' reactions on the well-being of women with abusive partners. *Violence Against Women*, 9, pp. 347–373.

Goodman. L. A., & Smyth, K. F., 2011. A call for a social network-oriented approach to services for survivors of intimate partner violence. *Psychology of Violence*, 1 (2), pp. 79–92.

Goffman, E., 1959. *The Presentation of Self in Everyday Life*. New York: Doubleday.

Gregory, A. C., 2017. "The edge to him was really, really nasty": Abusive tactics used against informal supporters of domestic violence survivors. *Journal of Gender-Based Violence*, 1, pp. 61–77.

Gregory, A. C., Williamson, E. & Feder, G., 2017. The impact on informal supporters of domestic violence survivors: A systematic literature review. *Trauma, Violence, & Abuse*, 18 (5), pp. 562–580.

Hardesty, J., Campbell, J., McFarlane, J. & Lewandowski, L., 2008. How children and their caregivers adjust after intimate partner femicide. *Journal of Family Issues*, 29, pp. 100–124.

Harris, B. A., & Woodlock, D., 2019. Digital coercive control: Insights from two landmark domestic violence studies. *British Journal of Criminology*, 59 (3), pp. 530–550.

Hasbullah, M., Kahar, R. & Ahmad, S., 2016. *A preliminary study of instrumental, emotional, and social support for domestic violence survivors in Selangor, Malaysia*. Proceedings of the 3rd World Conference on Integration of Knowledge, Malaysia, 28–29 November 2016. Langkawi, Malaysia: WorldConferences.net.

Hayes, S., & Jeffries, S., 2016. Romantic terrorism? An auto-ethnographic analysis of gendered psychological and emotional tactics in domestic violence. *Journal of Research in Gender Studies*, 6 (2), pp. 38–61.

Hertz, M. F., Prothrow-Stith, D., & Chery, C. (2005) Homicide survivors: Research and practice implications. *American Journal of Preventive Medicine*, 29 (5S2), pp. 288–295.

Hobart, M., 2002. *"Tell the World What Happened to Me": Findings and Recommendations from the Washington State Domestic Violence Fatality Review 2002* [online]. Washington, DC: Washington State Coalition Against Domestic Violence. Available at: https://www.baylor.edu/content/services/document.php/29323.pdf [Accessed 19 March 2025].

Jackson, C. L., Margolius, S. & Browning, S., 2022. The impact of intrafamilial homicide on the family system. *Journal of Family Violence*, 37, pp. 573–583.

Kerr, K. J., Beech, A. R. & Murphy, D., 2013. Sexual homicide: Definition, motivation and comparison with other forms of sexual offending. *Aggression and Violent Behavior*, 18 (1), pp. 1–10.

Kelly, L., 1988. *Surviving Sexual Violence*. Cambridge: Polity.

Klein, R., 2012. *Responding to Intimate Violence Against Women: The Role of Informal Networks*. New York: Cambridge University Press.

Kocsis, R. N., Cooksey, R. W., & Irwin, H. J., 2002. Psychological profiling of sexual murders: An empirical model. *International Journal of Offender Therapy and Comparative Criminology*, 46 (5), pp. 532–554.

Latta, R., 2008. Struggling to define my role: The experience of network members who intervened in intimate partner violence [online]. Ph.D. thesis, Boston College. Available at: https://www.proquest.com/openview/a7a88ceb2692e7eba34dfc1b539f3b5d/1?pq-origsite=gscholar&cbl=18750 [Accessed 3 January 2025].

Latta, R. E., & Goodman, L. A., 2011. Intervening in partner violence against women: A grounded theory exploration of informal network members' experiences. *The Counseling Psychologist*, 39 (7), pp. 973–1023.

Liang, B., Goodman, L., Tummala-Narra, P. & Weintraub, S., 2005. A theoretical framework for understanding help-seeking processes among survivors of intimate partner violence. *American Journal of Community Psychology*, 36 (1/2), pp. 71–84.

Levin, J., & Fox, J. A., 2008. Normalcy in behavioral characteristics of the sadistic serial killer. In: Kocsis, R. N., ed. *Serial Murder and the Psychology of Violent Crimes*. Sydney, Australia: Humana Press, pp. 3–14.

MacVane S. L., Miranda A. O. & Molina, B., 2003. Coping with the murder of a loved one: Counseling survivors of murder victims in groups. *The Journal for Specialists in Group Work*, 28, pp. 48–63.

Marshall, T., 1999. *Restorative Justice: An Overview* [online]. London: Home Office. Available at: chrome-extension://efaidnbmnnnibpcajpcglclefindmkaj/http://www.antoniocasella.eu/restorative/Marshall_1999-b.pdf [Accessed 7 January 2025].

McFarlane, J. M., Campbell, J. C., Sachs, C. J., Ulrich, Y. & Xu, X., 1999. Stalking and intimate partner femicide. *Homicide Studies*, 394, pp. 300–316.

McGlynn, C., & Westmarland, N., 2018. Kaleidoscopic justice: Sexual violence and victim-survivors' perceptions of justice. *Social & Legal Studies*, 28 (2), pp. 179–201.

McLachlan, F., & Harris, B., 2022. Intimate risks: Examining online and offline abuse, homicide flags, and femicide. *Victims & Offenders*, 17 (5), pp. 623–646.

McNamara, P., 2008. Changed forever: Friends reflect on the impact of a woman's death through intimate partner violence. *Journal of Family Studies*, 14, pp. 198–216.

Meloy, J. R., 2000. The nature and dynamics of sexual homicide: An integrative review. *Aggression and Violent Behavior*, 5, pp. 1–32.

Melton, H. C., 2007. Closing in: Stalking in the context of intimate partner abuse. *Sociology Compass*, 1 (2), pp. 520–535.

Monckton Smith, J., Williams, A. & Mullane F., 2014. *Domestic Abuse, Homicide and Gender*. London: Palgrave Macmillan.

Morris, A., 2009. Gendered dynamics of abuse and violence in families: Considering the abusive household gender regime. *Child Abuse Review*, 18 (6), pp. 414–427.

Munk, T., & Kennedy, M., 2024. *Victimisation in the Digital Age: An Online/Offline Continuum Approach*. London: Routledge.

Nahm, E., Resnick, B., Orwig, D., Magaziner, J. & Degrezia, M., 2010. Exploration of informal caregiving following hip fracture. *Geriatric Nursing*, 31, pp. 254–262.

Pain, R. 2014. Everyday terrorism: Connecting domestic violence and global terrorism. *Progress in Human Geography*, 38 (4), pp. 531–550.

Persons, R., 1990. Psychotherapist and widower. *The Psychotherapy Patient*, 6, pp. 71–80.

Petric, D., 2018. Gaslighting and the knot theory of mind. *Medicine*, 4, pp. 1–4.

Prigerson, H. G., Shear, M. K., Jacobs, S. C., Reynolds, C. F., Maciejewski, P. K., Davidson, J. R., Rosenheck, R., Pilkonis, P. A., Wortman, C. B., Williams, J. B., Widiger, T. A., Frank, E., Kupfer, D. J. & Zisook, S., 1999. Consensus criteria for traumatic grief. A preliminary empirical test. *The British Journal of Psychiatry*, 174, pp. 67–73.

Rietdijk, N., 2018. (You drive me) crazy: How gaslighting undermines autonomy [online]. Master's thesis, Utrecht University. Available at: chrome-extension://efaidnbmnnnibpcajpcglclefindmkaj/https://studenttheses.uu.nl/bitstream/handle/20.500.12932/31075/RMA%20Thesis%20Natascha%20Rietdijk.pdf?sequence=2&isAllowed=y [Accessed 31 July 2024].

Riger, S., Raja, S. & Camacho, J., 2002. The radiating impact of intimate partner violence. *Journal of Interpersonal Violence*, 17, pp. 184–205.

Rinear, E. E., 1988. Psychosocial aspects of parental response patterns to the death of a child by homicide. *Journal of Traumatic Stress*, 1, pp. 305–322.

Rose, L. E., Campbell, J. & Kub, J., 2000. The role of social support and family relationships in women's responses to battering. *Health Care for Women International*, 21, pp. 27–39.

Salari, S., 2007. Patterns of intimate partner homicide suicide in later life: Strategies for prevention. *Journal of Clinical Interventions in Aging*, 2, pp. 441–452.

Scarr, L., & Kennedy, M. C., 2023. "They didn't want to upset the client": Stalking in hands-on occupations. In: Mellins, M., Wheatley, R. & Flowers, C., eds. *Young People, Stalking Awareness and Domestic Abuse*. Cham, Switzerland: Palgrave Macmillan, pp. 201–223.

Schlesinger, L. B., 2004. *Sexual Murder: Catathymic and Compulsive Homicides*. Oxon: CRC Press.

Solot, D., 1997. Untangling the animal abuse web. *Society and Animals*, 5 (3), pp. 257–265.

Spencer, C. M., & Stith, S. M., 2020. Risk factors for male perpetration and female victimization of intimate partner homicide: A meta-analysis. *Trauma, Violence & Abuse*, 21 (3), pp. 527–540.

Spencer-Carver, E., 2008. Social support for children who had a parent killed by intimate partner violence: Interviews with mental health workers [online]. Ph.D. thesis, Kansas State University. Available at: chrome-extension://efaidnbmnnnibpcajpcglclefindmkaj/https://krex.k-state.edu/server/api/core/bitstreams/a8f91cf7-191c-4e3e-9df3-a9bc05285e38/content [Accessed 3 January 2025].

Stark, E., 2007. *Coercive Control: How Men Entrap Women in Personal Life*. New York: Oxford University Press.

Stark, E., 2023. *Coercive Control: How Men Entrap Women in Personal Life*. 2nd ed. New York: Oxford University Press.

Stewart, D. E., MacMillan, H. & Kimber, M., 2021. Recognizing and responding to intimate partner violence: An update. *The Canadian Journal of Psychiatry*, 66 (1), pp.71–106.

Storer, H., Casey, E. & Herrenkohl, T., 2016. Efficacy of bystander programs to prevent dating abuse among youth and young adults: A review of the literature. *Trauma, Violence, & Abuse*, 17 (3), pp. 256–269.

Stretesky, P. B., O'Connor Shelley, T., Hogan, M. J. & Prabha Unnithan, N., 2010. Sense-making and secondary victimization among unsolved homicide co-victims. *Journal of Criminal Justice*, 38, pp. 880–888.

Suler, J., 2004. The online disinhibition effect. *Cyberpsychology & Behavior*, 7 (3), pp. 321–326.

Swanberg, J., & Logan, T., 2005. Domestic violence and employment: A qualitative study. *Journal of Occupational Health Psychology*, 10, pp. 3–17.

Swanberg, J., Macke, C. & Logan, T., 2006. Intimate partner violence, women, and work: Coping on the job. *Violence and Victims*, 21, pp. 561–578.

Swanberg, J., Macke, C., & Logan, T., 2007. Working women making it work: Intimate partner violence, employment, and workplace support. *Journal of Interpersonal Violence*, 22, pp. 292–311.

Sweet, P. L., 2019. The sociology of gaslighting. *American Sociological Review*, 84 (5), pp. 851–875.

Sylaska, K., & Edwards, K., 2014. Disclosure of intimate partner violence to informal social support network members: A review of the literature. *Trauma Violence Abuse*, 15 (1), pp. 3–21.

Trotter, J. L., & Allen, N. E., 2009. The good, the bad, and the ugly: Domestic violence survivors' experiences with their informal social networks. *American Journal of Community Psychology*, 43, pp. 221–231.

Tyner, J. A., 2012. *Space, Place, and Violence: Violence and the Embodied Geographies of Race, Sex and Gender*. New York: Routledge.

UNODC and UN Women, 2023. *Femicides in 2023: Global Estimates of Intimate Partner/Family Member Femicides* [online]. Bangkok, Thailand: UN Women. Available at: chrome-extension://efaidnbmnnnibpcajpcglclefindmkaj/https://www.unwomen.org/sites/default/files/2024-11/femicides-in-2023-global-estimates-of-intimate-partner-family-member-femicides-en.pdf [Accessed 31 December 2024].

Walby, S., & Towers, J., 2018. Untangling the concept of coercive control: Theorizing domestic violent crime. *Criminology & Criminal Justice*, 18 (1), pp. 7–28.

Warshaw, C., Lyon, E., Bland, P. J., Phillips, H. & Hooper, M., 2014. *Mental Health and Substance Use Coercion Surveys: Report from the National Center on Domestic Violence, Trauma, & Mental Health and the National Domestic Violence Hotline* [online]. Chicago, Illinois: US Department of Health and Human Services. Available at: chrome-extension://efaidnbmnnnibpcajpcglclefindmkaj/https://www.thehotline.org/wp-content/uploads/media/2024/07/2012-Mental-Health-Coercion-Survey.pdf [Accessed 6 August 2024].

Williamson, E., & Hester, M., 2009. *Evaluation of the South Tyneside Domestic Abuse Perpetrator Programme (STDAPP) 2006–2008: Final Report* [online]. Bristol: University of Bristol. Available at: chrome-extension://efaidnbmnnnibpcajpcglclefindmkaj/https://www.bristol.ac.uk/media-library/sites/sps/migrated/documents/finalreport1.pdf [Accessed 31 December 2024].

Wilson, M., & Daly, M., 1985Competitiveness risk taking and violence: The young male syndrome. *Ethnology and Sociobiology*, 6, pp. 59–73.

Wolf, M., Holt, V., Kernic, M. & Rivara, F., 2000. Who gets protection orders for intimate partner violence? *American Journal of Preventive Medicine*, 19, pp. 286–291.

Woodlock, D., 2017. The abuse of technology in domestic violence and stalking. *Violence Against Women*, 25 (5), pp. 584–602.

Woodworth, M., Hancock, J., Porter, S., Hare, R., Logan, M., O'Toole, M. E. & Smith, S., 2012. *The Language of Psychopaths: New Findings and Implications for Law Enforcement* [online]. Quantico, Virginia: FBI Law Enforcement Bulletin. Available at: https://socialmedialab.sites.stanford.edu/sites/g/files/sbiybj22976/files/media/file/woodworth-fbi-the-language-of-psychopaths.pdf [Accessed 19 March 2025].

World Health Organization (WHO), 2021. *Violence Against Women Prevalence Estimates, 2018: Global, Regional and National Prevalence Estimates for Intimate Partner Violence Against Women and Global and Regional Prevalence Estimates for Non-Partner Sexual Violence Against Women* [online]. Geneva, Switzerland: United Nations Inter-Agency Working Group on Violence Against Women Estimation and Data. Available at: chrome-extension://efaidnbmnnnibpcajpcglclefindmkaj/https://iris.who.int/bitstream/handle/10665/341338/9789240026681-eng.pdf?sequence=1 [Accessed 31 December 2024].

6 Concluding Thoughts

Introduction

Co-victims' knowledge and experiences of abuse are hugely valuable. While existing research highlights how this can inform the wider intimate partner abuse literature in terms of the abusive tactics used by perpetrators towards the primary victim(s), these tactics can also extend to surviving relatives in intimate partner homicide cases. This book has demonstrated contemporary understandings of offline and online harm pertaining to victims and co-victims of intimate partner homicide. The book chapters have focused on three main areas: offline harm, online harm and the overspill of abuse to victims' families specifically. Having analysed these areas, it is apparent that approaches to harm need further attention in order to involve those who largely fall outside of the victim-perpetrator dichotomy.

Research with Co-victims

To date, research with co-victims continues to be limited with the victim-perpetrator dichotomy receiving much more attention across a number of different academic disciplines. The importance of co-victim accounts, particularly from victims' families, friends and co-workers, can provide understandings of offline and online harm, and a wealth of knowledge in terms of risk factors for intimate partner homicide. The relationship they have with the victim is pivotal to appreciating the reality of their loved one's abuse and in identifying abusive tactics used by perpetrators. In addition, co-victims can also provide insight into newer forms of harm. Such harm extends the web of abuse to those informally supporting victims (Gregory, 2017; Gregory et al., 2017; Hobart, 2002; Latta, 2008; Morris, 2009; Riger et al., 2002; Stark, 2007, 2023). However, as mentioned in Chapter 2, what constitutes family differs significantly worldwide. These co-victims can include an array of different people within the victim's community so it is necessary to look beyond Western views of family, instead considering more flexible conceptualisations (Crosbie-Burnett & Klein, 2009; Georgas et al., 2006; Holt, 2021; Pasternak et al., 1976; Swanson et al., 2022).

DOI: 10.4324/9781003464488-6

This book's approach has enabled the literature to be extensively reviewed in terms of offline and online harms linked to intimate partner abuse and homicide. It has also allowed for case studies to be incorporated, from the author's empirical qualitative research with victims' families, to illustrate the diversity of methods used by perpetrators. New findings have underscored the mechanisms of harm which have ranged from overt physical abuse to more subtle forms of harm such as the use of gaslighting through the medium of social networking sites. The harms experienced have been carefully unpacked, taking into account at what point these harms were perpetrated and to whom.

Continuum of Online-Offline Harm and Intimate Partner Homicide

Further Perspectives on Offline Harm

The central tenet of Chapter 3 is to provide a comprehensive discussion of existing risk factors for intimate partner homicide, with older literature being updated and newer perspectives being highlighted. The unique appeal of this discussion is that the case studies included throughout this chapter are from the perspective of victims' families. They are reflections on their loved ones' abusive experiences and based on unstructured interviews, providing first-hand accounts of perpetrators' webs of abuse. As such, Chapter 3 begins by discussing the web of abuse, detailing the historical underpinnings of this concept and how it relates to the wider issues of coercive control (Faver & Strand, 2003, 2008; Solot, 1997). Stark's (2007, 2023) work is thoroughly discussed considering the four overarching elements of coercive control, including the presence or absence of physical injury, intimidation, isolation and control. Within these subsections, other areas of interest are examined.

While physical injury occurs within abusive relationships, it is not always perpetrated within the context of coercive control (Kennedy, 2022; Stark, 2007, 2023). However, in cases where physical injury is present, there are a number of tactics used towards victims including physical assault, physical neglect, sexual abuse/coercion and the withdrawal of sex or intimacy. As discussed in Chapter 3, the purpose of physical injury is to dominate the victim (Stark, 2007). However, Little (2023) disagrees, suggesting that physical injury is the literal embodiment of intimate partner abuse. Injuries may be seen to prevent others from interfering or may be unseen to hamper the victim's agency (Hellman & Hurley, 2023; Sanderson, 2008). This can extend to sexual abuse or coercion where victims are forced to have sex with the perpetrator, or expected to engage in sexual contact which makes them feel uncomfortable or humiliated (Logan et al., 2007; Rees et al., 2006; Stark, 2007, 2017). Other mechanisms such as physical neglect or food insecurity may also be contingent on whether or not a victim performs a particular sexual act (Thiel de Bocanegra et al., 2010). Withdrawal of sex or intimacy can be another means of control, making the victim feel more isolated (Kennedy, 2022; Mitchell and Raghavan, 2019; Raghavan et al., 2014; Rees et al., 2006; Stark, 2007, 2012, 2017). One study identifies this as a risk factor for intimate partner homicide, particularly where the victim is refusing sexual contact (Adinkrah, 2017). However, much of the research in this area tends to focus on victims being pressured into sex rather than the withdrawal of sexual contact being another means of control. This requires further empirical research. Jealousy and envy have also been discussed in Chapter 3. Despite envy being overlooked as a risk factor for intimate partner homicide, substantial literature shows that jealousy can be the rationale for fatal abuse (Aloyce et al., 2023; Wilson & Daly, 1993; Martinez, 2015; Vatnar et al., 2017). This is often where infidelity or possible infidelity is considered the motivation for abuse. Moreover, a previous history of abuse of any kind can predict future harm (Andrews & Bonta, 2006; Dobash et al., 2009) but the link is stronger where perpetrators have abused previous partners (Campbell et al., 2007; Jayasuriya et al., 2011; Kivisto, 2015; Monckton Smith et al., 2014; Spencer, 2018; Spencer & Stith, 2020; Vatnar et al., 2017).

It should be noted that studies concerning precursors to intimate partner homicide tend to omit a critical discussion of jealousy and envy. Jealousy is often considered a singular construct with envy receiving little attention in the academic community (Kivisto, 2015). As such, jealousy is almost always coupled synonymously with sexual jealousy which is a broad generalisation (Wilson & Daly, 1992). The case study in the "Jealousy and Envy" section of Chapter 3 refutes this generalisation by providing an example of familial jealousy within the context of intimate partner homicide. Indeed, this suggests that jealousy can occur in other contexts outside of the sexual and romantic notions discussed previously. Within Table 3.1, there is also a suggestion that economic jealousy may be another potential risk factor for intimate partner homicide which, again, has been neglected in the literature. While the qualitative research used for this example is limited to one isolated case, it still warrants further attention. This shows one significant contribution this book makes in terms of risk factors for intimate partner homicide when it comes to offline harm.

A range of behaviours can be attributed to intimidation including threats, gaslighting, stalking, microregulation, degradation and shaming. This tactic is used to scare victims into compliance using their previous experiences as leverage for future harm (Karakurt and Silver, 2013; Kennedy, 2022; Salari and LeFevre Sillito, 2016; Stark, 2007, 2023). Threats can be active or passive, meaning that they can involve direct threats of harm or the possibility of the perpetrator withdrawing from the victim (Campbell et al., 2007; Cavanagh et al., 2001; James & Farnham, 2003; Liem & Roberts, 2009; Monckton Smith et al., 2014; Pain, 2014; Stark, 2007, 2023; Stewart et al., 2021; Walby & Towers, 2018). The contribution of Table 3.2 in Chapter 3 consolidates literature on active and passive threats, placing examples of each threat type in their respective categories, which is unprecedented. Gaslighting is another form of intimidation considered in Chapter 3 which impacts victims' sense of self (Dorpat, 1994, 1996). It can be coupled with threats or other degrading behaviour such as telling lies or embarrassing the victim. However, prior research has failed to take into account social intersections which may impact the effectiveness of gaslighting (Sweet, 2019). Surveillance has also been reported as a mechanism of intimidation which diminishes victims' privacy. This can involve direct or indirect means of monitoring, with many perpetrators employing stalking behaviours to follow the victim (Logan & Walker, 2009; Stark, 2007, 2023). The perpetration of stalking within abusive relationships has been linked to fatal abuse (Kennedy, 2022; Monckton Smith et al., 2017; Scott et al., 2010; Stark, 2007, 2023). Microregulation is a further thread in the anatomy of coercive control. While this method is not directly measured or recorded, it impacts every part of victims' lives (Stark, 2007, 2023). Shaming and degradation are other ways in which victims' self-worth is depleted. Often name-calling or verbal abuse is linked to gendered expectations, with women's body image and/or weight being commented on (Stark, 2007, 2023).

Isolation is integral to coercive control with it being the perpetrator's main purpose and/or a consequence of abusive acts. It can prevent victims from divulging abuse and seeking support as the perpetrator becomes the overriding fixture in the victim's life (Arnold, 2009; Rose et al., 2011; Stark, 2007, 2012, 2023). This leads many victims to separate themselves from informal and formal support mechanisms (Stark, 2007; Fontes, 2015). Isolation is a complicated phenomenon which can occur on different levels and in different ways (Baldwin et al., 2015; Duron et al., 2021; Stark, 2023). As such, support is vital for victims to make sense of their abuse. However, access to support can be hindered by perpetrators. Support can be divided into informal and formal support, with much of the literature pointing towards victims engaging with informal support structures prior to victims seeking support outside of their immediate social network (Stark, 2007, 2023). In situations where victims are employed, isolation can also extend to their workplace where perpetrators may also interfere with this part of victims' lives (Stark, 2007, 2023; Munteanu, 2021).

Control is the overarching mechanism of coercive control where social structures within society aid the unequal standing of women in abusive relationships. This disproportionality, enabled by patriarchy, is used by perpetrators, forcing women to adhere to traditional gender roles (Stark, 2007, 2023). This factor is more prevalent in cases of abuse than physical violence (Adams, 2007; Stark, 2007; Websdale, 2010). While control over bodily functions was mentioned earlier in Chapter 3, the main focus of this section was economic abuse. This type of abuse is not limited to financial abuse, but also has significant emotional consequences for victims (Littwin, 2012; Sharp-Jeffs, 2015, 2021). Perpetrators can prevent victims' access to money, including their own money, and can commandeer their finances (Adams et al., 2008; Pollet, 2011; Sharp-Jeffs, 2022). This can impede victims' ability to support themselves economically, meaning that many may stay in relationships as they have no other option (Dutton & Goodman, 2005). In recent years, economic abuse has received more attention but still requires further study.

As a result of consolidating literature concerning the web of abuse, its connection to coercive control and the myriad of abusive tactics involved in the deployment of coercive control, this book has provided a critical appreciation of the research conducted in these areas. It draws on both the strengths and weaknesses of said research and identifies gaps for further study. Case studies have also been incorporated into this extensive narrative literature review to add a fresher perspective on these risk factors from the perspective of co-victims of intimate partner homicide.

New Insights into Online Harm

The focus of Chapter 4 is to provide a detailed account of harms which occur across the online environment with the use of the internet and mobile technologies. These harms are associated with intimate partner abuse. As such, this chapter uses the concept of coercive control to inform more contemporary understandings of online harm by drawing on the work of Harris and Woodlock (2019), and what they term digital coercive control. Coercive control is not without its issues, which are further highlighted in Chapter 4. Its inclusivity of different populations is limited due to the heterosexual and patriarchal undertones of this concept (Harris & Woodlock, 2023; Hester & Donovan, 2009; Renzetti, 1992). Similarly, the concept of coercive control cannot be connected to Indigenous populations as they do not hold the same views as Western societies when it comes to the victimisation and perpetration of harm (Harris & Woodlock, 2023).

As mentioned, research has shown the link between digital media and coercive control, particularly within intimate relationships (Abdul Aziz, 2017; Bailey et al., 2021; Douglas et al., 2019; Dragiewicz et al., 2018; Fraser et al., 2010; Harris & Woodlock, 2019, 2023; Hand et al., 2009; Leitão, 2021; McLachlan & Harris, 2022; Reed et al., 2017; Rees et al., 2011; Reyns et al., 2013; Woodlock, 2017). This research emerged in the 21st century with the focus being on the perpetration of harms through online means. This allowed researchers to describe how perpetrators used digital media to enact victimisation. Part of this book's unique contribution is that few studies have considered online harm in relation to intimate partner homicide (McLachlan & Harris, 2022). The connection between online harm and intimate partner homicide appears to only have been made with secondary research, which fails to recognise the nuance involved in individual cases. Although McLachlan and Harris's (2022) study is groundbreaking, there are some issues in their data collection. As they relied on coroner and police files, they were only able to make assumptions based on the information reported and recorded. Due to the dark figure of crime, differences in reporting and recording mechanisms, and understandings of digital coercive control, it is likely that a significant amount of relevant information was excluded from these files. As such, there is likely to be merit in further research using the qualitative paradigm to investigate this topic. Part of this book's appeal is that it does just that. The qualitative research employed to construct the case studies included in this book has provided personal testimonies from victims' families. These personal testimonies have highlighted the relationship between digital coercive control and intimate partner homicide. They have effectively filled the gap within McLachlan and Harris's (2022) study and progressed this research further. While this research is still in its infancy, it is the author's opinion that online harm should be considered a risk factor for intimate partner homicide. Similar assumptions were drawn in McLachlan and Harris's (2022: 629) study with risk factors relating to online harm being termed "homicide flags".

Within their discussion, McLachlan and Harris (2022: 629) expand on some of the issues related to online harms being considered "homicide flags". For example, only 33% of their sampled cases reported digital coercive control victimisation. As there is a range of definitions related to online harm and inconsistencies in the measures implemented, awareness in terms of the reporting and recording mechanisms for this type of harm may be limited (McLachlan & Harris, 2022). In Queensland, Australia, this means that the rates of victimisation may be much higher. By the same token, there is a lack of regulation in place relating to instances where digital coercive control occurred post-separation (McLachlan & Harris, 2022). As mentioned in earlier discussions, pending or actual separation is already considered a risk factor for intimate partner homicide (Hand et al., 2009; McLachlan & Harris, 2022; Markwick et al., 2019; Spencer & Stith, 2020). However, when coupled with digital coercive control, it can also have fatal consequences (Hand et al., 2009; Markwick et al., 2019). The digital environment allows for continued contact even when the victim is no longer physically present. These risks are not currently taken into account (McLachlan & Harris, 2022). Arguably, the same holds true for countries across the globe, including the UK. There is also a suggestion, from data analysed in McLachlan and Harris's (2022) study, that the presence of other risk factors are linked to online harm and, as such, could predict the presence of online harm in potentially fatal cases.

Applying the Overspill of Harm to the Continuum of Online-Offline Harm

As a consequence of high rates of intimate partner abuse worldwide, it can be concluded that many will likely support someone experiencing abuse at some point in their lives (Gregory, 2017; WHO, 2021). The collective term given to these individuals is co-victims, as discussed earlier in this chapter and in other chapters. However, they have also been called "informal supporters" by others scholars (Gregory, 2017: 63; Gregory et al., 2017). As a large proportion of studies concentrate on the initial target of harm, they fail to acknowledge or document the harms which are perpetrated towards those beyond the initial victim. Co-victims are, therefore, at increased risk of harm due to their ties with the victim. This can include physical harm (Gregory, 2017; Gregory et al., 2017; Latta, 2008; Latta & Goodman, 2011; Riger et al., 2002); the possibility of fatal harm (Gregory, 2017; Gregory et al., 2017; Hobart, 2002); and behaviours akin to coercive control such as threats of harm, intimidation and/or harassment (Goodkind et al., 2003; Gregory, 2017; Gregory et al., 2017; Hobart, 2002; Latta, 2008; Latta & Goodman, 2011; Riger et al., 2002; Swanberg & Logan, 2005; Swanberg et al., 2006; Wolf et al., 2000).

However, these studies are not without their issues. For example, only two of the studies' participant samples include those considered co-victims such as friends and family of the victim (Gregory, 2017; Latta & Goodman, 2011). One of these studies pertains to Latta's (2008) doctoral research. More than half of these assumptions are made based on interviews with women who are experiencing intimate partner abuse (Riger et al., 2002; Swanberg & Logan, 2005; Wolf et al., 2000), with one considering secondary employment data (Swanberg et al., 2006) and another examining domestic violence fatality cases from a quantitative perspective (Hobart, 2002). This shows that while research on co-victims is becoming more prevalent, the participant samples used to ascertain this data are not necessarily fit for purpose. As such, victims of intimate partner abuse are not the best placed individuals to explain the victimisation of their family and friends. Instead, further research in this area should concentrate on collecting qualitative and quantitative data from co-victims directly.

In addition, the continuum of online-offline harm is not considered in terms of co-victim narratives. From the limited research on co-victims, only offline harm is recognised and recorded (Gregory, 2017, Gregory et al., 2017). This tends to cover the impact of physical and emotional harm on this group of individuals (Gregory, 2017, Gregory et al., 2017). These impacts are often complicated by a change in caring responsibilities (Spencer-Carver, 2008), differences in processing grief (Connolly & Gordon, 2015; Costa et al., 2017; Stretesky et al., 2010; Persons, 1990; Prigerson et al., 1999) and inadequate support from the criminal justice system (Armour, 2003; Casey, 2011; Clements & Vigil, 2003; Duggan, 2012; Gregory et al., 2017; Spencer-Carver, 2008; Van Wijk et al., 2016). This book, therefore, shows that the continuum of online-offline harm also applies to co-victims of intimate partner homicide which no other research has highlighted. Furthermore, it provides empirical evidence from victims' families that suggests the harm perpetrated offline can also move online. To reiterate, this book maintains a further contribution to knowledge concerning the overspill of harm, suggesting that this harm can transcend physical barriers shifting to the online environment. This novel convergence perspective has not yet been explored in other research.

Moving Forward

Research in the field of intimate partner abuse and homicide is only likely to progress further, especially with the evolution of digital media and mobile technologies. Current perspectives have already started to move beyond heterosexual relationships, considering digital coercive control victimisation in relation to other intersections, including in the LGBTIQA+ community (Fileborn & Ball, 2023; Hester & Donovan, 2009; Renzetti, 1992). Similarly, others have embarked on research seeking to understand how digital coercive control operates in communities which do not follow normative family structures, where language and culture differs significantly, and where legacies of colonial violence impact experiences and responses to digital coercive control (Carlson & Day, 2023). This research has also extended to women with disabilities and those within rural or remote areas (Harris & Woodlock, 2023).

In addition, research with perpetrators continues to dominate the academic landscape with scholars seeking to unpick the motivations for intimate partner abuse. This has led to discussions related to perpetrators' extended families, and how they may play a part in abuse towards the victim (Chowdhury & Winder, 2022; Douglas et al., 2019). However, much of this discussion appears to be coupled with the Muslim community where cultural context is important, and where family structures sometimes have the potential to enable further abuse (Chowdhury & Winder, 2022). Similar to other arguments relating to intimate partner abuse, context still continues to be central to victimisation and perpetration of harm (Monckton Smith et al., 2014; Stark, 2007, 2023).

Research on intimate partner homicide has existed for decades but, understandably, this focus has largely considered a small subset of victims. This victim pool tends to include perpetrators' partners, ex-partners and acquaintances (Dobash & Dobash, 2015; Monckton Smith, 2012). Until recently, co-victims were also acknowledged as part of this victim pool within the academic community. However, this research was linked to intimate partner abuse rather than considering the full spectrum of abuse with the inclusion of homicide (Gregory, 2017; Gregory et al., 2017). With that being said, there appears to be more interest in the co-victim community in the past five years with researchers providing guides relating to healing strategies (Pollard, 2020), improvements to death notice protocols (Reed, 2022), effects of homicide on co-victims from Black and Latinx communities (Edwards et al., 2021; Werner, 2022), the impact of co-victims not fitting the 'ideal victim' narrative (Sharo, 2024), and the ways in which co-victims use domestic violence helplines (Gregory et al., 2021). With that being said, more research needs to consider co-victim narratives in relation to online harm, particularly given that this area of research has been neglected.

Moreover, the author is currently engaging in a further project relating to resistance strategies in regards to victims of intimate partner homicide and digital coercive control. However, this book's scope does not allow for this to be discussed further. Nevertheless, the aim of this book is to contribute to the limited knowledge and understanding of co-victims of intimate partner homicide, highlighting perspectives relating to offline and online harm. In addition, it has established that co-victims, particularly victims' families, hold significant value in terms of conceptualising intimate partner abuse. Furthermore, it draws attention to the overspill of harm which extends to victims' families. The hope of this book's author is to encourage other researchers to explore further co-victim narratives, recognising the value and lessons to be learned from those witnessing and experiencing abuse beyond the primary victim.

References

Abdul Aziz, Z., 2017. *Due Diligence and Accountability For Online Violence Against Women* [online]. Boston, Massachusetts: Association for Progressive Communications. Available at: chrome-extension://efaidnbmnnnibpcajpcglclefindmkaj/https://esem.org.mk/pdf/Najznachajni%20vesti/2018/1/DDP-OVAW.pdf [Accessed 12 November 2024].

Adams, A., Sullivan, C., Bybee, D. & Greeson, M., 2008. Development of the scale of economic abuse. *Violence Against Women*, 14 (5), pp. 563–587.

Adams, D., 2007. *Why Do They Kill? Men Who Murder Their Intimate Partners*. Nashville, TN: Vanderbilt University Press.

Adinkrah, M., 2017. When a wife says "no": Wife sexual refusal as a factor in husband–wife homicides in Ghana. *Journal of Interpersonal Violence*, 34 (3–4), pp. 1–27.

Aloyce, D., Mshana, G., Peter, E., Malibwa, D., Buller, A. M., Mchome, Z., Kapiga, S. & Stöckl, H., 2023. Pathways of romantic jealousy to intimate partner violence in Mwanza, northern Tanzania. *Family Relations*, 73 (2), pp. 843–857.

Armour, M., 2003. Meaning making in the aftermath of homicide. *Death Studies*, 27 (6), pp. 519–540.

Andrews, D. A., & Bonta, J., 2006. *The Psychology of Criminal Conduct*. Toronto, Ontario: Anderson Publishing.

Arnold, G., 2009. A battered women's movement perspective of coercive control. *Violence Against Women*, 15, pp. 1432–1443.

Bailey, J., Flynn, A. & Henry, N., 2021. *The Emerald International Handbook of Technology-Facilitated Violence and Abuse* (Emerald Studies In Digital Crime, Technology and Social Harms). Leeds: Emerald Group Publishing.

Baldwin, S. B., Fehrenbacher, A. E., & Eisenman, D. P., 2015. Psychological coercion in human trafficking. *Qualitative Health Research*, 25, pp. 1171–1181.

Campbell, J., Glass, N., Sharps, P., Laughon, K. & Bloom, T., 2007. Intimate partner homicide: Review and implications of research and policy. *Trauma, Violence & Abuse*, 8 (3), pp. 246–269.

Carlson, B., & Day, M., 2023. Technology-facilitated abuse: The need for Indigenous-led research and response. In: Harris, B., & Woodlock, D., eds. *Technology and Domestic and Family Violence: Victimisation, Perpetration and Responses*. Oxon: Routledge, pp. 33–48.

Cavanagh, K., Dobash, R. E., Dobash, R. P. & Lewis, R., 2001. "Remedial work": Men's strategic responses to their violence against intimate female partners. *Sociology*, 35 (3), pp. 695–714.

Casey, L., 2011. *Review into the Needs of Families Bereaved by Homicide* [online]. London: Commissioner for Victims and Witnesses. Available at: https://samm.org.uk/wp-content/uploads/2021/01/Review-needs-of-families-bereaved-by-homicide.pdf [Accessed 19 March 2025].

Chowdhury, R., & Winder, B., 2022. A web model of domestic violence and abuse in Muslim communities – A multi perspective IPA approach. *Social Sciences*, 11, p. 354.

Clements, P. T., & Vigil, G. J., 2003. Child and adolescent homicide survivors: Complicated grief and altered worldviews. *Journal of Psychosocial Nursing & Mental Health Services*, 41, pp. 30–39.

Connolly, J., & Gordon, R., 2015. Co-victims of homicide: A systematic review of the literature. *Trauma, Violence, & Abuse*, 16 (4), pp. 494–505.

Costa, D. H. de., Njaine, K. & Schenker, M., 2017. Repercussions of homicide on victims' families: A literature review. *Ciência & Saúde Coletiva*, 22 (9), pp. 3087–3087.

Crosbie-Burnett, M., & Klein, D. M., 2009. The fascinating story of family theories. In: Bray, J. H. & Stanton, M., eds. *The Wiley-Blackwell Handbook of Family Psychology*. Chichester, West Sussex: Wiley-Blackwell, pp. 37–52.

Dobash, R. E., Dobash, R. P. & Cavanagh, K., 2009. "Out of the blue": Men who murder an intimate partner. *Feminist Criminology*, 4, pp. 194–225.

Dobash, R. P., & Dobash, R. E., 2015. *When Men Murder Women*. New York: Oxford University Press.

Dorpat, T. L., 1994. On the double whammy and gaslighting. *Psychoanalysis & Psychotherapy*, 11 (1), pp. 91–96.

Dorpat, T. L., 1996. *Gaslighting, the Double Whammy, Interrogation, and Other Methods of Covert Control in Psychotherapy and Analysis*. Northvale, New Jersey: Jason Aronson Inc.

Douglas, H., Harris, B. A. & Dragiewicz, M., 2019. Technology-facilitated domestic and family violence: Women's experiences. *British Journal of Criminology*, 59 (3), pp. 551–570.

Dragiewicz, M., Burgess, J., Matamoros-Fernández, A., Salter, M., Suzor, N. P., Woodlock, D. & Harris, B., 2018. Technologies of coercive control: Digital domestic violence and the competing roles of social media platforms. *Feminist Media Studies*, 18, pp. 609–625.

Duggan, M., 2012. Using victims' voices to prevent violence against women: A critique. *British Journal of Community Justice*, 10 (2), pp. 25–37.

Duron, J. F., Johnson, L., Hoge, G. L., & Postmus, L. L., 2021. Observing coercive control beyond intimate partner violence: Examining the perceptions of professionals about common tactics used in victimization. *Psychology of Violence*, 11 (2), pp. 144–154.

Dutton, M. A., & Goodman, L. A., 2005. Coercion in intimate partner violence: Toward a new conceptualization. *Sex Roles*, 52, pp. 743–756.

Edwards, T., Sharpe, T., Bonomo, A. & Massaquoi, N., 2021. Exploring research on the coping strategies of Black survivors of homicide victims: A scoping review protocol. *BMJ Open*, 1 (11), pp. 1–5.

Faver, C. A., & Strand, E. B., 2003. Domestic violence and animal cruelty: untangling the web of abuse. Special section: Domestic violence and social work education. *Journal of Social Work Education*, 39 (2), pp. 237–248.

Fileborn, B., & Ball, M., 2023. Technology-facilitated domestic violence: Some queer considerations. In: Harris, B., & Woodlock, D., eds. *Technology and Domestic and Family Violence: Victimisation, Perpetration and Responses*. Oxon: Routledge, pp. 133–143.

Fontes, L. A., 2015. *Invisible Chains: Overcoming Coercive Control in Your Intimate Relationship*. New York: Guilford Publications, Inc.

Fraser, C., Olsen, E., Lee, K., Southworth, C., & Tucker, S., 2010. The new age of stalking: Technological implications for stalking. *Juvenile and Family Court Journal*, 61 (4), pp. 39–55.

Georgas, J., Berry, J. W., Van der Vijver, F. J. R., Kağitçıbaşi, C. & Poortinga, Y. H., 2006. *Families Across Cultures: A 30-Nation Psychological Study*. Cambridge: Cambridge University Press.

Goodkind, J., Gillum, T., Bybee, D. & Sullivan, C., 2003. The impact of family and friends' reactions on the well-being of women with abusive partners. *Violence Against Women*, 9 (3), pp. 347–373.

Gregory, A. C., 2017. "The edge to him was really, really nasty": Abusive tactics used against informal supporters of domestic violence survivors. *Journal of Gender-Based Violence*, 1, pp. 61–77.

Gregory, A., Taylor, A. K., Pitt, K., Feder, G. & Williamson, E., 2021. "… The forgotten heroes": A qualitative study exploring how friends and family members of DV survivors use domestic violence helplines. *Journal of Interpersonal Violence*, 36 (21–22), pp. 11479–11505.

Gregory, A. C., Williamson, E. & Feder, G., 2017. The impact on informal supporters of domestic violence survivors: A systematic literature review. *Trauma, Violence, & Abuse*, 18 (5), pp. 562–580.

Hand, T., Chung, D. & Peters, M., 2009. *The Use of Information and Communication Technologies to Coerce and Control in Domestic Violence and Following Separation* [online]. Sydney: Australian Domestic and Family Violence Clearinghouse. Available at: https://advocacy4oromia.files.wordpress.com/2015/03/stakeholderpaper_6.pdf [Accessed 28 October 2024].

Harris, B. A., & Woodlock, D., 2019. Digital coercive control: Insights from two landmark domestic violence studies. *British Journal of Criminology*, 59 (3), pp. 530–550.

Harris, B. A., & Woodlock, D., 2023. *Technology and Domestic and Family Violence: Victimisation, Perpetration and Responses*. Oxon: Routledge.

Hellman, A. N., & Hurley, S., 2023. Looking for the hidden hurts: When radiological findings suggest presence of intimate partner violence. *Journal of Radiology Nursing*, 42 (2), pp. 166–171.

Hester, M., & Donovan, C., 2009. Researching domestic violence in same-sex relationships – A feminist epistemological approach to survey development. *Journal of Lesbian Studies*, 13 (2), pp. 161–173.

Hobart, M., 2002. *"Tell the World What Happened To Me": Findings and Recommendations from the Washington State Domestic Violence Fatality Review 2002* [online]. Washington, DC: Washington State Coalition Against Domestic Violence. Available at: chrome-extension://efaidnbmnnnibpcajpcglclefindmkaj/https://www.baylor.edu/content/services/document.php/29323.pdf [Accessed 3 January 2025].

Holt, A., 2021. *Family Criminology: An Introduction*. London: Palgrave Macmillan.

James, D. V., & Farnham, F. R., 2003. Stalking and serious violence. *Journal of the American Academy of Psychiatry and the Law Online*, 31 (4), pp. 432–439.

Jayasuriya, V., Wijewardena, K. & Axemo, P., 2011. Intimate partner violence against women in the Capital Province of Sri Lanka: Prevalence, risk factors, and help seeking. *Violence Against Female*, 17 (8), pp. 1086–1102.

Karakurt, G., & Silver, K. E., 2013. Emotional abuse in intimate relationships: The role of gender and age. *Violence & Victims*, 28 (5), pp. 804–821.

Kennedy, M. C., 2022. Digital coercive control: A male perspective. In: Gavin, H., ed. *Women and the Abuse of Power*. Leeds: Emerald Publishing Limited, pp. 105–122.

Kivisto, A. J., 2015. Male perpetrators of intimate partner homicide: A review and proposed typology. *Journal of the American Academy of Psychiatry and the Law*, 43, pp. 300–312.

Latta, R., 2008. Struggling to define my role: The experience of network members who intervened in intimate partner violence [online]. Ph.D. thesis, Boston College. Available at: https://www.proquest.com/openview/a7a88ceb2692e7eba34dfc1b539f3b5d/1?pq-origsite=gscholar&cbl=18750 [Accessed 3 January 2025].

Latta, R., & Goodman, L. A., 2011. Intervening in partner violence against women: A grounded theory exploration of informal network members' experiences. *The Counseling Psychologist*, 39 (7), pp. 973–1023.

Leitão, R., 2021. Technology-facilitated intimate partner abuse: A qualitative analysis of data from online domestic abuse forums. *Human-Computer Interaction*, 36 (3), pp. 203–242.

Liem, M., & Roberts, D. W., 2009. Intimate partner homicide by presence or absence of a self-destructive act. *Homicide Studies*, 13 (4), pp. 339–354.

Little, J., 2023. Violence, the body and the spaces of intimate war. In: Carter, S. & Woodyer, T., eds. *Domesticating Geopolitics*. London: Routledge, pp. 74–93.

Littwin, A., 2012. Coerced debt: The role of consumer credit in domestic violence. *California Law Review*, 100 (4), pp. 951–1026.

Logan, T. K., Cole, J. & Shannon, L., 2007. A mixed-methods examination of sexual coercion and degradation among women in violent relationships who do and do not report forced sex. *Violence and Victims*, 22 (1), pp. 71–94.

Logan T., & Walker R., 2009. Partner stalking: Psychological dominance or business as usual? *Trauma, Violence, and Abuse*, 10, pp. 247–270.

Markwick, K., Bickerdike, A., Wilson-Evered, E. & Zeleznikow, J., 2019. Technology and family violence in the context of post-separated parenting. *Australian and New Zealand Journal of Family Therapy*, 40 (1), pp. 143–162.

Martinez, C. T., 2015. Engendered expressions of aggression: The role of gender, proprietary behaviours, and jealousy in intimate partner violence. *Violence and Gender*, 2 (2), pp. 112–118.

McLachlan, F., & Harris, B., 2022. Intimate risks: Examining online and offline abuse, homicide flags, and femicide. *Victims & Offenders*, 17 (5), pp. 623–646.

Mitchell, J. E., & Raghavan, C., 2019. The impact of coercive control on use of specific sexual coercion tactics. *Violence Against Women*, 27 (2), pp. 187–206.

Monckton Smith, J., 2012. *Murder, Gender and the Media: Narratives of Dangerous Love*. London: Palgrave Macmillan.

Monckton Smith, J., Szymanska, K. & Haile, S., 2017. *Exploring the Relationship between Stalking and Homicide* [online]. Gloucester, England: University of Gloucester. Available at: chrome-extension://efaidnbmnnnibpcajpcglclefindmkaj/https://eprints.glos.ac.uk/4553/1/NSAW%20Report%2004.17%20-%20finalsmall.pdf [Accessed 12 August 2024].

Monckton Smith, J., Williams, A., & Mullane F., 2014. *Domestic Abuse, Homicide and Gender*. London: Palgrave Macmillan.

Morris, A., 2009. Gendered dynamics of abuse and violence in families: Considering the abusive household gender regime. *Child Abuse Review*, 18 (6), pp. 414–427.

Munteanu, V., 2021. Examining the impact of domestic abuse survivors on employee performance and recommendations for the employer [online]. M.A. thesis, National College of Ireland. Available at: chrome-extension://efaidnbmnnnibpcajpcglclefindmkaj/https://norma.ncirl.ie/5336/1/violetamunteanu.pdf [Accessed 28 August 2024].

Pain, R. 2014. Everyday terrorism: Connecting domestic violence and global terrorism. *Progress in Human Geography*, 38 (4), pp. 531–550.

Pasternak, B. E., Ember, C. R. & Ember, M., 1976. On the conditions favoring extended family households. *Journal of Anthropological Research*, 32, pp. 109–123.

Persons, R., 1990. Psychotherapist and widower. *The Psychotherapy Patient*, 6, pp. 71–80.

Pollard, G., 2020. Examining the experiences of homicide co-victims to inform a survivor's guide to healing [online]. Honors Research Project, Williams Honors College. Available at: https://ideaexchange.uakron.edu/honors_research_projects/1091 [Accessed 13 January 2025].

Pollet, S. L., 2011. Economic abuse: The unseen side of domestic violence. *New York State Bar Journal*, 83 (2), pp. 40–44.

Prigerson, H. G., Shear, M. K., Jacobs, S. C., Reynolds, C. F., Maciejewski, P. K., Davidson, J. R., Rosenheck, R., Pilkonis, P. A., Wortman, C. B., Williams, J. B.,

Widiger, T. A., Frank, E., Kupfer, D. J., & Zisook, S., 1999. Consensus criteria for traumatic grief. A preliminary empirical test. *The British Journal of Psychiatry*, 174, pp. 67–73.

Raghavan, C., Cohen, S., & Tamborra, T., 2014. Development and preliminary validation of the Multidimensional Sexual Coercion Questionnaire (MSCQ). *Journal of Sexual Aggression*, 21, pp. 271–289.

Reed, L. A., Toleman, R. M. & Ward, L. M., 2017. Gender matters: Experiences and consequences of digital dating abuse victimization in adolescent dating relationships. *Journal of Adolescence*, 59, pp. 79–89.

Reed, M., 2022. The administration of death notifications in murder cases: Retelling the secondary victimization experiences of homicide co-victims [online]. Georgia State University: CJC Publications. Available at: https://scholarworks.gsu.edu/cj_facpub/47 [Accessed 13 January 2025].

Rees, A., Agnew-Davies, R. & Barkham, M., 2006. Outcomes for women escaping domestic violence at refuge. In: *Society for Psychotherapy Research Book of Abstracts*. Edinburgh: University of Edinburgh, 21–24 June 2006.

Rees, S., Silove, D., Chey, T., Ivancic, L., Steel, Z., Creamer, M., Teesson, M., Bryant, R., McFarlane, A. C., Mills, K. L., Slade, T., Carragher, N., O'Donnell, M. & Forbes, D., 2011. Lifetime prevalence of gender-based violence in women and the relationship with mental disorders and psychosocial function. *Journal of the American Medical Association*, 306, pp. 513–521.

Renzetti, C. M., 1992. *Violent Betrayal: Partner Abuse in Lesbian Relationships*. London: Sage.

Reyns, B. W., Burek, M. W., Henson, B., & Fisher, B. S., 2013. The unintended consequences of digital technology: Exploring the relationship between sexting and cybervictimization. *Journal of Crime Justice*, 36, pp. 1–17.

Riger, S., Raja, S., & Camacho, J., 2002. The radiating impact of intimate partner violence. *Journal of Interpersonal Violence*, 17, pp. 184–205.

Rose, D., Trevillion, K., Woodall, A., Morgan, C., Feder, G. & Howard, L., 2011. Barriers and facilitators of disclosures of domestic violence by mental health service users: Qualitative study. *British Journal of Psychiatry*, 198, pp. 189–194.

Salari, S., & LeFevre Sillito, C., 2016. Intimate partner homicide suicide: Perpetrator primary intent across young, middle, and elder adult age categories. *Aggression and Violent Behavior*, 26, pp. 26–34.

Sanderson, C., 2008. *Counselling Survivors of Domestic Abuse*. London: Jessica Kingsley.

Scott, A. J., Lloyd, R. & Gavin, J., 2010. The influence of prior relationship on perceptions of stalking in the United Kingdom and Australia. *Criminal Justice and Behavior*, 37 (11), pp. 1185–1194.

Sharo, C. A., 2024. The experiences of homicide co-victims: the impact of not being an "ideal victim" [online]. Ph.D. thesis, University of Delaware. Available at: chrome-extension://efaidnbmnnnibpcajpcglclefindmkaj/https://udspace.udel.edu/server/api/core/bitstreams/ec4340a6-94ca-47f4-8734-d310c903638b/content [Accessed 13 January 2025].

Sharp-Jeffs, N., 2015. *A Review of Research and Policy on Financial Abuse Within Intimate Partner Relationships*. London: CWASU.

Sharp-Jeffs, N., 2021. Understanding the economics of abuse: An assessment of the economic abuse definition within the Domestic Abuse Bill. *Journal of Gender-based Violence*, 5 (1), pp. 163–173.

Sharp-Jeffs, N., 2022. *Understanding and Responding to Economic Abuse*. Leeds: Emerald Publishing Limited.

Solot, D., 1997. Untangling the animal abuse web. *Society and Animals*, 5 (3), pp. 257–265.

Spencer, C. M., 2018. A meta-analysis of risk factors for intimate partner homicide: Examining male perpetration and female victimization [online]. Ph.D. thesis, Kansas State University. Available at: https://krex.k-state.edu/server/api/core/bitstreams/dbd914ee-c187-4cde-8f6f-73d9775e0cfc/content [Accessed 14 May 2024].

Spencer, C. M., & Stith, S. M., 2020. Risk factors for male perpetration and female victimization of intimate partner homicide: A meta-analysis. *Trauma, Violence & Abuse*, 21 (3), pp. 527–540.

Spencer-Carver, E., 2008. Social support for children who had a parent killed by intimate partner violence: Interviews with mental health workers [online]. Ph.D. thesis, Kansas State University. Available at: chrome-extension://efaidnbmnnnibpcajpcglclefindmkaj/https://krex.k-state.edu/server/api/core/bitstreams/a8f91cf7-191c-4e3e-9df3-a9bc05285e38/content [Accessed 3 January 2025].

Stark, E., 2007. *Coercive Control: How Men Entrap Women in Personal Life*. New York: Oxford University Press.

Stark, E., 2012. Looking beyond domestic violence: Policing coercive control [Special issue]. *Journal of Police Crisis Negotiations*, 12, pp. 199–217.

Stark, E., 2017. Foreword. In: McOrmond-Plummer, L., Levy-Peck, J. Y. & Easteal, P., eds. *Perpetrators of Intimate Partner Sexual Violence*. Oxon: Routledge, pp. xx–xxv.

Stark, E., 2023. *Coercive Control: How Men Entrap Women in Personal Life*. 2nd ed. New York: Oxford University Press.

Stewart, D. E., MacMillan, H. & Kimber, M., 2021. Recognizing and responding to intimate partner violence: An update. *The Canadian Journal of Psychiatry*, 66 (1), pp.71–106.

Stretesky, P. B., O'Connor Shelley, T., Hogan, M. J. & Prabha Unnithan, N., 2010. Sense-making and secondary victimization among unsolved homicide co-victims. *Journal of Criminal Justice*, 38, pp. 880–888.

Swanberg, J., & Logan, T., 2005. Domestic violence and employment: A qualitative study. *Journal of Occupational Health Psychology*, 10, pp. 3–17.

Swanberg, J., Macke, C. & Logan, T., 2006. Intimate partner violence, women, and work: Coping on the job. *Violence and Victims*, 21, pp. 561–578.

Swanson, S., Nygård, R. H. & Saus, M., 2022. Native American social work – Including family and community. *Journal of Social Work*, 22 (3), pp. 615–636.

Sweet, P. L., 2019. The sociology of gaslighting. *American Sociological Review*, 84 (5), pp. 851–875.

Thiel de Bocanegra, H., Rostovtseva, D. P., Khera, S. & Godhwani, N., 2010. Birth control sabotage and forced sex: Experiences reported by women in domestic violence shelters. *Violence Against Women*, 16 (5), pp. 601–612.

Van Wijk, A., Van Leiden, I. & Ferwerda, H., 2016. Murder and the long-term impact on co victims: A qualitative, longitudinal study. *International Review of Victimology*, 23 (2), pp. 1–13.

Vatnar, S., Friestad, C. & Bjerkly, S., 2017. Intimate partner homicide in Norway 1990–2012. *Psychology of Violence*, 7 (3), pp. 395–405.

Walby, S., & Towers, J., 2018. Untangling the concept of coercive control: Theorizing domestic violent crime. *Criminology & Criminal Justice*, 18 (1), pp. 7–28.

Websdale, N., 2010. *Familicidal Hearts: The Emotional Styles of 211 Killers*. Oxford: Oxford University Press.

Werner, S., 2022. A review on the effects of homicide on co-victims: Mental health, coping, and race. *Oregon Undergraduate Research Journal*, 21 (1), pp. 22–39.

Wilson, D., & Daly, M., 1992. The man who mistook his wife for a chattel. In: Barkow, J. H., Cosmides, L. & Tooby, J., eds. *The Adapted Mind: Evolutionary Psychology and the Generation Of Culture.* New York: Oxford University Press, pp. 289–322.

Wilson, D., & Daly, M., 1993. An evolutionary psychological perspective on male sexual proprietariness and violence against wives. *Violence and Victims*, 8 (3), pp. 271–294.

Woodlock, D., 2017. The abuse of technology in domestic violence and stalking. *Violence Against Women*, 25 (5), pp. 584–602.

Wolf, M., Holt, V., Kernic, M. & Rivara, F., 2000. Who gets protection orders for intimate partner violence? *American Journal of Preventive Medicine*, 19, pp. 286–291.

World Health Organization (WHO), 2021. *Violence Against Women Prevalence Estimates, 2018: Global, Regional and National Prevalence Estimates for Intimate Partner Violence Against Women and Global and Regional Prevalence Estimates for Non-Partner Sexual Violence Against Women* [online]. Geneva, Switzerland: United Nations Inter-Agency Working Group on Violence Against Women Estimation and Data. Available at: chrome-extension://efaidnbmnnnibpcajpcglclefindmkaj/https://iris.who.int/bitstream/handle/10665/341338/9789240026681-eng.pdf?sequence=1 [Accessed 31 December 2024].

Index

Note: Page numbers in **bold** indicate tables in the text

abuse *see* intimate partner abuse; sexual abuse
active threats 64, **65**, 101–103, 120–123, 135
actual victim 20
Adams, A. 76
Advocacy After Fatal Domestic Abuse (AAFDA) 8
affordability 96
Al-Alosi, H. 97
Alcoff, L. M. 7
anonymity 10, 35, 96
attention problems 5

Bahrami, M. 64
Bastomski, S. 3
Belfrage, H. 57
Bion, W. R. 52
body, as "site of violence" 61
Bostock, J. 64
Bowstead, J. 67
Boyle, K. 20, 38
Bradford, L. 29
branding 71
brittle family 4
Brown, C. 100
bystanders 118

Campbell, J. 57
Carrabine, E. 26
Casey, L. 30
Christie, N. 26, 27
Code of Practice for Victims' of Crime (Victims' Code) 32–33
coercive control 1, 9, 20, 35, 36, 51, 60–78, 92; abuse and 11; control in 75–78; digital 39, 70, 92–94, 100–106; digital media and 137; intimidation and 63–71; isolation and 60, 71–75, 136; online harm and **101**; physical injury and 60–63
Cohen, L. J. 4
"collateral killing" 120
communicating abuse mediums 101–103
Community Safety Partnerships (CSPs) 33
contemptuous family 4
continuum thinking 38–39
control: in coercive control 75–78, 136; and economic abuse 76–78
Copelon, R. 64
courting compassion 24
co-victims 1–2, 3–6, 29–30, 78, 117, 138–139; informal support 118–119; offline harm 120–121; Prisoners Bill 2015 35–36; research 133–134
Crime Survey for England and Wales (CSEW) 19, 76
criminology 2, 29; cultural 24–25
critical victimology 23–24
Crown Prosecution Service (CPS) 93
culpability 21
cultural victimology 21, 24–25

Daly, M. 54, 120
death 5, 8, 119
de Certeau, M. 93
degradation 71, 100, 135–136
DeGue, S. 62
Department of Work and Pensions (DWP) 75
designated victim 21
digital coercive control 39, 70, 92–94; and technologies of abuse 100–106
"digital detox" 97
digital dualism 50, 91

digital media 95, 106, 137
digital technologies 95–97; and abuse 100–106
digital voyeurism 98
direct monitoring behaviours 67
Discola, K. L. 3
distress 5, 31
Dobash, R. E. 120
Dobash, R. P. 120
Domestic Abuse Act 2021 11, 32, 36–37, 60, 76
Domestic/Family Death Review panels/committees 33
Domestic Homicide Reviews (DHRs) 8, 33–35
domestic homicides 11, 19, 34
Domestic Proceedings and Magistrates' Court Act 1978 30–31
Domestic Violence and Matrimonial Proceedings Act 1976 (DVMPA) 30–31
Domestic Violence, Crime and Victims Act 2004 (DVCVA) 32
Domestic Violence Fatality Review (DVFR), in US 33–34
Douglas, H. 97
Dragiewicz, M. 107
drive-bys 69–70
Duane, M. 3
Dutton, D. G. 57
Dutton, M. A. 67

economic abuse 76–78, 136
economic jealousy **53**, 135
emotional anaesthesia 5
emotional isolation 72
emotional support 72
enduring family 4
envy 51–53, 135
Equal Credit Opportunity Act 76
Equal Pay Act 1970 76

Facebook 99
familial jealousy case 52–53, **53**, 135
family(ies) 27–30; as co-victims 29–30; criminology 29; homicide victims 11, 19; and litigation 4; member loss 5–6; non-Western 28; research 6–10
Family Law Act 1996 31–32
fatal abuse 8, 19, 51, 54, 56, 135, 136
fear: chronic 97; "female" 63; and threats 122
femicide 11
feminism 7; and victimology 25–26
filicide 107
forced sex 62
Foucault, M. 67
French, J. R. P., Jr. 67
functional family 4
Furedi, F. 26

gaslighting 65–66, 99, 122–124, 135
Gekoski, A. 30
gender 7, 66; inequalities 7, 64, 92
Global North 28
global positioning systems (GPS) 98
Goodman, L. A. 67
Gosse, C. 50
Gregory, A. C. 3
Gregson, N. 93
grief 3, 24, 119
grieving 6
Guerrero, L. K. 51
guilt 119

Hand, T. 97
Harding, S. 7
harm 2–3, 23, 29, 31, 64, 91, 99, 104; continuum of 38–39, 50; and homicide 134–139; overspill 120–126, 138–139; *see also* online harm; offline harm
Harris, B. 92–94, 100, 107, 137–138
Hartmann, H. 74
hashtag activism 96
Hegarty, K. 100
Hertz, M. F. 3
Hester, M. 92
hierarchical family 4
Hindelang, M. J. 22
Hinduja, S. 102
Hobart, M. 120
Hogg, R. 93
Holtzworth-Munroe, A. 62
home space 93–94
homicide adaptation hypothesis 54

ideal victim 26–27
image-based sexual abuse 38, 98, 101
'Independent Public Advocate' scheme 35
indirect monitoring behaviours 67
infidelity 51, 55, 63, 98, 135
informal support 72–74, 118–119, 138
instrumental support 75
intimate partner abuse 1–2, 8, 5, 18–19, 11, 30–37, 57, 60, 64, 95, 102, 118–119, 139–140; communicating 101–103; continuum thinking 38–39; co-victims 4, 117–127; and digital media 95, 106; economic 76–78, 136; fatal 8, 19, 51, 54, 56, 135, 136; gendered nature 19, 77;

history 56–58, 135; and physical injury 134; resistance 97; social 117; technologies 97–100; verbal 136; victims' experiences of 7; web of 59; *see also* coercive control; physical abuse; sexual abuse
intimate partner homicide 9, 51, 11, 18, 54, 119; consequence of male desire 54; continuum thinking and 38–39; co-victims of 3–6; as criminal offence 32; family of victims 29–30; female oppression and 55; gendered nature 19; harm continuum and 134–139; impact on women 18; implications 106–108; incidence 5; jealousy and 51; legal remedies 30–37; online harm and 137; precursors 51–58; prevalence 20; refusal of sex in 62–63; risk factors 9–10, 39, 50–51, 59, 78, 107–108, 135, 138; threats 64
intimidating behaviour 100; degradation and shaming 71; gaslighting 65–66; microregulation 70–71; stalking 68–70; surveillance and monitoring 67–68; threats 64, **65**
isolation: coercive control and 60, 71–75, 136; from formal support 74–75; from informal support 72–74; intimidation and 100; from work 74

jealousy 51–53, **53**, 135
Johnson, H. 55
Jones, C. 34
Jurgenson, N. 50, 91

Kaighobadi F. 54
Kauzlarich, D. 23
Kelly, L. 20, 38, 39
Kennedy, M. 39, 50
Kenney, J. S. 29
Kerry, G. 57
"killing the competition" phenomenon 120
Kivisto, A. J. 51, 52, 57
Klein, M. 52
Kotzé, J. 2

Latta, R. 4, 139
Little, J. 61, 134
Logan, T. K. 62
loss 5–6
Lowe, M. 93

MacVane S. L. 3, 4
male desire 54
Malone, L. 6
Married Women's Property Act 1964 76
Marshall, A. D. 62
Martinez, C. T. 54
Mawby, R. 23
McGarry, R. 30
McGlynn, C. 38
McLachlan, F. 94, 107, 137–138
Melander, L. A. 99
memory loss 5
Mendelsohn, B. 21, 22
methodology 6–8; limitations 10
microregulation 70–71, 136
microsurveillance 105–106
Miller, L. 4
misogyny 95
monitoring behaviour 67–68, 99; mediums 103–106
Multi-Agency Risk Assessment Conferences (MARACs) 34
Munk, T. 39, 50
Murdock, G. P. 27
Murphie, A. 92

neglect and sexual abuse 61–63

offline harm 50–51, 120–122, 134–137; convicted perpetrators 57–58; history of abuse 56–58; homicide precursors 51–58; jealousy 51–53; neglect and sexual abuse 61–63; physical abuse 60–63; proprietary behaviours 54–56; threats overspill case 121–122; 'web of abuse' 59–60; *see also* coercive control; intimidating behaviour; support
omnipresence 106
online disinhibition effect 124
online harm 122–124, 137–138; communicating abuse 101–103; digital coercive control 92–94, 100–106; digital technologies importance 95–97; digital technologies in abuse 97–106; risk factors 91–92; gaslighting 123–124; and homicide implications 106–108; legal responses 37–38, **37**; monitoring 103–106; total digital surveillance case 104–106; victimisation and perpetration 100
Online Harms White Paper 37, **37**
Online Safety Act 2023 37
Online Safety Bill 37, **37**

panopticism 106
passive threats 64, **65**, 135

Patchin, J. W. 102
perpetrators 11, 19–21, 31, 56, 61–62, 65, 68, 73, 75–76, 96, 108, 117, 125–126; abusive tactics 62–75, 100, 125; gaslighting 66, 123–124; history of abuse 56–58; microregulation 70; mobile technologies and 103, 107; and online tools 97–99; of sextortion 102; of sexual coercion 62; stalking 68; of surveillance and monitoring 67, 99
Persons, R. 5
physical abuse 134; and coercive control 60–63; injuries 60–61; neglect and sexual abuse 61–63; withholding sex/intimacy 63
physical assaults 61, 134
physical isolation 72
physical neglect 61–62, 134
physical support 75
physical violence 31
Police and Criminal Evidence Act 1984 32
Popenoe, D. 27
positivist victimology 22
postmodernism 7; postmodern feminism 26
post-traumatic stress disorder (PTSD) 4, 5, 119
Potts, J. 92
prior offences 58–58, 135
prison communications 124–126
privacy 93
private crime 102
property rights 77, 106
proprietary behaviours 54–56, 106
Protection from Harassment Act 1997 31

qualitative feminist research 6–8; limitations 10
Queensland Domestic and Family Violence Death Review Unit (DFVDRU) study 107
Quinney, R. 22

Radford, J. 11
radical victimology 22–23
Rajah, V. 74
rape 62–64
Raven, B. 67
refusal of sex 62–63
rejected victim 20
Richards, B. 52
Richards, L. 69
Ristock, J. 94
Rock, P. 30
Rothe, D. 23
Russell, E. H. 11
Rying, M. 57

safety zone 74
Salari, S. 120
Scott, J. 93
secondary victimisation/victims 6, 8, 30
self-respect 71
separation, potential/actual 59, 107–108
Serious and Organised Crime and Police Act 2005 32
Serious Crime Act 2015 36, 60, 92
sextortion 101–103
sexual abuse 122, 134; image-based 38, 98, 101; neglect and 61–63; rape and 63
sexual jealousy 51, **53**, 54
sexual violence: continuum of 38–39; Kelly on 59; and sexual coercion 61, 62, 134
shaming 71, 100, **101**, 135–136
sleep disturbance 5
social abuse 117
social harms 2
social power theory 67
social support types 72
Southworth, C. 99
space and place 93
stalking 68–70, 98, 103–104
standpoint theory 7
Stanley, L. 10
Stark, E. 56, 60, 61, 64, 68, 70, 74, 75, 92, 93, 100, 103, 125
state crime victims 22–23
Strobl, R. 20–21
suicide 19–20, 71, 77, 78
Suler, J. 124
support: formal 74–75; informal 72–74, 118–119, 138; physical 75; types 72
surveillance and monitoring behaviour 67–68, 136
Suzy Lamplugh Trust 68
Sweet, P. L. 65–66, 122

technologies of abuse 97–100; digital coercive control and 100–106
Thiel de Bocanegra, H. 62
threats: active 64, **65**, 101–103, 120–123, 135; death 120; fear and 122; overspill case 121–122; passive 64, **65**, 135; of sexual abuse 122; verbal 122
Tolman, R. 71
total digital surveillance case 104–106
"tweet and delete" behaviours 97

Van Wijk, P. 26
Vesper, J. H. 4
victimology 20–25; critical 23–24; cultural 21, 24–25; feminism and 25–26; positivist 22; radical 22–23
victim(s) 20–25, 56, 61, 62, 65, 68, 73, 75, 76, 10: designated 21; family as 29–30; friends of 3; hierarchy of victimisation 26; history of abuse and 57; ideal 26–27; of international crimes 26; isolation 72; microregulation 70; minority groups 21; responsiveness 23; status 26–27, 29–30;
Victims and Prisoners Bill 2015 35–36
Victims' Charters 33
Victims' Code 32–33
victims' families, interviews with 9–10
Viñas-Racionero, R. 70
Von Hentig, H. 21
vulnerability 26

Walklate, S. 23, 30
white-collar/corporate crime victims 23
Wilson, D. 54
Wilson, M. 120
Wise, S. 10
withholding sex/intimacy 63, 134
Wolak, J. 102
Wolf, M. 120
Woodlock, D. 92, 93, 100

zemiology 2–3

MIX

Papier | Fördert gute Waldnutzung

FSC® C083411

Kolibri 360 GmbH
Ferdinand-Jühlke-Straße 7
99095 Erfurt, Deutschland
produktsicherheit@kolibri360.de